Elephants

Elephants

Up Close and Personal

ELLEN GREENE STEWART

Toplight

Jefferson, North Carolina

A portion of the author's proceeds from this book will be donated
to the Knysna Elephant Park/AERU Research.

All photos are from the author's collection.

LIBRARY OF CONGRESS CATALOGUING-IN-PUBLICATION DATA

Names: Stewart, Ellen Greene, author.
Title: Elephants : up close and personal / Ellen Greene Stewart.
Description: Jefferson, North Carolina : McFarland & Company, Inc.,
Publishers, 2022 | Includes bibliographical references and index.
Identifiers: LCCN 2022004503 | ISBN 9781476687797 (paperback : acid free paper ∞)
ISBN 9781476645933 (ebook)
Subjects: LCSH: African elephant—South Africa—Knysna. | African elephant—
South Africa—Knysna—Anecdotes. | African elephant—Conservation—
South Africa—Knysna. | BISAC: NATURE / Animals / Mammals
Classification: LCC QL737.P98 S743 2022 | DDC 599.67—dc23/eng/20220218
LC record available at https://lccn.loc.gov/2022004503

BRITISH LIBRARY CATALOGUING DATA ARE AVAILABLE

ISBN (print) 978-1-4766-8779-7
ISBN (ebook) 978-1-4766-4593-3

Front cover photograph by Matt Ratcliff (Shutterstock)

Printed in the United States of America

Toplight is an imprint of McFarland & Company, Inc., Publishers

Toplight

Box 611, Jefferson, North Carolina 28640
www.toplightbooks.com

This book is dedicated to the memory of Shepherd Chuma whose loving kindness and radiant smile enlightened the lives of so many. It is also dedicated to every elephant who has ever graced our planet with their mammoth hearts, their gentle spirits, ancient wisdom, and their amazing elegance.

Acknowledgments

I could not have written this book without the help, support, and encouragement I received from Dr. Maud Bonado, Shepherd Chuma, Sharon Cuccinata, Dumisani Dube, Julie Ford, Sue Fritz, Lilly Golden, Laurie Greene, Sylvia and Ken Greene, Mac Juwa, Davison Mbaura, Joan Medsker, Nicki Milachowski, Ndyebo Momsenge, Charles Moyo, Wilfred Nyamazunza, Fanwell Nyoni, Clare Padfield, Nikki Perosino, Kristen Artz Rendler, William Rendler, Kathy Schroeder, Arnie and Carol Schwartz, Noleen Skinstad, Bob Stewart, Lacey Peace Stewart, Anique Taylor, Michael Teitelbaum, Elliot Tembo, Christina Tholander, Sias Van Rooyen, Alex Vipond, Dr. Debbie Young.

Table of Contents

Table of Contents

Part Three

Preface

I remember the tipping point in which my love for elephants became an integral part of me. I rode high on the back of an elephant at the Bronx Zoo at the ripe old age of four and have remained drawn to them ever since. As I touched the elephant's rubbery skin and bristly hair with my small hand, she reached me with her tender spirit. After years of reading about elephants in books, watching them on television and seeing them in the news, I was determined to find a place where I could interact with them up close and personal, experience their majesty firsthand as an adult. I quickly came upon the renowned volunteer program at the Knysna Elephant Park (KEP) on the southern coast of South Africa, and the rest fell into place.

My decision to visit KEP in South Africa was a long time in the making, however. This was an outsized leap of faith; I would have to travel alone, halfway around the world, to spend three weeks volunteering to assist with research and caring for the elephants—all with a group of people I'd never met. I am not at all athletic and didn't know if I was physically fit enough for this adventure. I could hardly afford the trip, and I would have to take time off from work without pay in order to make the trip work. I'd been to South Africa before to visit an orphanage for children whose parents died of HIV/AIDS in Durban on the east coast of South Africa with a dear friend. I was well aware of the long travel time and the jet lag as well as the expense and culture shock. It seemed like a long way and a lot of logistics to navigate just to interact with elephants firsthand. But that first trip to South Africa had changed me in ways that are difficult to articulate. Although the language, accents, native garments and culture are all unfamiliar to me, they felt strangely comforting, and I quickly realized that Africa is the cradle of life, both human and animal. Being back on South African soil felt like a homecoming to me in some unexplainable way.

On the long flight, I read the brochure on KEP's ten elephants, memorizing their names, identifying characteristics, studying their pictures and their personality descriptions. It is not easy to tell the elephants apart, so study is necessary. I could hardly believe I was going to see them in a matter of hours, the excitement preventing me from sleeping through the 16-hour overnight flight. By the time I arrived in Cape Town, I was exhausted and elated and still had another flight to take along the southern coast to George at the heart of the Garden Route.

When I finally arrived at the elephant park, I felt so welcomed by the staff, the guides and the elephants. My time there flew by, and I savored every minute of being out in the field with the elephants. These elephants had much to teach me, and all that was required of me was the willingness to learn from them. The following is the story of my trips to the park and tales of what the elephants taught me, up close and personal.

Any quotations without attribution are a result of the interviews conducted by the author.

1

South Africa's Garden Route

"Africa changes you forever, like nowhere on earth. Once
you have been there, you will never be the same. But how
do you begin to describe its magic to someone who has
never felt it? How can you explain the fascination of this
vast, dusty continent, whose oldest roads are elephant
paths?"—Brian Jackman, *The Last Elephants*

South Africa: Land of Hope

South Africa, the country at the southernmost tip of the African continent, is diverse in its people, its wildlife, habitats and in its
languages. Its pristine coastlines, which include three sides of South
Africa, face great stretches of completely open water. At the southern tip two vast seas of completely different character come together,
blurring the boundaries between the Atlantic and Indian oceans. This
meeting of two oceans in the Cape areas creates a unique microcli-
mate—with its own idiosyncratic weather and its own unique flora—
one that played a critical role in both human and animal evolution.
South Africa is of colonialism and Zulu warfare fame, Nelson Mandela, apartheid and Truth and Reconciliation Commission fame. It is
rich with mineral deposits of diamonds, gold and other jewels and is
home to more than 56,000,000 people. Of the more than 1,000 languages spoken on the African continent, South Africa alone employs
11 official languages. Among them are English, Afrikaans, Zulu and
Xhosa (sometimes spelled Khosa). South Africa borders on Mozambique to the northeast, Zimbabwe, Namibia and Botswana to the north
and west, and it wholly envelops the countries of Lesotho and Eswatini
(formerly Swaziland). Cape Town, one of the largest cities, is the southernmost African settlement before Antarctica. South Africa's topogra-
phy ranges from lush mountainous stretches to the flatter wine country,

The meeting of the Atlantic and Indian oceans creates a unique climate and biosphere known as the Garden Route. Pictured is the beach area at Plettenberg Bay, a 15-minute ride from the Knysna Elephant Park. The Garden Route is one of only six botanical "hotspots" on the planet housing more than 8,000 unique plant species.

hilly sugarcane fields, and pristine beaches. It is approximately the size of the state of Texas.

The Garden Route

The Garden Route is a popular, scenic stretch of highway N2 on the southern coast of South Africa. It lies within the Western Cape Province and stretches from Mossel Bay in the Western Cape to the Storms River toward the Eastern Cape Province. Cape Town, at the westernmost part of the southern tip, is the "Mother City" of South Africa and is famous for its grand-scale Table Mountain which hugs the city at its perimeter. The name Garden Route is derived from the fertile and ecologically diverse vegetation encountered here and the numerous lagoons and lakes dotted along the coast. It includes towns such as Mossel Bay,

1. South Africa's Garden Route

Knysna, Oudtshoorn, Plettenberg Bay and Nature's Valley. George, the Garden Route's largest city and main business area, is the flight destination when visiting the Knysna Elephant Park. It is a short flight from either Cape Town or Johannesburg. From there, KEP is an hour and a half car ride.

There are two main seasons in the Garden Route. One is the rainy season between April and September in which the weather is cooler, in the 50s and 60s, and the dry season between October and March in which the weather is quite warm and often humid. Because South Africa is in the southern hemisphere, the seasons are opposite to that which North America and Europe are experiencing.

Within just 70 years from the time they arrived, the settlement of the Dutch colonizers forever changed the South African culture and landscape. When European settlers first reached the shores of South Africa, the country is estimated to have had 26,000,000 elephants living within its borders. The indigenous copper-skinned Khoi were reduced to half their original population, their economic and political bodies collapsing under Dutch rule. Some Khoi succumbed to smallpox. The rapid decline of the Khoi nation was as mysterious to the colonists as it remains for us. The two groups of settlers battled frequently, and the Dutch continued to poach elephants throughout that period. By the early 1900s, only a few small populations of elephants remained in the area, and in 1919, Major Pretorius shockingly commanded that all the remaining elephants be executed. It is a sad story with many villains, no heroes. By 1931, only 11 elephants remained.

In order to survive, the Khoi needed to maintain possession of their livestock, retain their traditional pastures, be free to make their own decisions, and maintain their own standard of living. The Dutch rendered any of that impossible by absorbing livestock, encroaching on pastures and fields, and forcing indigenous people to live under Dutch (Boer) law while they took advantage of local labor. Without their herds, leaders were looked down upon, and many were forced to work in the colony for food, tobacco and liquor. Thus began the takeover and dissection of Africa by European countries. It is a similar fate to that of the Native American population in the United States, who were senselessly killed, were relegated to live on reservations and continue to be given little assistance or the respect they so deserve for the amazing cultures they developed.

Similarly, several thousand miles north in Kenya, dictator Jean-Bédel Bokassa openly claimed the entirety of the country's elephant population and ivory his personal property, vowing to physically punish to death anyone who came between himself and the elephants and ivory. The profits from his ivory sales to France funded his catastrophic decade-long control of that country.

Khosa, Afrikaans, and English are the languages most commonly spoken in the Garden Route region of South Africa. Listening to the spoken word in Xhosa is an unforgettable experience of rhythmic syllables intermingled with startling clicks and clacks. Mouthfuls of these explosive sounds actually boil down to five distinct clicks and about 140 distinct sounds. Many Khosa words consist of a single syllable, their meanings derived from the order of the clicks rather than from the inflection. The clicks and clacks, unique to the Xhosa language, are represented in written form by symbols. For example, Tsk, is represented in Xhosan writing as a forward leaning slash (/). Pop is a click on the palate of the mouth and is represented as (l). Clip and clop are modified pops called alveolar clicks (consonant that is sounded with the tongue touching or close to the ridge behind the teeth of the upper jaw); or clicks are made when the tongue is near the upper tooth ridge and is recorded as a slash across an equal sign; and Gee is the lateral click, shown as a double slash (///). The smack of a kiss is the labial click, written as a dot inside a zero.

The Afrikaans language is based on Old Dutch but incorporates many words borrowed from local languages and was developed as the Dutch colonized South Africa. The South African nation was the first African country to achieve independence from colonizers. Freedom for black South Africans would have to wait another 84 years.

The Garden Route region is rich with dinosaur fossils and unusual geologic formations. The Heathlands or Fynbos are a unique biome characterized by small or medium-sized bushes growing on the sandy, low-nutrient soil of mountains and flatlands. The fynbos is one of only six botanical "hotspots" on the planet housing more than 8,000 unique plant species. These include many types of giant lobelia, the protea, South Africa's gorgeous national flower, many varieties of lilies, orchids, daisies, verbena, hibiscus, morning glory, jasmine, hyacinths, a myriad of wildflowers and bulbs. Common trees in the area include different kinds of yellowwood, ironwood, stinkwood, several kinds of alders, and blackwood. There are many indigenous animal species, including elephants. Heathland rests on the summit of the Drakensberg mountain chain, the same as the upper levels of Kilimanjaro, Mount Kenya and the Rwenzoris, but the diversity of plant life is far richer in the Cape Fynbos.

2

Loxodonta Africana

"The generation that destroys the environment is not the generation that pays the price. That is the problem."
—Wangari Maathai, *The Last Elephants*

A Brief History of Elephants in Africa

Primitive drawings of elephants appear on ancient cave walls throughout South Africa. Proof of their existence goes back to 55,000,000 years ago on the plains of northern Africa. There were many evolutionary offshoots from this ancestor, and some scientists believe that over 300 different species of trunked animals once roamed the Earth. While all the others have become extinct, today's elephants are the only trunked survivors. Many native tribes regard elephants as a totem animal, displaying an almost religious zeal for these regal creatures. In many myths and religions around the world, the elephant is an important symbolic figure, evident in the countless paintings, carvings and drawings, and other artistic tributes created throughout human history. Elephants are symbolic of strength, determination, peacefulness, and family life. For over 55,000,000 years humans have been their only consistent predators, which, sadly, is still true today.

Elephants are a keystone species, meaning that they are essential in order to maintain the integrity of their ecosystem. They contribute to biodiversity by dispersing seeds through their dung, opening thickets by browsing, making plants and seeds more available to smaller herbivores, promoting nutrient recycling, and making water accessible in dry riverbeds by digging with their tusks and feet.

The Legend of the Knysna Elephants

In the 1600s, European settlers arrived in the Cape area (now Cape Town) of South Africa where elephants roamed free for thousands of years and have been a part of the mystique and magic of this thickly forested land. By 1910, there were fewer than 200 elephants living in the Cape area in four separate herds.

Not more than a few years ago, rumor and occasional sightings indicated there may be one left roaming the dense, hilly forests in Knysna. The forests on the Garden Route are so thick with vegetation that it has been difficult to verify if the lone elephant is still alive. The results of the 2019 study reached the heartbreaking conclusion that there was only one surviving elephant in the Knysna Forest, who is approximately 45 years old and is believed to be the last truly wild, free-roaming elephant in South Africa and most likely the southernmost elephant on planet Earth. The study was conducted by Professor Graham Kerley from the Centre for African Conservation Ecology at Nelson Mandela University. He explains, "There has been a debate for years now about how many Knysna elephants are left, as they are difficult to see or locate. To have it confirmed that there is only one Knysna elephant left is a shock to many as they are surrounded by a deep aura of mystique and mythology, fueled by their elusiveness, and by world famous stories like Dalene Matthee's classic book *Circles in a Forest.*"[1]

To conduct the survey, 72 cameras were deployed at 38 locations within the forest determined to be within the established elephant paths, with a two-second delay between video clips. They were fastened to trees within ten feet of the well-worn elephant paths. The cameras remained in use for 15 months and covered the range evenly, ensuring there were no areas where elephants might hide undetected.[2]

Lizette Moolman, one of the researchers on the study, broke the bad news. "The brutal reality is there is no longer a population of Knysna elephants. All the mystique of the Knysna elephant is reduced to a single elephant left in rather tragic circumstances. Female elephants are not meant to be alone—they spend their lives in family units of related adult females with their calves." She added that the remaining elephant appears to be in reasonably good condition with the exception of her swollen temporal glands with excessive temporal streaming, a kind of sweating related to extreme emotions, suggesting that she is stressed, very possibly the result of being alone. The research study concluded that since the population of the Kynsna elephants is almost extinct, the way scientists manage the last elephant is a very emotional and very serious matter, as she is "a symbol of how we treat biodiversity as a whole."[3]

When interest in the forests was first roused by explorers and travelers, all shipping to the east went around what is now Cape Town. Lumber was in demand for spears and ship repairs. Knysna was geographically able to meet that need, and in 1776, with the Dutch settlers running wood processing facilities, Forestry Department posts were established at George, Knysna and Plettenberg Bay, which lie in successive order from west to east on the southern coast where the Indian and Atlantic oceans meet.

The giants of the animal kingdom are elephants, but they are dwarfed by plant giants, the soaring yellowwood trees with elegant crowns of branches bearing narrow, elliptic dark green leaves draped with gray-green lichen. The largest specimen recorded stands at 140 feet tall and measures almost 30 feet around its trunk, and it is said to be about 800 years old.

For centuries wild elephants lived in these forests undisturbed; today they roam no more. Development in the area and poaching has eliminated them almost completely from the wild. Elephant sanctuaries, such as KEP, have taken a few in. But I repeat: They roam wild no more.

Elephants were viewed as a resource to be exploited. Many believe that any attempts to preserve them were made with an eye toward future exploitation. The Knysna Forest, which lies in the hills surrounding the town of Knysna, is a dense, moist forest, often referred to as a high forest, where the rainfall enables swarming vegetation.

The Knysna elephants avoid areas where they have had a bad experience, say, for example, where their relatives were killed or died. They have always moved directionally and seasonally, preferring to travel well-defined paths between food supplies and watering holes when moving around. Indeed some of the oldest roads in the region are elephant paths. How they can walk through such dense forest is a mystery to me, but they have done so for centuries.

As white settlers began to arrive, with them came woodcutters, farmers, and inevitably hunters. Prior to the arrival of white settlers, the only inhabitants were from the Khoi tribe and some Bushmen. They lived among the elephants without harming the environment until they got the idea to set fires in order to drive large game away from the area. This had a serious effect on the entire ecosystem. White settlers hunted the blue antelope into extinction, and by the late 1880s wiped out the great buffalo herds from this densely forested land.

In the 1970s the Wildlife Society of South Africa made a public statement announcing plans for the conservation of the entire ecosystem in the Knysna area under their control and that all 67,000 acres of the indigenous forest would be classified as a nature reserve. This was very welcome news and made a hopeful case for the remaining Knysna elephants at that time.

The South African governmental groups working on elephant issues considered various options for future management. After much deliberation, the following recommendations were agreed to unanimously. It was felt that because the Knysna elephants are not a distinct subspecies and therefore not scientifically unique, and because the Knysna Forest is of prime importance for conservation since it is the largest indigenous forest in southern Africa, the elephants should be conserved as part of the whole Knysna Forest and fynbos ecosystem. So, the elephants were safe to continue to roam free, but they came in a close second to the group's desire to save the forest. Better to be an afterthought than not a thought at all.

When I asked Noleen Skinstad, daughter of Knysna Elephant Park's (KEP) founders, about the status of the wild Knysna elephants, she clarified with excitement, "A researcher recently found elephant dung on the forest floor and called KEP for our expertise in estimating an elephant's age according to the size of a dung sample. We supplied them with samples of dung from elephants of various ages. There is reportedly at least one wild Knysna elephant with sightings as rare as four-leaf clovers. The study concluded that the identified elephant has been in her forties based on the size of her dung." Noleen continues, "Twenty years ago a helicopter tragically crashed in the Knysna Forest. To this day no one has found the remains of the chopper or its passengers. That shows how dense the forest really is, and adds to the mystery of the Knysna elephants."

The trick to figuring the age of an elephant by measuring its dung is to measure the circumference. If it measures four inches or less, it's definitely a young calf. If the dung ball measures about five inches, you're looking at a young or adolescent elephant. Likewise, if the dung ball measures more than about five inches, it's from a mature elephant. It seems simple enough.

I longed to see the Knysna Forest, to feel its mysteries, take in its dense forestation, and smell the earthy forest scent. Christina Tholander, KEP's volunteer coordinator and lab technician at the on-site Laboratory at KEP, was ready to escort me on the way back from the Sedgefield Farmer's Market. She said it's one of her favorite places in the world. That's saying a lot for Christina, a Danish native who came to South Africa to work at KEP.

2. *Loxodonta Africana*

It was going to be an exciting day away from the park, the first one in two weeks for me. We drove in her small, compact car straight down the coastal N2 highway to the Sedgefield Market, which was fairly large and full of locally grown food, handcrafted items and gift shops. After a delicious breakfast of fresh yogurt with fig sauce, a homemade pastry and coffee, we were ready to walk the market. It was fun to see folks walking around in native clothing and hairstyles, always colorful and beautifully patterned fabrics.

We continued on to the Kynsna Forest. As we drove deeper and deeper into the forest, I began feeling we were dwarfed by the height of the towering yellowwood trees, the thickness of the vegetation, and the grand scale of the forest as a whole compared to the woodlands in my rural home in upstate New York. I tried to imagine elephants walking through this dense forestation. I felt the harsh reality of their absence as we drove the rough dirt road, endlessly winding through 20 miles of tangled forest. It was even bumpier than riding the tractor out into the field at KEP. An elephant could have kept up with Christina's small car, which chugged valiantly uphill, ever deeper into the forest. I felt like I was riding in *The Little Engine That Could*.

And we did! At the top was a small, old house. It had been made into a museum which housed artifacts, an elephant skeleton, and some documents from the 1700s and 1800s related to wood gathering and lumbering in the region. The museum, the size of a two-room house, looked like a relic from the early 1900s. It provided a historical perspective of the forest and the elephants who made it their home for centuries. We signed the register before heading back down the trail, still marveling that elephants could navigate such denseness. As we drove the narrow, rutted road, another car approached us. We had to quickly find two trees spaced far enough apart for us to pull between in order to let the other car pass, not an easy maneuver in the thick Knysna Forest. Back on the road we hoped to be the only car for the rest of the ride downhill, and, luckily, we were.

My parting thoughts when leaving the forest were of what environmentalists call empty forest syndrome. This straightforward name is just that: a forest emptied of the fauna that once lived within its borders. How profoundly sad I am to realize that elephants will never again thrive in these luscious, wooded acres.

Once out of the forest, the sky was bright even though it was an overcast late afternoon, and I realized how much the forest foliage blocked light. We returned to the park by dinnertime feeling satisfied and wrinkled. I was happy to eat my frozen dinner and retire early. My plan was to spend the next day, Sunday, out in the field with the elephants where I could act as a tourist, feeding them by hand and getting closer to them. As I drifted off to sleep, I tried to imagine the park in the early days when Harry and Sally, the park's first elephants, were youngsters tromping about chasing guinea fowl and doves, trumpeting to each other across the large fields. They must have been such beautiful youngsters. The thought of their antics lulled me to sleep.

3

Knysna Elephant Park
(KEP) Is Founded

The Knysna Elephant Park (KEP) was founded in October 1994 by husband and wife team Ian and Lisette Withers. Ian grew up on the family farm near what is now KEP, surrounded by the forest's myths and legends as well as the famous Knysna elephants. Lisette grew up in a suburb of Johannesburg. Sadly, by the time Ian and Lisette settled on their farm just outside Knysna, the elusive Knysna Forest elephants were all but extinct, with fewer than five animals thought to still survive in the thick, tangled woods. At the time of its founding, KEP was the only free-range, controlled elephant facility in all of southern Africa.

It was important to Ian and Lisette that the foundation of the Knysna Elephant Park reflect the struggles of the elephants in the Knysna Forest. Then, in 1994, the young couple heard of two young elephant calves rescued from a cull in the Kruger National Park who were in need of a safe home. Ian took this as an important opportunity to return elephants to the Knysna area. Lisette, a highly spirited, determined woman, was always devoted to animals. She was quick to come to the rescue of these young orphans. There was no question in her mind that they would live on the family farm. This young elephant pair highlighted the conservation needs of elephants in the nearby forests. The rest is history.

Harry and Sally, named for the 1989 movie *When Harry Met Sally*, starring Meg Ryan and Billy Crystal, arrived at the park in October 1994. Little did Ian and Lisette realize how this small family would blossom. It did not take long for word to spread throughout South Africa that the Knysna Elephant Park was a sanctuary that would take in elephants in need of a good home.

More than a quarter of a century later, more than 40 elephants have passed through the gates of the park, which has developed from a small field shack into a world-class elephant facility with a research laboratory on the premises that offers vital information on captive elephants, their behavior, needs, and well-being in the spirit of helping all elephants. Also on the premises is a world-class, four-star hotel which overlooks the night camps where the elephants stay for the night, restaurant, AERU volunteer and research center, curio shop, housing for some employees, and a wedding chapel. And hundreds of acres of land for grazing.

"I was terrified of Harry and Sally when they first arrived," admits Alex Vipond, Lisette's younger brother. He remembers, "None of us knew anything about elephants, and Harry would go chasing ostriches on the farm next door. I would often play hide and seek with Harry and ride on his back as he trumpeted, running into the field. We had such fun!" Alex's deep love for Harry is apparent in his wistful smile. "Among the elephants that have passed through this park are calves rescued from culls, elephants relocated from reserves where conflicts with rhino threatened their survival, a tiny calf searching for milk after losing her mother in a translocation, orphaned and abandoned calves from reserves and zoos, animals no longer wanted by their owners as they were seen to be unworkable—they have all found a home with the Knysna Elephant Park 'family.' The KEP family extends well beyond the physical borders of the park, in fact it extends internationally. Some of the elephants have settled here, becoming part of our resident herd. Others have moved on to less restrictive facilities and reserves where they now roam more freely and can start their own new families," Alex reminisces.

"Our management style is what we call a 'controlled, free-range environment,' which allows our elephants as much freedom and choices as possible, within the borders of the Park," Alex continues. "Our elephants know they can gather at specific points should they want to feast from the snack buckets filled with fruit that guests bring. Following this feeding session, the elephants are free to move away and graze, browse, wallow, or play. Guests are then invited to follow the elephants and enjoy their time in amongst the herd observing and learning about elephant biology and behavior. This type of management is unique and is not found anywhere else in South Africa," Alex states proudly.

KEP plays a leading and vital role in formulating regulations and guidelines for captive elephants throughout South Africa. They even work toward challenging and changing traditionally accepted management practices to better suit the welfare of captive elephants. Alex concludes, "The Park has strict guidelines which steer all tourism activities, so that animal welfare is never compromised, and insures that the impact of tourism on the elephants is a positive one. The handling of elephants at KEP is conducted according to internationally recognized standards. All activities are conducted ethically and responsibly, in line with Best Practice Guidelines for captive elephants."

How do you measure the welfare of elephants in a free choice yet captive environment? Part of evaluating well-being involves determining behavioral and physiological responses to stressors which reflect an elephant's state of mind and things external to the animal that we might assume will affect them by causing stress. Researcher J. Veasey suggests, "An absence of proof of suffering cannot be viewed as a proof of an absence of suffering, and as a result, it may be reasonable to take a precautionary approach to welfare in certain circumstances."[1] Animal welfare advocates created what they call the Five Freedoms in Animal Welfare. Developed to help simplify adequate welfare standards, they were originally developed for farm animals. These five freedoms are freedom from pain, injury and disease; freedom from hunger, thirst and malnutrition; freedom to express most "normal" behaviors; freedom from discomfort; and freedom from fear and distress. Clearly these standards ought to apply to all living creatures.

＊　＊　＊

Noleen also has so many fond memories of young Harry and Sally and of her mother, who all but slept outside with the young ones until they were acclimated. Noleen explains that Harry and Sally were survivors of a cull at Kruger National Park. But there was a third musketeer, Willie, whom Sally was very bonded to. Willie died of malnutrition before the transport was able to take place, and Sally grieved deeply. In addition to the loss of Willie, both elephants probably witnessed their mothers killed before their very eyes. "You see, my parents were in the construction business for a long while and when building slowed down, they lost the business. So here I was at 10 years old, suddenly these adorable baby elephants appeared, while not one of us knew anything about taking care of them! We had to build a boma (shelter area) in order to keep them comfortable and in a large but restricted daytime area until they became comfortable with their new surroundings—and the people. They had no trust in people after their traumatic ordeals. Mom was with them morning until night and gradually built up a sense of trust with both Harry and Sally."

Noleen continues, "One day mom announced in her characteristically sudden way 'today is the day we're letting them out,' and so they were let out first for an hour or so, then two hours, then four, and so on. Mom amazed me. She hadn't developed skills to deal with elephants, but she forged bonds between herself and these two babies, they had everything they needed—food, love, and a safe environment."

"Perhaps the wild isn't always free," Noleen stated sadly and softly. She spoke of an elephant she knew called Tandora who was set free from a Bloemfontein Zoo after decades of confined space and living alone. "She lost the ability to care for herself and she just died. In 2005 there was a controlled burn in nearby Pilanesberg. The burn got out of hand and ended up killing some disoriented elephants. Mom was called away to help those elephants who had burns and she stayed for 3½ months, living on site to care for these wounded victims. She left her own elephants home in order to care for these burn victims. After her return, the park began providing homes to ellies in need. We had no fences back then," continued Noleen.

"When Harry was still a baby, we put him in a truck and took him to the beach, because ... well, why not! Harry walked along in the sand and a sea gull came near and startled him. It was the funniest thing to watch! Mom brought the ellies to school, a sort of show and tell, in order to educate teachers and students about elephants. Harry has even travelled in order to breed. The park's first visitors were school groups on educational trips. When the children would come to the park, they could buy a small bag of snacks such as fruit and popcorn for the elephants, the size bag my licorice came in, for 10 rand (about $.70). As a child, I painted the original sign for the ticket office all by myself," she boasts.

Noleen recalls one elephant they had at the park named Satara, who would get jealous when Noleen got too close to Lizette because, after all, he believed Mrs. Withers was *his* mother. "He insisted on standing in between mom and I," Noleen recalls with a smile.

Several years later, Alex went to the Riddles' school of elephant handling in Arkansas. There he was taught about the use of tethers to help control elephants. Independent-minded Alex believes, however, that if elephants are taught at a young enough age, tethers are unnecessary. "The best way to be successful in training elephants," according to Alex, "is by using positive reinforcement." It's much like the limbo bar to teach an elephant to lie down using a horizontal item like a yardstick or cane, gradually lowering it while verbalizing the command loud and clearly, then rewarding the elephant with food every time it listens. He firmly trusts that if they are rewarded with food, reassurance and patience, they will eventually learn what you are teaching them. "It may take a bit longer than other methods, but it's the only humane way. The trainer should always stand on the left side. The elephants are trained with touch and voice commands. The voice commands are mostly in English, but our elephants understand a few Xhosa words," Alex shared.

When asked about some of the parks where elephants are said to be "wild," Alex responded, "Even immense parks like Kruger, South Africa's largest national park, aren't truly wild. They are managed by humans and have fences surrounding them. Although Kruger is larger than the countries of Wales and Israel, it is not truly wild."

He lists a few of the commands Sally's herd of elephants know: turn right, turn left, stretch down, get up, back up, trunk up, trunk down, flap ears, cross feet (both ways) and head up. He also believes in the importance of each guide having a firm bond with each elephant in case the preferred handler isn't there on a given day. And he believes that daily training is not only beneficial for the elephants to practice commands but for elephants to strengthen the bond with their handlers and vice versa.

He leaves me to return to the field with the thought, "Those who work with elephants are family to each other. We all have to know how to read the elephants. Some days you can see that an elephant is not up to training for some reason. If you give them love they will love you back. They won't attack unless provoked."

Noleen reminisces, "Mom's mission has always been to give a home to elephants in need. She studied at a place called Riddles in Arkansas, prior to Alex studying there, where she learned some practical handling skills, elephant care and behavioral strategies. It was then that she realized the serious lack of research available on captive elephants. For our family it was never about this being a business, but at the end of the day someone has to pay for what they (the elephants) need." Noleen and her Uncle Alex have taken a more active role in managing the park as Mr. and Mrs. Withers begin to step back. From listening to their adventures while growing up with elephants, it is clear that they consider Harry and Sally as family members, siblings in a sense, whom they have known most of their lives.

The family has welcomed thousands of visitors to the park over the years, giving them highly unique insight, knowledge and priceless interactions with elephants. Guests are privileged to have an up close and personal encounter with these gentle giants and leave with a healthy admiration for these amazing animals, as well as a better understanding of the African elephant and its plight across the continent and through history. The Knysna Elephant Park has dedicated more than a quarter of a century to elephant welfare and research; and it is both nationally and internationally recognized as one of the best captive elephant facilities in the world.

KEP has been a leader in the formulation of regulations and guidelines for captive elephants throughout South Africa as well as other African nations. The park has had a profoundly positive effect on elephants everywhere. The management team has even worked toward challenging and changing traditionally accepted management to better suit the welfare needs of captive elephants. And it provides employment for almost 100 people in an area where poverty is prevalent, educational opportunities for students, volunteer opportunities and allows these ten elephants to be ambassadors to the world for their species.

African Elephant Research Unit (AERU) Is Born, October 2009

Mrs. Withers realized that in order to better understand her elephants' behaviors and what is needed for their ultimate best welfare, research was the answer. Together, the Withers founded AERU under the umbrella of the Knysa Elephant Park. AERU was the first elephant research unit dedicated to optimizing the welfare of captive elephants in South Africa. AERU's mission is to promote ethical and non-harmful research of captive elephants, guide the management of captive elephant operations through science and research, and provide information relevant to wild elephants to improve their protection and conservation. Their slogan is, "Conservation through Education." The unique collaboration between the Park and AERU is unusual and translates to research guiding elephant management, a welfare-based concept. The AERU now collaborates with local and international researchers on a variety of elephant issues, from nutrition and reproduction to communication, behavior and welfare and conducts its own groundbreaking research into elephant behavior, welfare and husbandry. It is a nonprofit research trust dedicated to the advancement and dissemination of information relating to all aspects of the biology, behavior and husbandry of African elephants, with particular reference to their welfare and management in captive facilities.

Enter Dr. Debbie Young, affectionately called Dr. Debbie by all who

3. Knysna Elephant Park (KEP) Is Founded

know her. Debbie was working with whales in the Eastern Cape area and suddenly found herself out of a job. An acquaintance knew that KEP was looking for someone with her type of zoology degree and put them touch. She has been the senior researcher from 2009 until 2019. She admits that switching animal expertise was a big adjustment at first but doesn't regret it for a second. Under her direction, the park has taken in needy elephants and discharged some to a more open living situation, completed pioneering research on elephant behavior, hormones, husbandry, food and nutrition, and interfaced with park management, regional and national entities on behalf of improving elephant wellness. A slight woman with an auburn ponytail and a field jacket at all times, she can be seen walking around the park at a fast clip, always on a mission and always smiling. She is clearly a woman who loves her work. At the end of the workday, she pauses to feed the dozens of ducks, black and white swans and speckled guinea hens in the pond on site, and they run toward her quacking up a storm, flapping their wings in glee. There is no doubt she is able to communicate with all kinds of animals.

When it was clear that the research unit needed more of a workforce, Debbie set out to find a research officer. Enter Clare Padfield, who studied at Exeter University in the United Kingdom and came to KEP to do research after working with Griffon Vultures in Croatia. Among her challenges was to research whether interaction with tourists during the day affects elephant behavior at night. Elephant researchers being as rare as pink elephants, Debbie pulled Clare into AERU, much to Clare's delight. A true scientist at heart, Clare will greet you with a brilliant smile and explain the most difficult research in totally understandable terms, with a large dollop of humor and a wry smile on the side.

Ongoing AERU projects include collecting information on captive elephants based at KEP and sister facilities. This includes records of biological, anatomical, veterinary, physiological, behavioral and dietary data for each individual animal in its care. AERU researchers and volunteers collect these data, not only to establish values for all elephants but also to coordinate and assimilate multidisciplinary research on the behavior, ecology, anatomy and physiology of these mammoth mammals. Several studies have followed the progress of animals as they are prepared for and moved to new facilities.

Researchers and volunteers observe the elephants out in the field or in the boma, taking data throughout the day and often at night. These activities provide insight into all aspects of elephant life. AERU uses an ethogram (which is behavioral by definition), a study plan of a people or culture, specifically developed by AERU staff for captive or domesticated elephants. The data are not only used to establish baseline values for all elephants but also to coordinate and assimilate multidisciplinary research on the behavior, condition, and physiology of these outsized mammals, particularly in relation to the tourism activities conducted within various facilities.

What does AERU do with a database as enormous as an elephant? They investigate long-term patterns of change in elephant behavior, which may evolve over time as they age and mature, and they build up longitudinal records of every aspect of the lives of these ten individual elephants who live at KEP. And they also establish, test and refine research protocols which can then be applied dynamically to address new hypotheses. Through the collection of these data, AERU is able to develop a type of "welfare index for elephants," placing emphasis on balancing the welfare needs of the elephants with the tourism activities of the captive facilities in the best possible way. AERU provides a platform from which to guide management via research, giving regular feedback and assessments to management. Not only do these data provide valuable insight into all African elephants; they allow for unparalleled insight into individual elephants, within specific facilities, under varying management styles.

All captive elephant owners in SA are subject to regular governmental inspections and must adhere to strict norms and standards. AERU's vision is to promote data collection sessions to any elephant facility that may be interested in learning more about the elephants in their care. AERU can conduct research sessions at elephant facilities throughout southern Africa with the aim of providing baseline data pertaining to those elephants and how the animals respond to management within their own unique environments.

Research on captive elephants is particularly valuable for a number of reasons. It provides us with a valuable opportunity for participation in research and education programs, often allowing for the collection of data not readily available from wild animals. From a research perspective the value of the KEP elephants and others AERU has interacted with includes two main factors. The first is that they are not captive animals as they maintain a free-ranging nature, showing a certain degree of "choice" in what they eat, where they move, who they socialize with and how they behave. The age-size-sex composition of the group allows for vital insight into assessment of behavior, socialization, physiology, and other biological factors for a wide spectrum of animals. The nature of the elephants at KEP allows for them to be closely observed and monitored, consequently allowing for research initiatives not easily carried out on elephants in the wild. This allows the formulation of a variety of research protocols for both wild and captive elephants.

Secondly, sampling and data collection have been implemented and standardized first at the KEP facility. Following this, there are opportunities to expand the research program to include other captive elephant facilities which would allow them to include and compare a larger number of animals in a wider variety of habitats. The ultimate goal is for AERU's research to provide valuable insight into the lives of elephants and provide information that may be used to improve and upgrade the management of elephants who live in reserves and promote the protection as well as conservation of wild elephants.

The hands-on nature of AERU's research makes it possible to make ongoing contributions to elephant welfare on a daily basis and ensure that elephants receive the best possible care. In a world where more and more emphasis is being placed on responsible tourism and ethical wildlife interactions, this type of research and interactive science is vital to the well-being of elephants everywhere.

As an example of science informing welfare, KEP management has taken the advice of the research unit and made changes to many of the diet and feeding practices, changes in the way tourists interact with the elephants, the improvement of shelters, and improved handling and training techniques.

Visitors to the park enable KEP/AERU to give their elephants the best possible care, facilities, and nutrition. They also enable the park to offer a home to other elephants in need of a better life. And most importantly, visitors come away with in-depth knowledge and personal, up close experience of these special "ambassadors for all elephants" and can help spread the world about saving this endangered species when they return back to their homes and communities.

Among the activities tourists can participate in at KEP are walks with the elephants in which guests can walk alongside the footsteps of giants, daily tours during which they can hand-feed fruit to the elephants, all the while interacting with the elephants on the elephant's terms. Up close and personal is what the experience is about. The elephants have freedom to choose where they want to move, what they want to eat and who they want to interact with. There is also a lodge attached to the boma, or night shelter, where guests can stay and observe the elephants' nighttime behavior close-up from a balcony for as long as they wish. In a comfortably cozy lounge with a window separating the sleeping elephants from them, lodge guests can watch the elephants browse, feed and slumber under the red glow of ultraviolet light. It is an amazingly calming and fascinating experience.

Knowing the tractor schedule at the park is just as critical as if I were living in a big city with the need to navigate with punctuality, which is taken seriously here. In order to be in the field in time to relieve others, one has to plan to be ready for the tractor's arrival at the main building in enough time for the ride to the field. Some days the ellies are grazing at the farthest points of the park.

During daytime tours, tractors leave every half hour to and from the field. Guests are transported to see the elephants in the field by a tractor which pulls a trailer of seats. There they have the opportunity to interact, feed and walk among these gentle giants. Responsible and educational interactions enable guests to appreciate the awe-inspiring presence of these amazing creatures on the elephants' terms. The park setting encourages these elephants to behave naturally. Once out in the field, guests may linger as long as they wish to be among Sally and her herd. The views of the Outeniqua Mountains to one side of the park are as majestic as the elephants themselves as is the legendary Knysna Forest to the other side.

All About Ethograms

Ethograms are lists of behaviors specific to a species or culture being studied and the function of each behavior. They are in effect master lists of all known behaviors for that species. In the human world, we call these Functional Behavioral Assessments, or FBAs, in which we investigate the antecedent, the behavior itself and the consequence of the behavior in order to determine what the person gains from continuing the behavior. KEP developed its own ethogram, developed with captive elephants in mind. Clare says, "We've carefully developed the ethogram and created codes so that when taking data with the elephants in the field, the behaviors can be recorded quickly. We develop a hypothesis, test it, record the behaviors of interest and do correlational studies."

Clare continues, "An experimental ethogram is a refinement of this list into behaviors that are relevant to the hypothesis being tested. Experimental ethograms are usually constructed to be exclusive and exhaustive. An exclusive ethogram is one in which every behavior is performed by the animal and can be categorized as only one behavior in the ethogram. In other words, the animal can only be recorded as doing one thing at a time. An exclusive ethogram can define a behavior by exclusion. For example, the stances involved in the functions of standing, alert, and sleep are very similar, so the definitions for each involve exclusionary statements so that the observer can distinguish them."

In contrast, an exhaustive ethogram is one in which every behavior modeled by the animal has a category in the ethogram, normally achieved in an experimental ethogram by lumping all the behaviors that are not of relevance to the hypothesis. This greatly speeds recording of actions as behaviors irrelevant to the hypothesis can simply be discounted.

4

The Health and
Physiology of Elephants

"I have a memory like an elephant. In fact, elephants often consult me."—Noel Coward

"It is hard to believe that something weighing ten tons, carrying unwieldy columns of ivory over six feet long, breathing ten times a minute, having a seventy pound heart that beats every two seconds and a stomach fueled by three hundred gallons of methane a day, maintaining over two hundred square feet of rough skin in contact with the environment while dealing at the same time with another 300 pounds of restless trunk—could be very silent for even a second. But it can. We didn't move a muscle for what must have been several minutes, and never heard a sound."—Lyall Watson

Within the elephant kingdom on planet Earth, there are two types of elephants. The African and Asian elephants diverged from their common ancestor, the woolly mammoth, about 17,000,000 years ago. In comparison, humans diverged from our predecessor hominids about 6,000,000 years ago. The African elephants, which this book is about, have much larger bodies and ears and are less prone to have pink on their necks and ears than Asian elephants. Their ears are shaped like the African continent, while Asian elephants have smaller ears which resemble the shape of India. The ears of the African elephant are three times the size of the Asian elephant's. African elephants have a two-fingered tip to the trunk, allowing it to perform a pincer grasp, which for humans is putting the thumb and pointer fingers together. Asian elephants have only one finger at the tip of the trunk. Both male and female African elephants have tusks. The male's tusk is typically longer. Asian male elephants have tusks which are curvier and thicker than the African species, and female Asian elephants have very small tusks or none at all.

4. The Health and Physiology of Elephants

The skin of an Asian elephant is thinner and has less hair than an African elephant.

The African elephant, or *Loxodonta africana* as they are called in the scientific community, is listed as "vulnerable status" or endangered in animal conservation circles. There are two subspecies of African elephants: the savanna, or bush elephant, and the Forest elephant. Savanna elephants are larger than their forest cousins. Forest elephants are smaller, darker, and their tusks are straighter and point downward. Differences in the size and shape of the skull and skeleton also exist between the two subspecies. Forest elephants are uniquely adapted to the forested habitat of the Congo Basin, which is considerably farther north of South Africa but whose numbers are rapidly decreasing due to poaching for ivory. Estimates show that about one-quarter to one-third of the total African elephant population is made up of forest elephants.

* * *

It takes a sturdy skeleton to support the bulky weight of an elephant, a rib cage roomy enough to fit a four-wheeler, a skull the size of a generator, yet the elephant moves with a distinct plod, at times a striding gait. The skeleton of an elephant weighs about 16.5 percent of the total body weight, whereas a cow's skeleton only weighs about 10 percent of their total body weight. The backbone is the mechanism by which soft tissues are "hung," consists of sturdy vertebrae with high, strong neural spines in the chest or thoracic area. Like humans, the elephant has an almost vertical pelvis that is greatly expanded. Their enormous leg bones are placed directly above one another rather than at angles as in other mammals such as dogs and cats. They can be thought of as table legs rather than traditional mammalian legs. This design enables them to sleep standing up, which they do most of the time, with their legs rigidly locked.

According to Dr. Debbie, "The respiratory system of the elephant is quite exceptional in a number of ways. The elephant lacks a pleural cavity, and so the lungs are directly attached to the walls of the chest cavity and to the diaphragm. Thus, respiratory movements are solely dependent on the muscles of the chest, since there is no mechanism of inflating the lungs by negative pressure in the pleural cavity, as in all other mammals. As a result of this, the elephant would find it difficult to breathe if any restraint or pressure is placed on the movement of the chest and diaphragm, eventually suffocating from its own huge weight."

Debbie continues,

"The ribs extend along most of the backbone and form an enormous barrel-shaped cage. The limbs are composed of segments in direct line with one another resulting in a rigid pillar of support for the huge mass of the elephant. It is thought that an elephant walks on four thick and upright pillars, which are long in the upper segment and short in the lower. Also, the majority of the marrow cavities in the leg bones have been replaced with a spongy bone aiding in the leg's great strength without adding much weight. As in all mammals, elephants have seven neck vertebrae. Unlike other herbivores, the elephant's vertebrae evolved to have fused and relatively flat discs, which support the weight of the elephant's tusks and head. The neck is relatively short and has a huge double spine originating from the second vertebra. The head of the Asian elephant is the highest part of the animal due to the fact that it is held at a 45-degree angle to the neck. African elephant necks are positioned horizontally. Also, elephants do not possess a collarbone. The massive shoulder blades provide support for muscles from the forelimbs."

There are distinct differences between male and female African elephants. For example, Sally's forehead profile is angular, while the shape of Mashudu's profile is rounded at the forehead. Males (bulls) are heavier and taller, reaching up to 13 feet and can weigh up to eight tons, while females (cows) reach about eight and a half feet and weigh up to about six tons. Males also tend to have larger tusks.

The Fifth Appendage: An Elephant's Trunk

With tusks symbolizing aspects of power and dominance, an elephant's other most recognizable features are their oversized ears and their trunk, a highly unique feature in the animal kingdom. Their multipurpose trunks function to create a variety of trumpeting, squealing and screams, can lift hundreds of pounds, grasp a single piece of popcorn on the ground, inspect a stick, feather, or leaf, spray, scratch, sniff, caress to reassure their young, spar, fight, feed, drink, and take in and expel water. Since it has an astoundingly unlimited range of motion, an elephant can use its trunk for attack or defense and is capable of hurling a human 30 yards. The elephant's trunk can function as a snorkel during swims, a water hose to shower itself and others on a hot day, a hand, nose, or weapon strong enough to smash a lion or tiger to the ground.

Dr. Debbie explains that the elephant's trunk is formed by a combination of the nose, upper lip and some facial muscles. The trunk is boneless: the two nostril tubes are surrounded by approximately 60,000 "units" divided into six major muscle groups, which are responsible for the amazing dexterity of the trunk as well as its strength. By comparison, the human body has only 639 muscles in all! An elephant can lift 4.5 percent of its own weight with its trunk!

"Within the nasal cavity of an elephant are 7 turbinates which are scrolls of bones with sensitive tissues used to detect smell and which contain concentrations of millions of receptor cells. In comparison, dogs, known for their superior sense of smell, have only 5 turbinates. Elephants breathe through two nostrils at the end of their trunks as well as through their mouths," continues Dr. Debbie. "The trunk is also used to get water and food. To get water, the elephant sucks water into the trunk, then curls the trunk toward its mouth and squirts the water into it. Once an elephant is weaned, everything it eats or drinks is put in the mouth by the trunk. It can also retain water or dust in the trunk without having to hold its breath."

As we know, the African elephant has two small projectiles opposite each other at the tip of the trunk which function as fingers or opposable digits. They can pick up an item as small as a pine cone or peanut with their trunks because of this unusual dexterity. The elephant's trunk combines dexterity with a keen sense of touch and smell. It can bend or curve in any direction, providing an almost unlimited range of motion all coordinated by over 100,000 interconnected longitudinal and radial muscles. No, that was not a typo! That is more muscles in one appendage than in the entire human body! And yet it is highly sensitive.

Nicki Milachowski, AERU's former research assistant and volunteer administrator, adds that it takes baby elephants from six to nine months to learn to use their trunk optimally. They eat and nurse with their mouth until they master the use of those thousands of muscles in their trunks. Socially, elephants use their trunks to show affection and to comfort one another. When they greet each other, their trunks often enter the mouth of the other in an intimate but not sexual way, and often they stand face to face with trunks entwined, one of the most touching sights I've ever seen. It is truly breathtaking. Elephants also use their trunks socially for play-wrestling, caressing during courtship and for dominance displays. A raised trunk can be a threat, or raising the trunk up in the air and swiveling it like a periscope, an elephant can determine the location of fellow elephants, predators and food and water sources. A lowered trunk can be a sign of submission. The trunk is also used in communication. It not only helps to produce sound, but by laying it on

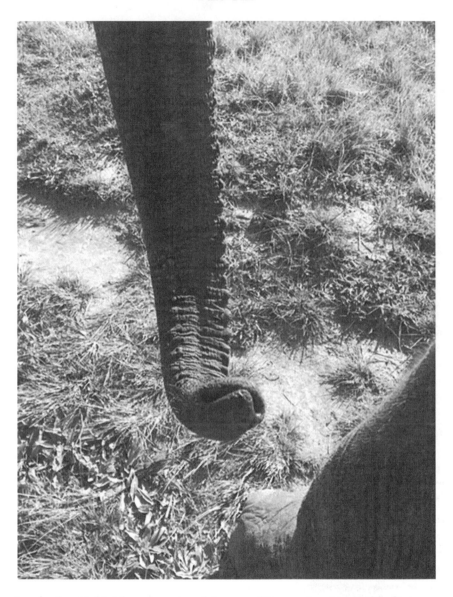

An elephant's highly unique trunk is one of its most recognizable features. An African elephant's trunk has two "fingers" at the end which are opposable digits that aid in picking up something as small as a peanut. The trunk combines dexterity with a keen sense of touch and smell. It can bend or curve in any direction, providing an almost unlimited range of motion all coordinated by over 100,000 interconnected longitudinal and radial muscles.

the ground, the elephant trunk is also able to pick up sensitive infrasonic messages, vibrations which travel through the ground from other animals. Elephants can also use their trunks to defend themselves by flailing it at unwanted intruders or grasping and throwing them like we might toss a napkin.

Trunk straight out is often a signal of the elephant sniffing for clues of activity in the environment or reaching for an object.

Trunk curled at the tip can be a nervous sign, self-soothing, or an "I'm thinking" gesture.

Behavior ecology is the study of the evolutionary basis for animal behavior. Geneticists have recently discovered that all current life on Earth evolved from a single organism or common ancestors which originated 3,500,000,000 years ago. The organism is referred to as the Last

Universal Common Ancestor or LUCA.[1] My how we've changed since then! Contrary to the adage that we look worse as we grow older, evolutionarily we are looking better all the time! Caitlin O'Connell points out in *Wild Rituals* that she shares 50 percent of her genes with the banana she had with her breakfast this morning and 98 percent of our genes with our nearest relatives, the chimpanzees.[2]

Speaking of evolutionary changes, Lyall Watson, a South African elephant expert and author, explains that elephants adapted through evolution so that as they became taller and larger, their trunks grew longer, enabling them to reach food and water at ground level yet also reach leaves in treetops. Similarly, giraffes solved their evolutionary tallness issue by growing longer necks so they too could reach food on the ground or high in treetops.

Watson notes that an elephant's trunk is even more dexterous than a human hand. He writes that the trunk of an elephant, when combined with an elephant's problem solving capacity, can pick up fronds of palm to use as a flyswatter or collect and prepare twigs small enough to remove ticks from between the folds of their wrinkled, leathery skin. Watson refers to the trunk as the "fifth limb" of the elephant, separating them physiologically from every hoofed animal and providing them with unbelievable dexterity. He was among the first to believe that this capability in turn created complicated brain adaptations that mirror the complexity of the human brain.[3]

As an elephant grazes or feeds, its trunk is in continuous motion. Their trunk enables them to select parts of plants or specific leaves, clean food by grasping it and wiping it on grass or other vegetation to tease out dirt particles, fold and manipulate food items into rolls or bundles, much like making burritos. Elephants can even use fibrous material to plug up holes made in search of water, access water in deep fissures, spray water and mud over their bodies (or ours if we are too close), manufacture tools by taking a rock, for example, and continuously rubbing it against hard tree bark or another rock, and manipulate the tools they create. Using branches as flyswatters and cleverly manipulating logs to neutralize electric fences is a demonstration of the extraordinary problem-solving ability of the elephant. It is pretty ingenious when you think about it. The elephant can use the strength of its trunk to push over sizable trees, strip bark with the help of its tusks, lift logs as heavy as a quarter of a ton, and they can use their trunks as deadly weapons to down an adult lion or a human. In *Elephant Destiny*, Martin Meredith writes about a man who witnessed an elephant cow pull a 15-foot-long crocodile from the water with her trunk wrapped around its tail, hurl it like a cowboy hurling a lasso and bash it against a tree trunk for five minutes. Given the huge range of functions performed by the trunk, if an elephant severs or severely injures its trunk, it may very well starve to death.[4]

Many zookeepers have reported elephants who, like Houdini, have figured out how to open locks and escape. Some trainers in Asia have reported that despite the fact that their elephants wear bells to assist in finding them in the dark, some elephants have figured out how to silence the bells by applying mud so they can sneak into a farm field in the dark to feast on fresh produce. Unfortunately for elephants, these capabilities make them useful to humans. In World War II, elephants were enlisted to help clear forests, harvest teakwood in Burma, and walk in caravans up and over steep mountains carrying heavy equipment and manpower.

The trunk of an elephant is also part of its extensive vocal tract and is critical to communication by making high-frequency sounds as well as loud trumpeting. We now have scientific proof that elephants are also capable of making sounds outside the spectrum of human ears. Elephants have been able to mimic sounds including the sound of a truck engine and some human sounds. Indian elephants have the unique ability to make a distinct chirping sound. When an Asian elephant was placed in a zoo with an African elephant, the latter was able to figure out how to make the same chirping sound as the former, one that is not native to them.

The elephant's trunk is sometimes used as an early warning system—at the first sign of danger or uncertainty, Sally's trunk is raised to gain information from scents in the air. Often other trunks follow suit. Since elephants have poor eyesight, their trunk provides them with much of the information they need to gather in order to negotiate their surroundings safely. Their keen sense of smell helps compensate for the elephant's generally poor vision. It takes infant and toddler elephants a very long time—years—to master the use of their ever-moving trunks and the musculature within them.

Elephants have a repertoire of more than 40 calls or vocalizations. Some are the high-frequency trumpets, for which they are famous; others are screams, bellows, roars and rumbles. Usually when matriarch Sally "rumbles," all it means is "let's go, let's move on from here," whereas at other times it can signal aggression. While humans with good hearing ability can pick up sounds with a frequency range as low as 20 Hz, many rumbles made by elephants occur within frequencies between one and 20 Hz, meaning that we humans cannot hear them. Forest elephants have been recorded as making calls to other elephants as low as five Hz, or two octaves below the lowest sounds that most humans can hear. When using infrasound, elephants often combine low-frequency calls with high sound pressure levels, as high as 115 decibels, close to the level of amplified rock and roll music. Because low-frequency sounds can travel greater distances than high frequencies of the same pressure level and are less affected by forests and other barriers, this gives elephants an effective means of long-distance communication of up to six miles, sometimes more depending on weather conditions. Elephants on the receiving end of the infrasonic messages pick up on their vibrations through the pads in their feet. Elephants generate and can detect the widest range of frequency sounds of any animal. A listening posture is standing with one foot up so the heavy side has more contact with the ground and can better pick up infrasonic messages. According to author Michael Garstang, the inverse relationship between the length and mass of an elephant's vocal folds proves that it is capable of producing lower-frequency sounds than any other animal on the planet.[5]

Elephants have an uncanny ability to detect impending danger. In 2004, Asian elephants showed evidence that they sensed a tsunami approaching 10 to 60 minutes prior to its arrival. On the beach in Thailand several Asian elephants were chained to stakes driven into the ground. They reportedly screamed, broke the restraining chains, pulled the stakes out of the ground and ran to high ground well in advance of the tsunami's arrival. Other studies have shown evidence that elephants may be able to detect TNT in leftover landmines in war-torn countries such as Angola, which warrants more research. Combining memory with sound making, scientists have proven that elephants have been able to recognize vocalizations or "voices" of about 40–60 other elephants. In one experiment, researchers found that when playing a recording of an elephant who had died a year prior, surviving family members reacted to hearing her call by stopping what they were doing and lowering their heads.

Incidentally, chemical communication is an important part of the elephant language. Secretions of fatty acids and pheromones are signals for herd mates to read how another elephant is feeling. It is a shorthand way of communicating emotion.

You may have heard about elephants producing paintings to be sold to raise money for their own conservation cause. Indeed, some elephants can and do paint in abstract ways. When not required to draw a prescribed image that they have been trained for, and allowed artistic freedom, painting should be a form of enrichment, an opportunity to reduce stress and provide stimulation through the use of color and shape. Many elephants have been cruelly trained to draw what their mahouts think the public wants to see. But some clearly enjoy painting abstract colors, lines and dots in freeform, and this practice should be encouraged.

Michael Garstang writes, in *Elephant Sense and Sensibility*, "The execution in which successive brushstrokes made with apparent confidence, combined to create a coherent composition, raises serious questions as to the origin and conception of the ultimate product. Does the elephant have such a completed image formulated in her mind? If so, such an achievement calls upon some of the higher forms of neural processes. Observing the actual creation of the image by the elephant strongly suggests that the equivalent of a mental picture preexists."[6]

Many elephants have been observed "drawing" with sticks or sharp pebbles in the mud. These can be classified as abstract or scribbling, but upon closer examination, those who were given paper and a pencil stayed within the paper boundaries and drew highly original compositions. The lines appear deliberate. The famous abstract artist Willem de Kooning said of some elephant drawings he was asked to evaluate that he was "struck by their flair, decisiveness and originality," adding that they were created by a "damned talented elephant."

The well-known American Psychologist Howard Gardner detected progress in the cognitive development of paintings done by Siri, an Indian elephant. Given a paper and pencil, Siri would create dozens of designs, all staying within the confines of the paper. Gardner, an expert in the development of cognition and creative ability extensively studied the development of children's drawings and the ways they mirror cognitive and emotional development. He reflected cognitive advancement in the quality of lines, shapes and overall designs in Siri's work.[7]

Regardless of whether or not you consider these works of art, there is intentional and vital engagement on the part of the elephants ... to say nothing of the healing value of working with color and form and just being creative. This is an area ripe for future study.

Tuskmania: The White Gold of the Infamous Tusks

The word "elephant" is derived from the Greek *elephas*, which originally referred to the ivory but became representative of the whole animal. An African elephant is born with four tiny deciduous incisors, which are the equivalent of milk teeth in human babies. The fairly small first and second teeth become visible shortly after birth, while the third and fourth remain below the gum line. These are replaced by permanent tusks at age 6 to 13 years old. Not for decoration, they have many highly important functions. Tusks are used as tools and as weapons, for digging, fighting, prying and resting one's trunk on. Although tusks are highly useful, some elephants can and do live without them. Sally, our matriarch, was born with only one tusk and will live her days as matriarch with little consequence.

Tusks grow continuously through an elephant's life at a rate of five to seven inches per year. They are composed mainly of dentin, the same substance which human teeth are made of, and like ours, are garnished with a dollop of enamel. Tusks begin to jut out when the elephant reaches about two or three years of age, coincidentally, and luckily for nursing mothers, the age a calf stops nursing. Only two-thirds of the elephant's tusk shows outside the body, leaving about a third, the tip of the iceberg, inside the socket to continue growing throughout the life span of the elephant. You may wonder why humans cannot just cut the tusks off to discourage poachers. The answer is the ivory is attached inside the head and attached to the skull, which has to be carved out of the head in order to be removed.

According to Clare, "The actual base of the tusk is hollow and contains the pulp cavity. This usually extends quite far, and in males may reach beyond the lip line. The tusk grows from its base as fresh dentine is slowly deposited over the surface of the pulp cavity. For females this cavity begins to fill in with age. Although both African elephant sexes have tusks, there are large differences in their size and weight. Typically, the male tusk has a larger circumference in relation to its length, is stouter, and much heavier. Interestingly, some elephants are born without tusks. This hereditary condition causes huge differences in the musculature and shape of the neck and the head. Also, the carriage of the head is different and the bones at the back of the skull are less developed. Elephants without tusks live normal elephant lives, learning to overcompensate and problem solve in other ways.

Tusks are used as digging tools, weapons, and for displays of power, however, some elephants loose them, and they also do not suffer because of the lack of tusks. Elephants are right- or left-tusked, just as humans are left-or right-handed. The tusk used most often tends to be shorter and more rounded and is called the 'master tusk.' When digging grass, an elephant will use its tusks for breaking off a divot of grass. Over time, this activity causes the dominant tusk to show wear near the tip and can appear shorter. The heaviest tusk on record weighed 258 pounds. The longest tusk ever measured was 3¼ yards."

Evolutionally, tusks are slowly disappearing. Sally herself was born with the makings for only one tusk, one of the features which helps us to recognize her easily in the field. Thato and Keisha have tusks smaller than their peers. This could be the beginning of an evolutionary gift: If elephants don't have tusks, there is no reason to kill or poach them. However, evolution is sluggish compared to poachers. If future elephants don't have tusks to help with defense and especially digging, they will have to problem solve another way of digging, perhaps by using sticks or other tools with their trunks. Mother Nature is clever, however, and may come up with something completely unexpected.

Dr. Debbie explains, "Elephants have six sets of molars, and they wear through them during their lifespan. As a tooth wears it is pushed forward to the front of the mouth and it slowly wears into a shelf of sorts as the roots are absorbed. The shelf will eventually break off and the remaining fragment pushed out of the mouth. Interestingly, the absorption of tooth roots is a phenomenon, which is found to take place after an injury or in old aged mammals. After the first two teeth are gone, parts of the two adjacent teeth are being worn down in each half of the jaw. This process continues until the last molar appears. This sixth molar weighs on average a stunning 8.8 pounds and has a maximum grinding length of 8¼ inches and a width of 2.75 inches. The sixth molar will be present for around 2/5 of the elephant's life. About 10% of elderly elephants will have an additional seventh molar, but it is never as developed as the former teeth. Very elderly elephants have been known to spend more time in marshy areas, where they can feed on the wet, softer grasses. Eventually, when the last teeth fall out, the elephant will be unable to feed at all. Tragically, these elderly elephants will virtually starve to death. Were it not for tooth deterioration, their metabolism would allow them to live for much longer than the approximately sixty five plus years. An elephant may live as long as 70 years and there are records of captive elephants living for over eighty years. As more habitats are destroyed, the elephant's living space becomes smaller and smaller, the elderly elephants will no longer have the opportunity to roam in search of more appropriate food and will, consequently, die of starvation at an earlier age."

4. The Health and Physiology of Elephants

In *Elephantoms*, Watson writes of an evolutionary shift that took place millions of years ago. "In that shake-up, ancestral elephants got a new set of teeth. Molars formed from hard grinding enamel and softer tooth cement, so that the two parts wore down at different rates, keeping the chewing surface from becoming too smooth. With such every-ready grinders, modern elephants are able to deal with tougher foods like woody shrubs, making it possible to live in more barren habitats."[8]

* * *

Unique to elephant ivory is an exclusive luster and craft-ability, making it even more desirable to humans. The cross section of a tusk is distinguished from the ivory of other animals by a pattern of intersecting lines and concentric rings that form cross-hatched, diamond-shaped designs, much like the rings in a tree trunk which mark the annual and seasonal growing phases. If abandoned to the elements, the ivory will eventually crack along these rings. Ivory has an unmistakable water absorbance quality. In fact, some African tribes stick tusks into the ground as barometers to predict coming rains. The actual composition of ivory has been found to change according to the region it is found in because concentrations of calcium, phosphate, magnesium, and amino acids vary from region to region. Elephant dentition expert Erich Raubenheimer proposed that by analyzing a poached piece of ivory forensically, we can track the origins of the ivory. This breakthrough could have huge implications in favor of elephants and the anti-poaching movement.[9]

Despite its whiteness, ivory has a long, dark history. According to Martin Meredith in *Elephant Destiny*, in the 19th century, African ivory was prized more than any other because it was finer-grained, richer in tone and larger than ivory from India.[10] East Africa ranked as the world's largest source of ivory throughout the century, producing what was known as "soft" ivory that was opaque, smooth, gently curved and easy to craft. At the time, West Africa produced "hard" ivory that was less white but glossy and more translucent.

With the industrial era overtaking the world, the uses for ivory became unlimited. Humans soon discovered that ivory could be cut, sawed, carved, etched, ground or worked on a lathe. It could even be stained or painted. Ivory was found to be so flexible that it was made into riding whips cut from the length of the tusk, sliced into paper-thin sheets so transparent that standard print could be read through it. One such sheet of ivory, exhibited in London in 1851, was 14 inches wide and 52 inches long. Meredith calls it the plastic of its day, possessing a creamy, lustrous beauty that was unique and sensuously appealing to the touch.[11]

Napoleon and his wife visited The Dieppe School of ivory carvers to stock up on all kinds of decorative items for themselves and as gifts. French royalty also patronized these ivory workshops. The work shown by members of The Dieppe School garnered great acclaim at the Paris Exhibition in 1834. In Germany, at Erbach in Hesse, carvers developed a unique style which became known as Biedermeier, taken from a fictional character that was thought to represent middle-class attributes of opulence. Erbach and Hesse became known for carving elaborate flowers from ivory, the flowers representing love and the ivory thought of as a romantic material. Europe produced many master ivory carvers who became famous for their statues and models of ships.[12]

In East Asia, Chinese carvers produced what became known as "devil's balls," which were concentric circles with a series of perforated ivory globes moving freely inside each other in decreasing size. Japanese carvers' specialty product was "netsuke," small toggles which were used with a string to hold pouches and boxes suspended from their waistbands, much like modern-day belt pouches.

Moving into the 19th century, huge quantities of ivory were imported from Africa by Europe and the United States. The volume of ivory needed in order to keep up with the world's demand continued to grow. According to Martin Meredith, in the 60 years spanning 1850 to 1910, Britain alone imported an average of 500 tons of ivory annually. World consumption in the later part of the century reached about 1,000 tons. Translated into elephant terms, this meant that 65,000 elephants were killed *each year* in order to quench the world's thirst for ivory. Slaughter on this kind of a scale began to incite international concern as it became evident that entire populations were in danger of being obliterated.[13]

During the 20th century, the late 1970s through the early 1980s saw the first postcolonial spike in demand for ivory emanating from Japan, Europe and North America. When legislation was put into place, declaring elephants an endangered species caused a sharp decline in poaching. But like a bad dream, demand spiked again in the early 21st century, reaching a peak around 2011 due to demand from mostly Asian markets. This spike caused the price of ivory to reach $2,100 per kg, or 2.3 pounds. The trade in illegal wildlife, including rhino horns, was worth an estimated $19 billion by 2018.[14]

The list of items manufactured from ivory is longer than a male elephant tusk and includes everything but the kitchen sink: buttons, bracelets, beads, napkin rings, knitting needles, doorknobs, snuff boxes, fans, shaving brush handles, picture frames, paper cutters, hair and hat pins, handles for teapots, canes and hairbrushes and much, much more. Ivory inlay work embellished a huge variety of items, including mirrors, furniture, and all kinds of other decorative items. In Aberdeen, Scotland, a labor force of 600 worked ten hours a day manufacturing ivory combs. Factories in Sheffield, England, used hundreds of tons of ivory to make handles for cutlery, and ivory was worked into a range of musical instruments. It was used for the frets and fingerboards of Spanish guitars, as pipe connectors for Scottish bagpipes, as bridges for violins, and stops for flutes. It is most famously used for piano keys so musicians can "tickle the ivories," a much admired skill, but one can't help but wish a pianist's fingers could tickle some other substrate. Ivory was also used to make scientific instruments. Because of its durability and ability to hold its form and finish under constant use, ivory was used to make navigational instruments, slide rules, telescopes, and microscopes.[15]

Game manufacturers quickly discovered that ivory was perfect for making dominoes, dice, chess pieces and billiard balls. This became its most popular use, as ivory pool balls bumping against one another had an unmistakably appealing "chink." No more than five balls could be made from one tusk because they had to be cut from the very center of the tusk in order for them to roll properly; the tusk's black nerve canal in its center was used as a guiding line. Scraps from this process were saved for smaller projects.

The ivory dust that resulted from manufacturing various items was boiled to make gelatin, hair dye, fertilizer, fabric sizing, and was burned to add to the recipe for Indian ink.

Sure-Footed and Silent

When we hear a very noisy procession, we often say it sounds like a herd of elephants. Nothing could be farther from the truth, though. I was shocked at how elephants lumber through fields and forests in utter silence. Here at KEP, I walked next to Shungu, gaping at the lack of clamor in his stride. Elephant feet have built-in "shock absorbers" made of fatty, fibrous tissue which cushion the impact of foot touching ground. An elephant's weight rests on the tip of each toe and the fibrous cushion under the heel. It is as if they are wearing high-heeled shoes. The elephant's foot bones point downward and forward, resting on a pad of fat and connective tissue that acts to spread its bulk evenly across their broad soles. In effect, they walk on their tiptoes. The sole of the foot is ridged and pitted, much like our palm and footprints, which contributes to their sure-footedness. The circumference of the forefoot is approximately equal to half the shoulder height, so an elephant's foot size can be used to judge the overall size of a particular animal and its age. Elephants use their feet in creating holes to collect water, for digging roots from the ground, and for navigating difficult terrain. Similar to human fingerprints, the pattern of ridges and fissures left behind by the sole of each animal is quite distinctive. In fact it is possible to judge the age of an elephant by its foot dimension and patterns. Generally, younger elephants have crisp designs, and older elephants have smoother ridges and worn heels. The front feet have a circular outline,

Sure-footed and silent is the best description of elephants walking in the field. Elephant feet have built-in "shock absorbers" made of fatty, fibrous tissue, which cushion the impact of foot touching ground. In effect, they walk on their tiptoes. Similar to human fingerprints, the pattern of ridges and fissures on the sole of each foot is unique to each elephant. At day's end, the guides walk the ellies back to the boma area. The elephants prefer to walk in a line. It is quiet except for the sound of shuffling stones on the path. Each guide's attention is vigilantly focused at all times. They know each elephant's personality, rank, typical body language. It is because of the guides' collective diligence that we get as close as we do to touch the elephants and look into their eyes at close range.

and the back foot is an oval shape. However, researchers have found that elongated oval footprints usually indicate an adult male. Bulls typically leave a double print because the rear leg often falls slightly to the side of the front leg. Elephants are surprisingly good at climbing steep hills, mountains, and even cliffs. As we saw earlier, during World War I elephants were used in Burma to help armies over steep mountains with narrow passes, making their sure-footedness a curse and a blessing.

Dr. Debbie explains, "An elephant's five toes are buried inside the flesh of the foot, but not all toes have toenails. The toenails are actually shields in the skin and are not attached to the fingers or digits. Overall, it is generally accepted that the African elephant has four toenails on the front feet and three on the back as opposed to the Asian elephants, which have five on the front and four on the back. Elephants are good swimmers and climbers but cannot trot, run, jump or gallop. Elephants have only one gait, a sort of gliding shuffle, but this can be stepped up to the speed of a human sprinter. An elephant normally ambles at a rate of about 3½ miles per hour but it can reach a top speed of 25 miles per when scared or upset. In spite of the fact that they can't run, there are few terrestrial animals that can travel further in a day than an elephant. Endurance and sure-footedness win out in the end."

Occasionally you can look into the field and spot an elephant lifting one foot so the other one is more firmly on the ground in order to receive the vibrations of infrasonic messages. We already know that an elephant's foot acts in effect as another ear, their feet acting as receptors to the infrasonic conversations which take place between elephants, sometimes at a frequency we humans are incapable of hearing.

Dumbo Had a Secret: The Elephant's Ears

African elephants have the largest ears in the world, period. These massive folds of flesh grow up to six and a half feet from top to bottom and up to five feet wide. The reason for the large ears, however, is not what you might expect. While their hearing is good, it is not superior. Those large, floppy ears are used as fans for elephants to cool themselves off under the hot African sun. The skin on the back of the ears is extra thin specifically for this purpose. Elephant ears are designed to shed heat. Inside the earflap there is a network of large blood vessels. Flapping the ears regularly cools an elephant in several ways. Each flap acts like a fan, blowing air over the body surface, as well as cooling the air around the blood vessels in the ear. The cooled blood returns to the main body. Three-quarters of heat buildup is lost through the ears while water and evaporative cooling is responsible for the rest. And by the way, each and every elephant ear is unique and is used as a type of fingerprint for identification in the wild.

Elephant ears are also a protective feature used to ward off potential threats. The underside is considerably softer to the touch; the outside feels like rubbery leather. They are particularly impressive when spread out in fear of threat. When Thandi, a member of Sally's herd who is Nandi's daughter, sticks her ears out close to her face, which she does sometimes just to show off, they are Mickey Mouse style, making her a natural model for advertisements and brochures for the park. When Thandi does puff her ears out and looks at you through those long, spiky eyelashes, there is nothing more endearing.

Sensory Superpowers and Other Interesting Elephant Info

Touch is an important way of emotional communicating in the elephant world. Through touch, Sally reassures a frightened family member or reprimands a naughty youngster by smacking it with her trunk. Some elephants, like Nandi, prefer to be touched only in certain places, while Shungu, Mashudu, and Thato can be touched all over.

The heart of an elephant weighs between 26 and 40 pounds, accounting for a normal percentage in mammals of total body weight at about a half of 1 percent. It differs from the hearts of other mammals in that it has a bifid, or double-pointed tip instead of the more typical single point. It beats about 28 times per minute or every one to two seconds, compared to the human heart beating about 70 times per minute.

Gazing into an elephant's eyes at close range is my favorite part of being with them. There is gentleness, a wisdom that exudes from their gaze, shrouded by the longest, thick, black wiry eyelashes I've ever seen. My breath slows while looking at an elephant's eye up close; their amber shade is soothing. But as stunning as the eyes of an elephant are, they are not one of an elephant's superpowers.

Clare explains the elephant's poor eyesight. "Elephant eyes are far larger than human eyes, at almost 2 inches in diameter. In bright sunlight elephants tend to travel with their eyes half hooded but where there is shade or shelter, the eyelids are nearly always open wide. Their pupils zoom in and out in direct relation to the emotional value of what is being seen. Because of the size of the skull, the distance between the eyes of an elephant is huge. In fact, they lie right on the edge of the orbit. This means that even though an elephant has little ability to turn its head, it has surprisingly good rear-view vision. To see forward and achieve binocular vision, an elephant must raise its head and look down its nose. In low light elephant eyesight is quite good; they have all the necessary retinal and optical equipment in addition to their 2 protective eyelids.

However, elephants have a third nictitating membrane that sweeps horizontally across the eyeball, lubricated by an internal gland. The secretion from this gland differs slightly from that of the human's lacthrymal gland, which produces tears, but when there is enough of this secretion, something similar to tears trickles down an elephant's face. An elephant's vision in bright light is poor, perhaps limited to about 160 feet, but they are very adept at gathering environmental information from body language such as ear flapping, raising or folding the trunk, gait, foot motion, swaying, the tilt of the head."

Elephants are able to differentiate most colors. Caitlin O'Connell, elephant researcher and author, writes of a fascinating experiment in which elephants were shown either a white garment or a red

Looking into the amber eye of an elephant is nirvana. There is gentleness, a wisdom that exudes from the gaze of an elephant, shrouded by the longest, thick, black wiry eyelashes I've ever seen. Looking into their eyes at close range, my breath automatically slows. In Keisha's case, she is the embodiment of calm and unconditional acceptance. Her gift to me is time to look deeply into her eyes. When she blinks, a feeling of profound calm overcomes me, and I am speechless.

one. White represented neutral, and red is the color traditionally worn by the Massai tribe, who are well known for hunting elephants. Elephants are dichromats, meaning they have the same color discrimination ability as a color-blind human. White and red are distinguishable from each other under these circumstances, and the elephants showed a significantly greater flight response to the red garment than the white one. In a more recent study, elephants were shown to recognize language differences between human groups and assess danger accordingly, even to the point of discriminating gender.[16]

O'Connell writes: "Scientists have long considered the ability to recognize oneself in a mirror to be an index of high cognitive ability and one that is associated with humans, apes, and other highly social animals. To pass the mirror test, an animal has to respond to its own reflection in ways that make it clear that it sees itself in the mirror, not seeing another animal of their same species. In the classic test, the experimenter surreptitiously applies a mark or sticker to the study subject, then presents the animal with a mirror. If on seeing its reflection the animal looks for the sticker or mark on its own body, it passes the test. Two such experiments were done on Asian elephants to determine whether just visible or both visible and concealed markings would be explored by elephants in front of a mirror.

Neither of the two elephants in the first study reacted to their reflections. In the second study, one out of three subjects explored visible markings on her forehead, an indication she knew she was looking at a reflection of herself and not at another elephant. Although not as incontestable as the responses of great apes, the results were significant enough to warrant further investigation. Perhaps future experiments affording the opportunity for elephants to explore the mirror outside of circumscribed testing times, such as incorporating mirrors into elephant enclosures, would allow more elephants to respond, thereby leading to a stronger conclusion. Such modifications may well demonstrate more quantitatively that elephants indeed do have a concept of self. In the meantime, these same researchers have proven the elephant's ability to empathize with the misfortune of another and console the other after a traumatizing event."[17]

* * *

On a quiet, relatively tourist-free afternoon, after an empty tractor pulled into the field, a grumpy Sally who, seeing the empty tractor knew she wasn't going to get any fruit, turned her attention back to grazing. A truck full of browse branches brought from a local farm entered the field. Sally's ears flared as she lifted her trunk to pick up scents. She began walking briskly toward the moving tractor, excitedly thinking she would sneak a juicy branch before the other elephants could reach it. When the driver saw her approaching, he sped up, and the men on the back trailer stood to discourage Sally from her quest. Ever-stubborn Sally reaches the tractor, sniffs, expecting something delicious, only to find it completely empty because they had already dumped it on the ground. She shook her large head, ears flaring, and gave a triple whammy of trumpeting disapproval, rumbling and streaming on the sides of her neck to be sure everyone knew her feathers were ruffled. You may be thinking that toddler tantrums work that way, and, well, you're right!

Going Through Life Thick-Skinned

"Elephants are pachyderms," explains Dr. Debbie. "The word pachyderm actually translates to 'thick-skinned.' The thickness of an African elephant's skin varies from .59 inch to .98 inch, thinner in areas like the inside of the ears, around the mouth and anus, and thicker on areas like the back and various spots on their head. The intricate network of wrinkles on an elephant's skin helps retain 5 to 10 times more moisture and therefore coolness under the hot African sun than smooth skin would. The cracks are formed when the elephant's skin thickens with new layers over time, placing pressure on the outer epidermis causing it to crack and wrinkle. Elephants lack the sweat glands we humans have which produce cooling perspiration.

The term "pachyderm" actually means "thick skinned." The intricate network of wrinkles on an elephant's skin helps retain five to ten times more moisture and coolness under the hot African sun than smooth skin would. Despite the thickness of the elephant's skin, it is highly sensitive.

Part One

Despite the thickness of the elephant's skin, it is highly sensitive. Elephant's often suck mud into their trunks to spray on their bodies, and sometimes they get down on the ground and roll around in the mud to trap it in the skin folds. This was priceless to witness. Picture a huge elephant lying on the ground rolling around in the mud with its four feet straight up in the air. I witnessed Shungu and Keisha do this late one steamy afternoon and they looked like mischievous kids caught getting muddy. The mud also acts as a sunscreen, protection against insect bites, moisture loss. Along with the flapping of its ears, these techniques help to keep the elephant cool in the severe heat of the day. The skin of an elephant is stippled with patches of wiry black hair, calves having a lighter color hair. Elephant skin is extremely sensitive to the sun and the mud acts as a sunscreen. Most calves take refuge in their mother's shadow to avoid sunburn. The overall color of the skin is grey, although when Shungu and Keisha finished rolling in the mud, their skin appeared coppery red from the gingery Garden Route soil.

5

The Behavior and Psychology of Elephants

"Some people talk to animals. Not many listen though. That's the problem."—A.A. Milne

An Elephant Never Forgets—Cognition and the Brain

Elephants are among the world's most intelligent species with a brain larger than all other land mammals. The brain of an African elephant weighs about 11 pounds, as compared to the human brain which weighs about two pounds. When born, an infant elephant's brain is 50 percent of its adult size. Elephant skulls are massive, having grown during the course of evolution to be able to support and anchor the weight of their heavy tusks and trunks. As in humans, the male elephant's brain is larger than the female's, weighing in at 12 pounds compared to the female elephant's brain at about ten pounds. The elephant brain is surrounded by a network of cavities or sinuses, rather than solid bone, which provides the skull volume and stability without the extra weight. The skull contains air cells known as diploe which also helps reduce its weight. The brain is located toward the back of the skull, away from the forehead. An adult elephant's brain is four times the bulk of a human brain and is highly convoluted, or rippled, filled with nooks and crannies. This they have in common with the human brain as well as dolphins and great apes. The brain of an elephant is half the size of a whale brain, which weighs 20 times more. A wide variety of behaviors, including exhibiting grief, play, use of tools, compassion, problem solving, self-awareness and the best memory in the entire animal kingdom is evidence of a highly intelligent species rivaled only by dolphins and primates.

Renowned elephant researcher Caitlin O'Connell explains that elephants have the largest temporal lobe, relative to body size, of all mammals. The temporal lobe is the portion of the cerebral cortex devoted to communication, language, spatial memory and cognition. Given the relative size of the temporal lobe in elephants, there is good reason to suspect that the elephant's cognition is even more sophisticated than we currently understand. Elephant brains contain as many cortical neurons as human brains and have larger pyramidal neurons than humans, which are specialized neurons thought to play a key role in cognitive functions. This suggests that elephants might have learning and memory skills superior to ours. The cortex constitutes the thin, outer layer of neurons or nerve cells that cover both cerebral hemispheres. It is closely associated with higher cognitive functions such as coordinated voluntary movement, integration of sensory information, sociocultural learning and memories that characterize an individual. Just for the sake of perspective, an elephant has approximately 5,600,000,000 neurons in the cerebral cortex, as compared to porpoises that have approximately 14,900,000,000. And where humans have about 86,000,000,000 neurons which make up the complete brain and nervous systems, the African elephant has 257,000,000,000.

Also according to O'Connell, within the realm of learning, elephants make use of both contextual learning, which is behavioral in context, and sequential positioning as well as production learning, which is based on experiential learning. Animals who utilize both methods of learning are theoretically capable of developing a more complicated communication system than species utilizing only contextual learning.

Both African and Asian elephants have a very large and highly convoluted neocortex, suggesting a high degree of similarity with humans, apes and certain species of dolphin. Many scientists view this as a sign of complex intelligence. Studies show that elephants are in the same category as great apes in their ability to create and use tools. A simple example of an elephant making and using a tool is Sally finding or pulling down a stick and using it to scratch her back. It's quite a sight to see!

Elephants have a large and highly convoluted hippocampus, part of the limbic system, larger than that of humans. The hippocampus is linked to emotion through the processing of certain types of memory, especially spatial memory. This is why I believe elephants like Keisha, who lost her mother as an infant, can suffer from psychological flashbacks that can be part of post-traumatic stress disorder. Like humans, elephants must be taught how to behave in their society just like human babies, both of whom are born without survival knowledge or the capability of being without their mothers. Elephant mothers must teach their babies how to feed, how to use tools and learn their place in the complex social structure of elephant herds. Without her mother to teach her, Keisha had a hard time learning how to behave within a herd of elephants.

Darwin viewed social structure as the bonds that hold a group together and represent the origins of morality. Spindle cell neurons believed to be responsible for social awareness have been discovered in elephant brains. Elephants live by social awareness, the ability to make quick decisions. Spindle cell neurons were previously thought to exist only in the human, great apes, and some dolphin species. Much more research is needed in this area.

Elephant researcher Jacobs writes, "In terms of cognition, my colleagues and I believe that the integrative cortical circuitry in the elephant supports the idea that they are essentially contemplative animals. Primate brains, by comparison, seem specialized for rapid decision-making and quick reactions to environmental stimuli."[1]

According to Wemmer et al. in *Elephants and Ethics*, "There is a growing amount of evidence that elephants may indeed be capable of both insight and theory of mind. Because of their propensity for empathy and sympathy, scientists assume they have mirror neurons, which are responsible for those same traits in humans. Mirror neurons responsible for empathy are, in effect, a theory of mind. Piles of anecdotal evidence suggest the presence of mirror neurons in elephants, as evidenced by the sight of several elephants using their bodies and trunks to rescue a drowning calf, or an elephant lingering at the site of a dead relative or friend, and even placing leaves and branches over the dead body."[2]

Renowned elephant researcher Cynthia Moss writes in *Elephant Memories* of many incidents during which she observed elephants touching the bones of dead elephants, particularly the skulls and tusks, as if they are trying to recognize whose bones they are touching and turning over, even carrying away. Much more research needs to be done in this fascinating area.[3]

The elephant's cerebrum handles motor control, while the cerebellum handles the coordination of muscles. The elephant's cortex is similar to ours; their cognitive processing leads to experiencing similar emotions.

Anecdotal evidence suggests the use of high levels of cognition by elephants in the wild in response to electric fences. Elephants frequently disable electric fences by dropping logs onto them (which prevent them from being shocked), or using their tusks, which don't conduct electricity. They also disable electric fences by uprooting or pushing over trees, causing live wires to sag to the ground.

Incidentally, Geoff and Mac, who have worked at the park since Harry and Sally arrived, recall that at the time of their arrival, there were no fences at all. According to elephant researcher Maud Bonato, between 1994 and 1997 there was a normal boundary fence around the park with just Sally and Harry there. As KEP received more elephants, they only added a single strand of electric wire fence around the perimeter of the park. As new regulations and norms and standards for keeping elephants were implemented, in 2013 KEP had to comply at great financial cost to erecting a new fence with three strands of wire on the inside in order to have an adequate fencing permit for keeping wild animals.

Back to the elephant's brain and its amazing social abilities. How, for example, can an elephant maintain meaningful social relationships with between 100 and 200 other elephants, similar to the capacity we humans have for meaningful contact with other humans? And it is probably no coincidence that this number is about the size of a human hunting/gathering clan, who spend most of their lives in smaller groups of relatives, separated from other clan, scouring the landscape for food, water and shelter.

A large part of an elephant's memory is taken up with spatial recall, which includes knowledge of sources for food and water, the seasons in which they are most plentiful, and the routes to navigate toward those resources. Some researchers hypothesize that the ability of the elephant to navigate and find specific locations is aided by natural seismic sound fields within the earth, which we humans cannot hear. They receive this information by interpreting vibrations felt in their feet.

According to Clare Padfield, "The organ of Jacobson or vomeronasal gland is an almost forgotten body part. It is a sense organ with the ability to detect chemical signals. In humans, the external evidence consists of a pair of tiny pits, one on either side of the nasal septum, approximately 3mm above the nostril. In no mammal is the opening to the Jacobson's organ obvious; it is tucked away somewhere on the edge of the air stream. In the elephant it is situated near the back of the palate, where the clearly visible marks in the bone can be observed. This organ communicates not only with the olfactory bulbs in the cortex of the brain where we organize what we know and can remember about particular odors, but also with the limbic system in the back of the brain, where basic emotions involved with sex and aggression seem to be coordinated."

It's a well-established fact that elephants are among the smartest creatures on our planet. But did you know there is evidence that they can distinguish between human languages? Researchers at the University of Sussex in the UK have discovered that African elephants can distinguish differences in human gender, age, and ethnicity purely by listening to the sound of someone's voice. If the voice emanates from a person who is more likely to pose a safety threat, the elephants switch into defensive mode. To prove this, these researchers found two Kenyan men from different ethnic groups, one from the Maasai and one from the Kamba. As we saw in the color experiments, the Massai have a long history of killing wild elephants, while the Kamba have lived in peaceful coexistence with elephants. The researchers recorded each man saying the equivalent of "Look, look over there, a group of elephants is coming." When the elephants heard the Maasai voice, they showed signs of fear, such as huddling together and moving away from the voice. The same phrase spoken by the Kamba man evoked no reaction from the elephants at all. The experiment suggests that they can differentiate between languages they have been exposed to. In addition, the same recordings were made by women and children of the two tribes, both of which left the elephants unfazed, which suggests that they can not only distinguish between languages but can also distinguish between age and gender.[4] Sally and her herd are accustomed to hearing mostly English and Khosa.

Elephants have an advanced capacity for problem-solving by thinking in abstract terms. One sign of high-level intelligence is the ability to solve problems by using tools. In 2010, a seven-year-old Asian elephant named Kandula impressed researchers by utilizing tools from his surroundings to reach fruit that had been strategically placed just beyond his reach. Kandula found a large plastic block, rolled it over, stepped on it and propped himself high enough to reach the fruit with his long trunk. And just in case you thought this might have been a fluke, he repeated the feat stacking blocks to reach even higher and used other tools such as branches to pry the fruit from the tree.[5]

Possibly the most astounding sign that elephants have a very high functioning brain is that they understand human body language. Researchers recently observed evidence that elephants might understand the human gesture of pointing. This hypothesis was tested by putting food hidden in one of two identical containers and observing which container a group of captive elephants approached. Granted they could smell the food but couldn't tell which bucket it emanated from. When the researchers pointed to the correct container, the elephants picked correctly 68 percent of the time. One-year-old human babies performed 5 percent lower on similar tests. When the researchers stood between the containers and did not point, the elephants approached them randomly.[6] Elephants are often seen using physical contact and vocalizations to comfort each other. They have long been known to exhibit fascinating responses to the dead bodies of their own kind by caressing the carcass with their trunks and standing near the body for hours or even days. At times they even make rudimentary attempts to bury the remains by throwing sticks, branches, leaves and dirt over it. One female elephant was seen to slowly wrap her trunk around the deceased elephant's trunk and remained in that position for hours.

More proof of an elephant's excellent memory is in the following amazing example. Shirley and Jenny knew each other when they were young companions in a circus. They were separated for 20 years before being reunited at The Elephant Sanctuary in Tennessee. Their reunion was full of joyful touching of trunks, trumpeting and streaming at their temporal glands. They recognized each other immediately and were clearly so joyful to be reunited. They remain there together today.

Psychologically, elephants are assumed to have an unconscious as well as a conscious mind. In humans and in elephants, most of the complex functioning of our bodies is carried out automatically by the unconscious. The unconscious is ultimately dependent on the conscious, and there is continuous feedback between the two. This is another area of elephant research ripe for exploration.

The Place of Ritual in Elephant Society

Rituals are part of the culture in all human as well as nonhuman societies in one way or another. Rituals are tools used to communicate, express intentions, emotions, soothe, and create a mutual language with which to facilitate connection between members of a society or culture. According to researcher Caitlin O'Connell in *Wild Rituals*, "Research shows engaging in ritual is temporarily appeasing and mitigates anxieties.... During the performance of a group ritual, personal fears or doubts are shared as a group, which has a calming effect. Engaging in ritual also has a profound impact on the hormone expression of all participants, which results in physiological, immunological, and behavioral changes. Ultimately, this helps to create cooperative relationships within complex societies…. Whether simple or elaborate, rituals can be transformative, both mentally and physically, and they connect us, strengthen bonds, create order, and ground us within a community. They *are* the glue that binds communities together into healthy societies for all social animals."[7]

In elephant society, a trunk-to-mouth greeting ritual, our equivalent of a handshake, involves a high degree of trust between elephants, since the risk of having one's trunk bitten is always there. But it is affiliative behavior at its best.

In her book, Caitlyn O'Connell reports, "Greeting rituals evolved within groups of social animals for three purposes. One is to reinforce bonds between two close associates or a group of associates or to welcome a new friend. Another is to reduce tension and foster reconciliation. The third is to signal submission to a dominant individual, which promotes cooperative and peaceful coexistence within a society."[8] Taking part in group rituals can produce endorphins that affect our brains, causing emotions such as happiness and even euphoria or reduce pain, increase group cohesiveness. Just as adrenaline, the flight-fight-or-freeze hormone is released under stress and danger, oxytocin is also known as the bonding hormone because it helps elicit feelings of trust and connection.

So, now that you know the hows, whys, whats and wheres of the African elephant, here are the stories, up close and personal, of the personalities and the behaviors of these majestic, gentle creatures and their caregivers. They are the true stars of the show.

6

Sally: The Matriarch

"I defy anyone to look upon elephants without a sense of wonder. Their very enormity, their clumsiness, their giant stature, represent a mass of liberty that sets you dreaming. They're ... yes, they're the last individuals.... No, mademoiselle, I don't capture elephants. I content myself with living among them. I like them. I like looking at them, listening to them, watching them move on the horizon. To tell you the truth, I'd give anything to become an elephant myself."—Romain Gary, *The Roots of Heaven*

"Sally" is Hebrew for "princess."
Identifying Characteristics:

One tusk on right side, none on left side
Long tail with lots of tail hair
Big knot-like fat lump above tail
Generally larger and rounder than the others
Born October 1989

She is the gentle, wise caretaker, the proficient matriarch of the herd, and she is also the bossy "I want to eat it all myself" bully. She is a favorite of visitors because she is so used to people that she allows them to touch her easily at close range and likes to show off for the crowd by picking up a branch and placing it on her back for comic effect. Born in October of 1989, Sally came to KEP in October 1994, having survived a cull at the Kruger National Park. Sally's mom was killed in that cull when Sally was only a few years old. Although she did not have a role model after her mother was killed, she is a role model to her herd in the truest sense of the word.

Sally is affectionately called "Big Mama" by all who know and love her. She is the largest of the herd by sheer girth. Sally is gentle but stern, always vigilant about the welfare of the elephants in her herd. In spite of the fact that she has never had calves of her own, nor any matriarchal training, she has all the motherly acumen needed to be an outstanding matriarch.

Since she has been around bulls of mating age and never been pregnant, the park has taken the stance that, in lieu of unnecessary testing, she is infertile. However, recent hormone test results do show that she has estrus cycles, muddying the waters. Hopefully, future hormone test results will shed light on the question of Sally's fertility. Matriarchs in the wild must be able to consistently guide their herd to adequate supplies of food and water, but living at KEP, Sally has been relieved of these duties. This frees her up to simply attend to her herd.

At the barrier, Sally rules, her four tons of bulk place her at almost full grown, although she is in her early 30s. Birds screech in excitement, and dust trails the tractor as it chugs toward her. She sways back and forth, throwing her weight from side to side in wild anticipation. Today she is a muddy, earth-toned giant, far rounder and taller than the others. From afar she appears as a large boulder but for her swaying. But even

Sally, the matriarch, is the oldest elephant and the largest of the herd. Note that she was born without a tusk on her left side.

6. Sally: The Matriarch

It is critical to life at the park to know the tractor schedule so you can be out in the field to relieve others on time or be back at the volunteer center when you are required to do other work.

Sally is dwarfed by the blue-gray mountains, the bright green valley and the broody sky, the heavens.

The rattle of the tractor bouncing with people and fruit buckets clangs its way over ruts and rocks in the packed dirt road. When the elephant herd returns to the field, opportunistic zebras snatch elephant scraps, grass, leaves, pellets, then scamper out of the way before the next tractor.

The sun pours itself over the park like some visible spirit. Doves sing arias, their refrain repeating over and over. Will they ever stop? Sally scans the horizon, her trunk partway in the air, making sure each member of her herd is accounted for. They stand at the barrier, a tangle of trunks beckoning food. Sally makes it look easy, with her sassy but loving, larger-than-life personality. Her herd has complete trust in her, an implicit contract that she will look out for all, and they will obey her. After the feeding session has ended, Sally and the others return to the field. Because she is the most experienced around humans, Sally is a good candidate for tourists to see up close. She is very tolerant of people gently stroking her and seems to bathe in the ooohs and ahhhhs just as she soaks in the fruit from the buckets. She knows she is beautiful and a good matriarch, sometimes playing the clown by taking a large, leafed branch from the ground and placing it over her back, leaving it there like a cloak. She appears to be smiling as people laugh at her antics, as if she understands the meaning of laughter.

Dr. Debbie laughs and recounts a story about a children's local TV show called *Roughing It*. When the TV crew came to the park to film an episode, unbeknownst to the park staff, some of the children had pellets in their pockets. Sally made her TV debut by sniffing their pockets and plunging her trunk into them, devouring the pellets.

* * *

Elephants live in what scientists refer to as a "fission-fusion" society, one in which the size and composition of the social group changes over time as animals move throughout the environment and merge into a group (fusion). Those of the herd who sleep together in one area are considered a split or fission, as is a small group foraging together. In fission-fusion societies, group composition and allegiances are dynamic, ever-changing. The change in composition, subgroup size, and dispersion of different groups are the main elements of a fission-fusion herd. Many natural phenomena can contribute to fission-fusion makeup, including the availability of food and water, weather, and the likelihood of predators in the same territory. At KEP, Sally starts her day out with the entire herd but may spend hours grazing with Thandi and Nandi before joining with some or all of the others for a swim and then spend overnight all together as a herd in the boma or night enclosure.

* * *

Mac Juwa has worked with Sally for 20 years. Born and raised in Malawi, he was brought in by Mr. and Mrs. Withers to help with Harry and Sally from the time they were young. Mac is lean but strong, with eyes that show a deep wisdom and love of life. Soft-spoken and shy, when Mac does speak, people listen. As I stand in the field with him, the elephants grazing nearby, I notice that Mac never takes his eyes off the elephants, monitoring their body language constantly. Mac recalls, "I remember once when Harry was taken away on a trip. Sally was so mad she couldn't sleep. She smashed the wooden boma. From the second night of Harry's absence on, Geoff, my friend and fellow guide then and now, calmed her. Sometimes she would trumpet and turn her bum in greeting. When Harry eventually left the park for good, it was done gradually so Sally had a chance to get used to him being gone." Mac explained, "Before Harry was taken to the Plett Game Reserve (PGR) a much larger tract of land, he was 'detrained' to some extent. We had people come up to him without food for a while, causing him to lose interest. By the time he headed out for PGR, he was really ready, and Sally was prepared for him to leave as well. He now has a new family of his own, with lots of calves, and a great deal more land to roam. Harry is toweringly massive with huge tusks, and he dwarfs any other elephant I've ever seen," boasts Mac. "I met Harry when I visited PGR. At almost 13 feet tall and weighing in at over 6,000 pounds, Harry is indeed the most foreboding-looking creature I've ever seen, with large thick tusks and a bulky girth. I was afraid of him at first sight, leaning tightly against the fence, but Charles, his main caregiver at PGR, sidled up to him and I could see how calm he actually is. He motioned me to approach them and I was able to greet Harry and touch him on his upper leg, which meant I was reaching up! Several of his calves meandered by and Harry reached his trunk out to them gently in reassurance."

Twenty years is a long time to get to know an elephant. To Mac its second nature to know that each elephant has his or her own personality. He loves the part of his job that allows him to get to know each one on very profound levels. "When something is wrong, the elephants always get together as a herd even if they don't like each other. They show trust and understand the role people play in their herd, that we're helping them live the lives they were supposed to live. They know we're a source of food and since we always use positive reinforcement, they have come to trust us, and even consider us as extended family. Building trust starts from the moment you meet an elephant, it builds from talking to them, feeding and touching them in ways that prove you don't pose a threat to them. When you give all you can from your end, their response will tell you whether or not they will trust you. People have to earn their trust from elephants."

"If we don't do enough for wild elephants, then the next best place for them is a place like this where they are in protected contact," Mac continues. "They express their natural behavior living in freedom. They need 4 things in order to be happy: space, food, each other since they are social creatures, and freedom. Elephants are like us—they have distinct emotions and need to be treated with love, care and passion. I believe with all my heart that if we humans learn from them the world will be full of harmony." Mac exudes a brand of calm that matches the elephants when they are grazing in the field. His smile is bright and sincere.

There are three newer girls in Sally's herd, who we'll get to know in a later chapter. Mac says of the new girls becoming integrated with Sally's herd, "We always use positive reinforcement. Eventually the three new girls will be fully accepted as part of Sally's herd. When there is food around, Sally bullies the others as they try to get some, but otherwise she's a good matriarch and really does care for each of the other elephants. She's letting them in slowly but surely."

Dumisani Dube, a guide who all affectionately call Dumi, hails from Zimbabwe. He is tall and slender, youthful and energetic. The wind blows wisps of clouds like a comb through the otherwise blue sky as we stand on the edge of the valley where Sally and the other elephants have chosen to graze today. The valley is a steep downward climb, which the elephants are more than capable of doing. When I saw the slope, I couldn't believe an elephant could work down and back, but once in the valley, they hobble upward to the main field at an angle.

Dumi says in his soft-spoken, poetic way, "Sally has a very good heart. She never had offspring of her own and so doesn't know what it's like to be pregnant. Yet she shows worry about young orphans, gives them confidence, helps them adapt easier. Many of the orphans came from life threatening situations, as did she, and Sally ensures that the young ones are well cared for. Sally also shows others in the herd how to display love and forgive each other, how to live peacefully as a group. It's the Ubuntu philosophy in action: I am therefore we are. Looking after calves is done communally because in the world of elephants, a calf is a child of the herd. I have observed that when problems need to be solved it strengthens the elephant family unit. She can be a bossy lady at times, especially when food is involved. She has been known to shove others out of the way at the barrier so she can have more fruit from visitors for herself."

Dumisani continues, "Elephants are humans in elephant bodies. It is touching to see how family-oriented they are, and to see them display loving behaviors such as embracing each other with their trunks, supporting each other. It is wired into their brains to live as loving families. They shed tears and sympathize with each other. I see this happen in the field so often."

Growing up Dumisani never dreamed of working with elephants. His love of elephants was born from a coincidence. "I worked with my uncle vaccinating lions against HIV and medicating them. He's my

Sally pauses between browsing and a swim to take a robust drink of water.

inspiration. I've realized animals are better off than humans. I studied animal behavior, flora and fauna and then came to South Africa to find work since jobs were difficult to find in my native Zimbabwe."

Dumi recounts the story of a herd of elephants in Pilanscape. "The juveniles there were orphans, both boys and girls, who had no matriarch to guide them. They began to become naughty, destroying the habitat, not staying in harmony with nature. They needed an older elephant to come and restore order. This same phenomenon has been seen in herds of young bulls who have no elder to guide them. Once an older bull is brought in, they are able to teach the younger ones about law and order. This is what Sally has done for the younger elephants here at KEP."

Duties of the Queen Mother

Royalty in the elephant family is not passed down in a bloodline. Many researchers have proven that the top position in an elephant family is passed on to the next oldest and wisest female rather than automatically to the children of the matriarch. She was not chosen to be matriarch because she is feared; she was chosen because she is the oldest and wisest.

The mind of the matriarch contains local elephant lore mysteriously handed down through generations. This places Sally in an even more admirable category, as she had no mentoring yet carries out her duties to the benefit of the entire herd. She makes being a matriarch look easy. Older matriarchs in the wild hold an advantage to younger ones given that the elders hold much more life experience. Since elephants are highly social, leadership is rarely contested, except perhaps by the occasional sassy, young elephant testing her boundaries. The conduct of the herd suggests a recognized pecking order and recognition of the group's norms and rules which benefit the group as a whole. This is the Ubuntu way of life: the whole is more important than any one part and involves mutual support from all for each other. It is ironic that although humans invented the concept of Ubuntu, they can't manage to live it, with prejudice, racism and hatred growing throughout the world at an unprecedented speed. Elephants are peaceful creatures who rarely fight. They live the worth of Ubuntu.

The matriarch's job relies heavily on her ability for spatial memory and recall. In order to ensure the survival of her herd, she needs to not only remember where water and food sources are located; she must also have a sense of the times of the year when she can find these available and the likelihood of encountering predators. She also needs to have maps stored away in her mind so she can recall how to pilot the herd to these resources. She must reason whether or not the food and water sources involve long walks in hot, humid climates, whether or not the elevations are steep and high, and whether or not everyone in the herd is up to making the trek. She is thought to have some advanced problem-solving capability. In other words, if she can sense rains approaching, she can also reason that they will provide water for drinking and bathing. She is also thought to have some knowledge of the drainage patterns of the landscape and to know that rain flows downstream. She will guide her herd away from the place where the rains fall to the downstream location where the water collects.

Altruism is another strong matriarchal trait, as well as a trait all elephant mothers strive to teach their calves. Altruism grows from empathy for those in need, blurring the lines between oneself and others and between being selfish or generous. To be altruistic is to give of oneself in order to benefit another. And while most elephants behave this way naturally, a matriarch has the added responsibility of holding the end of the line. The buck stops with the matriarch in any elephant herd. There are widely heard stories in which a blind elephant is being cared for by an unrelated female. The blind female depended entirely upon the other, staying close to her and vocalizing as soon as they lost contact. The sighted elephant knew that the blind elephant was dependent on her and accepted the role of caregiver.

Empathy is a trait restricted to mammals and originates from the mother/child bond. Garstang, in *Elephant Sense and Sensibility*, writes, "Empathy is, for an elephant, no conscious cognitive skill but manifested largely as an unconscious automatic response.... There are four components of elephant behavior—leadership, playfulness, gentleness, and constancy—which were tested and the results subjected to statistical verification. The results showed that elephants are highly affiliative and cooperative, and display infrequent overt aggression between family members ... leadership is shown in exerting influence rather than dominance."[1] Researchers Lee and Moss concluded, "leadership was manifest in terms of respect, which recognized problem solving and permissiveness.... Elephants are very sensitive to the emotional state of others and have multiple and subtle means, sound, smell, sight, taste, and touch, of detecting this state. The capacity of elephants to detect and read the state of others is critical to their survival."

Darwin regarded social interests as the bonds that hold a group together and represent the beginnings of morality. The exception is the males of the herd. As they move through adolescence, their hormones flare, altering their behavior. It becomes the responsibility of the matriarch to let these hormonal males know it is time for them to go off on their own. In the wild, they will either wander with other males in a "bachelor herd," or they will be lone rangers, and sometimes, they will alternate between the two. A matriarch instinctively tries to eliminate males between the ages of ten and 15 years old from the herd. Sometimes a matriarch realizes that the benefits of living together for protection outweighs the cost of actually sharing resources like food and water, providing another reason for these males to go off on their own. This is the elephant way.

A respectable matriarch also needs to have facial and olfactory recall for elephants she has encountered in her past. Almost every rank and file elephant can recall the scent of about 100 other elephants; most researchers agree that a matriarch can remember far more.

* * *

There is no doubt that each elephant has his or her own distinct personality. Dr. Maud Bonato, current Head of Research for AERU, has this to say about the subject. "From a young age, I always had a deep interest in animal behavior. But after 15 years spent in the field of research, I am even more fascinated by how animals have different personalities, just like humans, really. Yet this is often under-evaluated, under-appreciated and dare I say under-utilized in our comprehension of animals. I worked for 15 years with farmed ostriches, and even if most people see them as stupid birds, the way I worked with them made me realize how the way I could approach them safely involved a good understanding of their personalities, and the mood they were in at a specific moment in time. This is the same working with elephants. It does not take very long to see the cheekiness and boldness of Madiwa, the smallest elephant in the park; the stubbornness of 'bulldozer' Thato; the drama that comes with Thandi's movements; as well as the occasional need of 'me time' away from the herd for Keisha, Shungu, Amari and more recently Shanti. This is where I believe research is important for captive animals: we need to make sure that we understand and cover all the individual needs of these animals that were put into our care."

Maud is from France, where she completed all her undergraduate studies in animal biology. She explains, "In 1995, my dad came to South Africa for work and for the following five years I came to visit him twice a year during my school holidays. We travelled all around the country in our small car, covering province after province. After all these trips, I could just not see myself continuing to study in France. So I enrolled in a Master's program in African Mammalogy at the University of Pretoria in 2001, and then a PhD in Behavioral Ecology at Stellenbosch University in 2005. South Africa became my second home ever since."

Interestingly, even though Maud's story with KEP/AERU officially started in June 2020 in the midst of one of the greatest pandemics of all time, her first encounter with the KEP elephants took place in the late 1990s when she was traveling with her dad. Back then she met Sally, Harry and Duma. Maud says of that visit, "The memories are starting to fade but I can still remember this exciting yet frightening feeling of standing so close to these magical creatures." Little did she know that she would become the Head of Research at AERU more than 20 years later!

* * *

Scientists have recently identified four distinct personality types prevalent in a herd. They are the leaders, the gentle giants, the playful rogues and the reliable plodders. The theory goes that each of these types has evolved to help these mammoth creatures survive even in harsh environments, and scientists believe that these personality types are unique in the animal kingdom. A herd hopefully consists of a blend of these personality types to ensure their survival as a family. In the elephant world, the ability to influence others and sustain friendships is what makes the difference. In some other animal species, we often see aggression or dominance. Aside from the dominance factor being a key factor in herd behavior, so are neuroticism, agreeableness, curiosity and impulsiveness, which are easily studied with captive elephants.

Well-known elephant research pioneer Cynthia Moss, along with her associate, Phyllis Lee, analyzed data which was collected over a staggering 38 years of observations of one elephant family. Moss and Lee distinguished 26 elephant behaviors and bundled them into the four most common personality types. "The strongest of the personalities is that of the leader. These matriarchs tended to influence the physical movement of the group, are known and respected by their herd for being good problem solvers, and have a spatial map in their minds of where food, water, minerals and other resources can be found. They also had the loudest 'let's go' rumbles indicating that it is time to move on. In contrast, many other animal species have leaders who prove to be the most aggressive and dominant of the herd. Good elephant matriarchs live the African concept of Ubuntu, or together we are more important than any one of us."[2]

One blistering South African afternoon I observed Sally acting restless and unsettled when herd members returned from a distant pasture. She continued to glare back toward the forested area they had come from, her head shaking, her trunk poised upward in a sniffing stance. When the guides ambled over to the distant field to investigate, they returned with none other than a young Shungu. He was focused on a gathering of butterflies that were feeding on a patch of wildflowers, oblivious when the herd moved on. Once Sally saw Shungu approaching, she relaxed and went about her business. Even though he is the lowest in the pecking order, Sally had his back.

Moss and Lee wrote that while dominance is normally the way animal groups are governed; with elephants it is more about their ability to garner agreement among all involved. In human terms they act as a mediator. Lee wrote in *Telegraph*, "Leadership is not equal to power or assertion in elephants, but illustrates the respect accorded to individuals as a function of their problem-solving ability and their social permissiveness."[3]

As I've established, in order to ensure the survival of her herd, Sally must have a way to read the spatial perspectives of the landscape.

Part Two

Elephants, like other animals, do not use the landscape in a uniform way which helps vary their impacts on the landscape. One of the most important factors influencing the use of space is topographical relief. Although elephants are sometimes reluctant to climb slopes, they are adept at it when they decide to do it. KEP has an area with steep slopes that lead to a valley. Many are the times elephants like Mashudu or Keisha go off on their own for some alone time deep down in the valley. During the wildfires of 2017, which we'll come to soon, the guides led Sally and her herd into the valley in order to avoid the thick smoke that prevailed over higher ground.

Sally can be salty when she needs to be for the benefit of the herd's welfare, but she is a highly regarded matriarch by the other nine, the staff and all who meet her. It will be interesting to observe her as she ages, to see if she becomes pregnant and gives birth to her own offspring and to view the ways in which her matriarchal skills sharpen over time. Sally may wield her weightiness at times, but she is a delightful blend of wise, witty, empathetic and motherly. When she places a branch on her back or shows off at the barrier, she brings a big grin to everyone's face. She seems to thrive on human attention—as long as she has had her fill of fruit treats!

7

Nandi:
Mother of Thandi

"But perhaps the most important lesson I learned is that there are no walls between humans and the elephants except those that we put up ourselves, and that until we allow not only elephants, but all living creatures their place in the sun we can never be whole ourselves."—Lawrence Anthony, author of *The Elephant Whisperer*

"Nandi" means "a sweet thing" in the Zulu language.
Identifying Characteristics:

Crooked tail
Bite shape out of left ear
Extremely rough skin on forehead
Born February 1993

Nandi was named for the mother of the legendary Zulu leader, King Shaka, who was said to be a very strong-willed lady. So too is Nandi. She is the second oldest in the herd and the undeclared second in command. Nandi came to KEP from the Northern Province in 2002 and was the first elephant to give birth to a calf at KEP. Her daughter is Thandi, whom we will meet in the next chapter. Nandi is an exceptionally good mother, albeit a bit of a helicopter mother. In spite of her hovering style, she often fails to discipline Thandi when she misbehaves or takes chances, enabling Thandi's dramatic personality. Nandi, in her hypervigilance, can be heard roaring whenever Thandi is out of sight. They often share a branch, each with their mouth on an end, symbolizing their mother/daughter bond.

Nandi has an extremely rough patch of skin on her forehead and what appears to be a bite mark on her left ear, making her one of the easier elephants to identify. She and Sally are thick as thieves, often grazing together with Thandi away from the rest of the herd. Nandi is probably the most hesitant of the herd toward strangers, but since she trusts the guides, she will allow some to touch her as she grazes.

Fanwell Nyoni and Nandi have a special understanding. Born in the Hwange National Park in Zimbabwe where his family still resides, Fanwell began working with elephants 15 years ago and has been at KEP for the past five. In spite of the fact that he grew up being told that they were dangerous animals, he has loved working with elephants since he was a young man. He read books and studied about them with fascination. Fanwell says, "These animals are unpredictable. Nandi chose me, and likes me to be underneath her head. When I first arrived, I thought she was going to be difficult, so it was a nice surprise when after only a week she let me know she felt safe with me. She comes when I call and arrives begging for food," Fanwell says, as he flashes a smile bright as ivory. Fanwell is a well-respected elephant guide and is always full of information

Fanwell is pictured here with Thandi. He has a close bond with her mother, Nandi, but loves all the elephants. He marvels at the close bond between the two, knowing that Sally treats Thandi as her own and is the only one to discipline her.

about the elephants he clearly loves, when guiding tours.

Today, the guides' tan and green uniforms blend into the earth and trees in contrast to the jagged horizon of the plum-shaded Drakensburg Mountains in the distance. The spring grass the only brightness, the gray of the elephants matches the sky. Yesterday, the sun shone on their tail hairs, shiny and thick like strings of black licorice. Elephant tails make perfect flyswatters. The wiry hair on their heads and bodies bristles in the filtered sunlight. Day after day, all year round, the guides are out in these fields with the elephants, anticipating the next moves of each herd member, knowing their personalities inside and out and aware of the social rank of each. The guides appear calm but are always watching, watching, watching,

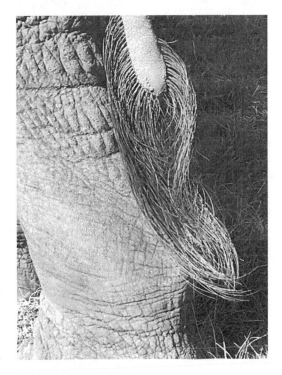

The tail of each elephant is unique. With thick hair like stalks of licorice, some have more hair on one side than the other or the hair forms different patterns. We know Shungu is easily recognizable partly by the kink in his tail with N shaped tail hair, more on the right side, and Thandi has a lot more hair on the left side of the tail than the right side. Thato has a noticeably short, stubby tail, and Mash has a long tail with lush hair.

reading and interpreting elephant body language, applying it to all situations. They often talk among themselves, the clicks and clacks of their native Xhosa music to my ears. Sure enough, Sally, Nandi and Thandi are grazing off in the distance to the right, and the rest of the herd is spread out on the hillside to the left.

* * *

Part Two

An Elephant's Reproductive Cycle

An important part of effective elephant population management involves monitoring reproductive and ovarian activity. In recent years, great strides have been made in endocrine and ultrasound monitoring techniques. There is a high need to develop new methods of controlling ovarian activity, both for enhancing and inhibiting pregnancy and birth in order to maintain elephant populations at levels that ensure survival of the species. Nutritional stress and the high metabolic and time cost of foraging when food is sparse can delay the mean age of the first conception in elephants and increase the average time between successive births.

The estrus cycle of both Asian and African elephants occurs every 15 to 16 weeks, or about every three months. Courtship may last anywhere from one hour to four days, during which the bull will stay near the cow and protect her from other bulls while occasionally mating with her. After one to three days, the cow will no longer be receptive to breeding or capable of conceiving, and voila, the courtship is over. It's much shorter than a summer romance.

The gestation period for elephants is a staggering 22 months, which translates to 659 plus or minus 30 days. It can be diagnosed by serial weekly serum samples screened for elevated progesterone or through urine samples containing higher-than-normal levels of luteal hormones. This method takes between 12 and 16 consecutive weekly samples to make a firm pregnancy diagnosis. Alternatively, a single blood sample taken from the ear, where the skin is thinner, can confirm a pregnancy by analyzing prolactin levels which increase exponentially after about 20 weeks of pregnancy. More recently, ultrasound has been used successfully to confirm pregnancy in elephants. These can be performed beginning around week eight after breeding; however, the fetus is not visible until nine to ten weeks after breeding. Elephants who live under the care of humans are fed highly nutritious, generally parasite-free diets and are free from having to walk long distances in order to find food, making them candidates for being overweight if not monitored carefully since this can cause the fetus to be large and potentially cause difficult births.

Speaking of births, C-sections have been attempted, unsuccessfully, in elephants undergoing difficult births. Most of the current population of adult females is unfamiliar with the birthing process. Some are not used to having infants around and, as a result, may be frightened of their newborn calves and attempt to harm or kill them out of fear. The *Elephant Husbandry Resource Guide* suggests, "Only the people with whom the elephants are familiar should be present during the birthing process. When the first signs of labor appear, it is recommended that the elephant handlers put the elephant on at least two and preferably four leg tethers. Typical signs of labor are stretching, leaning into walls, swaying, restlessness, crossing her legs, obvious contractions, going down on her knees, mucous discharge, vocalizations, pulling on teats, hitting her stomach with her legs and/or her trunk. Sawdust, or other safe absorbent material should be moved into an adjacent stall to avoid interfering with the handlers, but they should be able to observe the birth and the newborn calf. It is important for the other female elephants to witness the birth as this may be an invaluable learning experience. Tethering is recommended if the herd becomes agitated." These authors recommend that the elephant handlers remove the calf just out of trunk reach of the tethered female immediately after birth. The calf should be pulled a short distance from the mother so the mother can smell and touch the calf but not grab or step on it. The female should be allowed to calm down as she watches her infant being attended to. This period of separation gives the handlers time to clean and inspect the calf, the veterinarian time to perform the neonatal exam, and the calf time to become steady on its feet. The calf should attempt to stand on its own. They recommended that the calf is not rushed back to the mother until all conditions are controlled. If the calf is mobile and eager to nurse and the elephant manager is confident the female is calm, interested and is responsive to all of the handler's commands before the introduction is attempted, the calf should be allowed to find its mother's teat on its own. Ideally, successful nursing should occur within the first 12 hours to ensure the calf receives the necessary colostrum. As it is for humans, colostrum is high in calories and immunoglobulins which are critical for the development of the immune system and disease prevention.[1]

Dr. Debbie explains, "The mother and child should be kept separately from the rest of the herd in order to foster bonding between them, as well as to ensure that the mother demonstrates appropriate care of her newborn. Often when newborns arrive there is great celebrating amongst the herd with trumpeting and other happy sounds. After an initial and normal loss of weight in the first week or so, calves should gain approximately 2 pounds per day. The average calf weighs about 250 pounds at birth, so a healthy newborn should weigh 300 pounds in a few months. Calves need to nurse for two full years for optimal health, making orphaned elephants like Keisha highly susceptible to illness and even death, if they don't receive proper substitutions for their mother's milk." We'll see this in action in Chapter 9.

Calves need to be taught to tolerate medical examinations, blood collection, foot care, treatment of any injuries, trunk wash for tuberculosis (yes, elephants are susceptible to TB), and daily mouth examinations for early signs of the elephant herpes virus. It is good practice to teach the calf to tolerate brief separations from its mother in case it is in need of medical treatment. Some calves jeopardized their own safety by thrashing in an attempt to try to return to their mother. Because human contact is often unavoidable, the calf should be taught to respect the personal space of the handlers, no easy feat for a curious calf. They also must be taught the meaning of the command "NO" for safety reasons.

Controlling elephant populations is a key issue in the long-term survival of the species. When it comes to the use of contraception to control elephant populations, the ideal contraceptive must be efficient, allow remote delivery, be reversible, produce no negative short- or long-term side effects, cause no changes in social behaviors and herd integrity, must not pass through the food chain, should be safe during pregnancy, and be affordable. Contraception in elephants can be achieved through hormonal methods, surgery (vasectomy), or immunizations. The female immunization, called Porcine Zona Pellucidal (pZP) vaccine has proven successful thus far.

Much needs to be done through research efforts in order to use these available contraception methods effectively. Darting select females to inoculate with contraceptives would have to happen with some regularity. In areas like South Africa's Kruger National Park, animals can be difficult to locate, making contraception in female elephants highly labor intensive and expensive, not to mention potentially stressful to the animals.

Interestingly enough, a calf that is born to a mother under the age of 20 has an eight times lower mortality rate if the calf's grandmother lives in the herd with the calf and mom, as compared to calves living away from their grandmothers. Moms whose mothers lived with them had a decrease in the intervals between births by a full year, irrespective of whether or not the grandmother was still having her own calves. Hannah Mumby writes in *Elephants*, "From an evolutionary point of view, grandmothers increased their own fitness, or number of descendants, by enhancing the reproductive rates of their daughters and the survival of grandcalves."[2]

Incidentally, for those elephants who would rather not bother with the rituals of courtship, or for herds that are made up of only females, artificial insemination (AI) is a highly viable alternative, as it is with cows in the United States. AI can have many positive effects, such as increasing genetic diversity, in some cases increasing the numbers of elephants of reproductive age who can be impregnated and in reducing the need to move established female herds. It also is a tool for introducing new genetics into a fixed population without having to remove or translocate elephants for reproductive purposes only. This can be done by collecting semen from bulls to use in AI.

* * *

Sadly there are no babies at KEP, but both males, Mashudu and Shungu are reaching the age of sexual reproduction, so there's always hope. Madi and Mashudu have spent many flirtatious hours play sparring in the fields, while rumors of Thato following Shungu around tickle my fancy. Many of us imagined romances with the girls in Sally's herd, all of whom are eligible. Keisha, Thandi, Thato, Madiwa are the favorite fantasy contenders among staff and volunteers for becoming the next mothers, followed in later years by Amari, Shanti, and Thandi.

As we have seen, humans are the only predators for adult elephants; however, that is far from the truth for young elephants, who are in danger of being killed by any number of larger animals, lions and tigers being only a few. Living in a herd provides the advantage of collective defense against predators, especially with calves involved. While most lions, tigers, hyenas, or rhinos usually attack an adult elephant only as a last resort, they absolutely will attack young calves. Traveling in packs or prides, when a predator appears, the adult females charge the attackers in solidarity, and the young one is often saved, but occasionally, they lose the battle and forfeit the baby.

The Nandi/Thandi Phenomenon

Nandi and Thandi are often seen intertwining trunks and trumpeting for joy when they are reunited after being out of each other's line of vision. Nandi is the least likely in the herd to initiate contact with

Nandi and Thandi are pictured at the barrier awaiting their fruit buckets from tourists.

tourists or volunteers, but she is fine with them touching her side and taking photos when she has food available to distract her and a loving guide nearby.

Nandi's place at the barrier is next to Sally. Interestingly, Thandi

Nandi and Thandi are often seen with trunks entwined, a physical sign of the depth of their mother/daughter bond. When Thandi is out of Nandi's sight for more than a few minutes, she panics and shouts out for her. They often touch trunks when they are reunited.

stands on the other side of Sally for the ritual of visitors feeding fruit to the elephants. The elephants have either chosen their set place for this or worked it out with Sally, but they stand in the same spots reliably. They are creatures of habit, as we tend to be with our routines and structured time. Prepare to meet Thandi, whose personality is larger than life and whose own stint as a mother was tragically cut short.

8

Thandi: The Diva
with the Perfect Ears

"Of all African animals, the elephant is the most difficult
for man to live with, yet its passing—if this must come—
seems the most tragic of all. I can watch elephants, and
elephants alone, for hours at a time, for sooner or later
the elephant will do something very strange such as
mow the grass with its toenail or draw the tusks from
the rotted carcass of another elephant and carry them
off into the bush. There is mystery behind that masked
grey visage, and ancient life force, delicate and mighty,
awesome and enchanted, commanding the silence ordi-
narily reserved for mountain peaks, great fires, and the
sea."—Peter Matthiessen

"Thandi" means "love" in Zulu.
Identifying Characteristics:
> Lots of tail hair on left side
> Huge wrinkle on forehead
> Very large Dumbo-like ears
> Born October 16, 2003

Thandi, daughter of Nandi, was the first calf born at KEP. As such,
she is truly the pride and joy of all. In the first month or two of her life
she kept close to her mother's side. As she matured, she began taking
a particular interest in the youngest elephants at the park. The staff
believes she has been maintaining her mothering skills. She had a calf
when she was quite young who tragically did not survive. Fiela's story
will be revealed soon. Thandi can be quite bossy, full of drama and is
often referred to as a "diva" or drama queen. She has been known to
ignore Sally's "let's go calls" at times, and one day I saw her come to the
station and stand in Sally's place thinking she could get away with it.
Sally shoved her to the side. But since Nandi rarely disciplines Thandi,

Part Two

Sally often steps in and takes charge of that aspect of mothering Thandi. She continues to be very close to Nandi, and to Sally, whom she seems to consider a second parent or aunt. Sally truly treats Thandi as a daughter.

Physically, Thandi has exceptionally large ears, which when fanned

When Thandi spreads her ears out, it's as if she knows how beautiful she looks. She enjoys flapping them when people are watching, which is both beautiful and comical.

are picture-book beautiful. You might say Thandi is the epitome of what a female African elephant should look like. Like Dumbo the elephant, Thandi has a secret about those ears of hers. It's as if she knows people enjoy seeing her flap them, which is both beautiful and comical to watch.

Shepherd and Shungu are the first on the herd walks, Shungu preferring to lead the herd since none of the others want to. Shepherd, who has loved elephants since he was a small boy, is calm and confident around the ellies and has a good relationship with them all.

Another characteristic making her easy to identify is the large wrinkle over her eyes that crosses her forehead. It is prominent and unmistakable. Thandi is often "bratty," having been spoiled by her mother and Sally, as well as the rest of the herd and staff. She sometimes pretends not to hear commands if she isn't ready and at other times tries to force some lower in the pecking order away from fruit buckets and other goodies. Thandi's personality exceeds her size. She is currently in the prime of adolescence.

Shepherd Abednico Chuma, who has loved elephants since he was a small boy, enjoys the complexity and challenge of caring for Thandi, believing that with her it is especially critical to maintain a good relationship. I have had the pleasure of walking next to Shepherd and Shungu when the herd walks together. He is soft-spoken and funny, kindhearted and his eyes shine with love for these elephants. He explains, "It's important to read the body language of each individual elephant. Thandi believes she's the baby of the herd, the princess, and she knows she's pretty. She's the only elephant here who has virtually two mothers—Nandi, and Sally. Nandi often lets Thandi push her around. Many believe Nandi lacks the parenting skills to discipline her. Those who know Nandi well say it's because she steers clear of conflicts. Sally, on the other hand, doesn't tolerate that sort of behavior. I've seen her push her hip against Thandi to get her to listen or move, and I have also heard Sally rumble directly in Thandi's face as if to scold her. As the matriarch, she pushes back, putting Thandi in her place, teaching her necessary lessons."

Self-Directed Elephant Behaviors and the Roots of Personality

Clare Padfield explains that elephants engage in what scientists refer to as Self-Directed Behavior or SDBs. "A self-directed behavior is defined as having the potential to exert power, produce an effect, or influence the environment. These are individualized nervous behaviors that an elephant performs like putting its trunk out and curling the end, swinging the trunk back and forth, or otherwise fidgeting, much like we humans have our own individualized nervous behaviors such as nail biting, hair touching, or knuckle cracking. When Thandi places her trunk inside her mouth for a moment, it is like she is sucking on a pacifier or using a thumb-sucking gesture for self-comfort."

Clare continues, "A broad definition of personality is an observable pattern of thoughts and behaviors that an individual exhibits consistently over a period of time and in a variety of situations. Researchers generally agree that personality is largely a function of one's genes, and have defined factors that comprise personality in elephants. These are dominance, neuroticism, agreeableness, curiosity and impulsiveness. Much more research is needed on elephant personality in order for us to truly understand the depth and complexity of these many-faceted beings."

Shungu pictured here has his trunk in his mouth as a self-soothing, self-directed behavior akin to a human baby sucking on its thumb or a pacifier.

Fiela's Legacy Laboratory

Fiela's Lab honors the legacy of Thandi's baby who died as an infant. Thandi was young when she became pregnant. When Fiela was born, Thandi rejected her, possibly out of fear, trying to step on her as animal mothers often do when they know the baby has a serious defect and won't survive. Fiela was taken away from her and bottle fed. Soon, she began to thrive and run through the fields in sheer delight. At three months old, she suddenly became ill and passed away a few days later. An autopsy revealed organ failure, and the vet said he was shocked that she had lived that long.

Naturally, everyone at the park mourned Fiela's passing. Shiela and Garth Wheeler, a Canadian couple about to visit the park for the first time, donated money to pay for Fiela's special bottle formula, which was costly. Fiela passed away just before their arrival. They were so upset that they donated money to help build a laboratory on site with the hopes that it might help prevent tragedies like this in the future. The Wheelers made the laboratory a reality.

Enter Christina Tholander, who currently runs Fiela's Laboratory and is also a volunteer coordinator for AERU. The spring following Fiela's death, Christina, who studied biochemistry at the University of Copenhagen, decided to come to KEP to volunteer. As a very young child, she remembers seeing elephants in a parade and has loved them ever since. Christina blended with the staff and other volunteers like jam to peanut butter (elephants do love peanuts; it's really true!), and she was offered the position as a lab technician. South Africa is on the top five list of the most difficult places to obtain work permits, but she persevered from Denmark through a nail-biting process before finally getting approval. When it was finally granted, she returned to KEP and began the job she loves so much. Christina explains in her characteristically joyful way, "I still get chills going out into the field because I feel so lucky to get to work with elephants. I feel accepted here by them and by the other staff. I'll never forget the day Shungu put his trunk on my shoulder, and it's hard to explain I was so humbled and thrilled. Being here at KEP makes me feel like I'm part of something bigger."

"No two days here are the same," she continues. "We put in long days but in the end it's all for the elephants. My main focus is in the lab working with the dung samples collected twice a week on dung walks. And I also enjoy meeting people and showing them our elephants and this pearl of a place. I like to feel the small work I do will play into the big picture. We're all trying to make a difference."

I went on a dung walk early one morning with Christina. Samples are collected in a very specific way in order to be properly analyzed in the lab, which you'll read more about soon. A mature elephant produces up to 250 pounds of dung and 14 gallons of urine every day. Christina explains that looking at a dung sample under a microscope is like looking into a time machine, each sample unique. Once the samples are collected, they are labeled with the date, name of the elephant and the time of collection. Christina then freeze-dries the samples. The second step is to extract hormone samples by using dung dust from the freeze-dried samples. After that, she adds ethanol to extract hormones. She then spins it in a centrifuge. In the final step, Christina puts the sample into an oven to vaporize the liquid, and the remaining samples are sent to the University of Pretoria Endocrine Research Lab in Pretoria, the capital of

Named for Thandi's baby Fiela who passed away as an infant, the laboratory is used to process dung samples to profile hormone levels, including cortisol, a stress hormone. Here biochemist Christina Tholander processes a dung sample. Originally from Denmark, Christina started at AERU as a volunteer and has just as much enthusiasm and love for the ellies now as she did back then.

South Africa. Each dung sample costs $12 to analyze. This painstaking and expensive process is done for each elephant twice weekly. Through this extensive process, AERU gathers information about progesterone levels, which relate to reproductive health and estrus cycles, as well as cortisol levels, a hormone released by stress. Information on other hormones is in the reports that come back from the Pretoria lab which AERU compiles and uses in research.

Christina's future vision for the laboratory is to have the equipment for full hormone analysis here at the park, which would save a lot of time and money in the long run. She says, "Right now, I estimate I have over 8,000 samples that need to be analyzed. It costs a lot of money to ship the samples and pay the lab in Pretoria to do the analysis. If we could fully process the samples here, we would not only save money, but we could potentially perform the service for other facilities which would assist in covering our expenses. We would also be saving valuable staff time which could benefit the elephants in other ways." She adds with a smile as bright as sunshine, "We have to dream big. Volunteers are trained to prepare the dung samples for lab examination, which is a tedious process, requiring precise measurements and deep concentration to get each sample primed exactly right. Our volunteers are ambassadors for elephants whose support and willingness to help with anything and everything is overwhelming. If it wasn't for the volunteers, we could never gather the volume of information we amass. We rely so heavily on our volunteers and are so grateful for their dedication."

Also a highly talented fine artist, Christina has gathered the confidence to delve into her artwork in her spare time and has produced a line of drawings, postcards, magnets, tote bags and laser-cut items with each of the individual elephant's pictures on them. Her drawings are labors of love, so exquisite are they in their detail and the way they capture each elephant's personality. The sensitivity and detailing in her drawings reflect the profound love she has for these animals. Her work is sold at the park and online at Etsy.com.

Donate to Fiela's Lab via *www.aeru.co.za* using PayPal.

Sponsor an elephant—also through *www.aeru.co.za*

* * *

Late in the afternoon, Thandi stands near a wooded area which houses a tree full of weaverbird nests. Birds in the weaverbird category include some finches and sparrows who build their intricate woven houses communally, meaning there are many nests in the same tree, sometimes several to a branch. The nests are an amazing woven structure made of plant fibers such as leaf fibers, grass and twigs. The nests are roofed and enclosed with the entrance toward the bottom facing down in order to deter predators. Looking at these woven units is like looking at fine art, so intricately is the woven fabric and shape of the nests. It is up to the male weaverbird to weave and place the nest in order to attract a mate who is pleased with the structure as well as its location. Weaverbirds are the only birds known to have the ability to tie a knot, and when I looked at a nest closely, they indeed are tightly woven and include knots. Watching the birds fly in and out of the nests with so many nests in a single tree is a marvelous, joyous experience. It is as if each tree is a complete community.

9

Thato: All Kinds
of Adorable

"Ganesha, the elephant God in the Hindu religion, has
been revered for centuries. Buddhists of Tibet show similar reverence of elephants."—Michael Garstang, *Elephant
Sense and Sensibility*

"Thato" means "love" or "beloved" in Tswana and Zulu.
Identifying Characteristics:

Two short tusks that point downward
Short stubby tail
Looks "hunched"
Born February 2008

Thato came to KEP in May 2008 after her parents were killed on a
hunting farm in the North West Province. Still a baby, Thato loved being
bottle fed, often holding the bottle with her trunk as she sucked the milk
in through her mouth. She lives up to her name in every way: beloved or
loved. Thato has an ever-present youthfulness to her face, as she bats her
long, wiry eyelashes flirtatiously. Her sense of playfulness and sponta-
neity is priceless. She has known Mashudu her whole life, as she arrived
with him after his parents were killed on the same hunting farm.

Today her gray matches the clouds which shower rain on and off
like a faulty faucet. Verdant spring grass and an occasional dandelion are
the only brightness. The rumble and vibration of the tractor precedes
its sight, but she knows sweet fruit awaits her, like candy to a child. She
promenades to her place at the barrier, a thick metal pole mounted
horizontally, making it safe for the elephants to stand on one side, and
tourists stand on the opposite side in order to hand-feed the elephants
buckets of fruit. Thato, in her preadolescent defiance, decides to stand in
Sally's center spot. When Sally ambles over, she tosses her heavy weight
on Thato by nudging her firmly but gently with a shove of her massive

hips, and poor Thato is reminded of her place. Head down, she moves over as if to say, "I just wanted to see if I could get away with it." An elephant is constantly reminded of her status. She often doesn't get much fruit, as Sally demands her overwhelming share and obtains it by sticking her trunk out the farthest. Sally doesn't fool around when it comes to her fruit! Thato grabs a few pieces of fruit while Sally is chewing.

Shepherd was the first to work with Thato when she arrived at the park. "I spent many hours feeding and caring for her. Now she thinks I'm her father. We have a very special bond. With the elephants, it's all about having an individual relationship with each one. In order to accomplish that you have to love them, talk to them and feed them." Shepherd is well liked and well respected by the staff and the elephants, as are the other guides. They have each worked painstakingly to establish trust between themselves and each of the ten members of Sally's' herd. Shepherd won't admit it, but I see the twinkle in his eyes when he interacts with Thato that gives it away that she is indeed his favorite. Shepherd has a calming presence about him, and as he lifts his cap, it reveals a handsome traditional weave of rows that complement his serene face.

Back in the field an orange and black butterfly glides near Thato's head, tiny periwinkle wildflowers near her feet. Her skin is like rubbery leather to the touch with wrinkles deep as gorges, thick black hair accenting at intervals. She gazes at me with the longest tangle of eyelashes I've ever seen, and her deep amber-brown eyes somehow make me feel I'm looking into her heart. They are soft and moist and an ancient wisdom seems to emanate outward from this teenager. One night I observed her in the boma resting her tonnage by leaning on the iron poles along the wall. Another night, she was lying on her side in the soft sawdust looking angelic under the infrared light as she dreamed away.

Edison, who clearly loves all ten elephants, admits, when pushed, that Thato is his favorite. "She is cute, relaxed and funny. At the barrier she is mellow and polite. She and Shungu have come to realize 'if I don't get fed here, it's ok. I can just stand here and look cute.'" Edison finds Thato an interesting mix in her position within the herd. "She is part of the core group that includes Sally, Nandi and Thandi, but clearly stays away from their drama. She is in the middle of the hierarchy and gets along well with those above her and below her in stature." Edison, who is very talkative and warm, thinks Thato will retain her playful personality for life. There is a playful youthfulness about her as I watch her in the field fanning her ears to cool herself while loading her mouth with greenery. Like humans, young elephants like Thato tend to be more

Thato grazes with Sally (facing forward) in the field on a sparkling clear afternoon. The photograph angle here makes them appear to be of similar size, but Sally has more height and much more girth than Thato. The youngest and smallest of Sally's herd, Thato is a combination of funny and adorable. The combination of her small size and her stubby tail often gives her away in the field. She is allomothered by Sally as well as Keisha.

curious and playful. Some elephants retain this childlike tendency for life, as many humans do, while in others, playfulness declines with age. Along with Edison, my hope is that Thato retains her sense of play and lightheartedness as she grows into maturity. It is a beautiful thing to witness. Just thinking about her brings a smile to my face.

Understanding elephant behavior and body language is a tricky business. The guiding philosophy of an elephant herd is the South African concept of Ubuntu: I am what I am because of who we all are. But as individuals, each elephant has a distinct personality and unique behaviors. Clare gives a fascinating elephant behavioral presentation to each group of volunteers as part of their intensive training. In it, she explains, smiling and full of passion for her job, "Behaviors help elephants resolve their feelings by communicating them. Normal behaviors are scientifically referred to as state behaviors. Fascinating things happen daily within a herd of elephants making each day in the field a unique adventure."

Self-directed behaviors are the results of a living creature thinking and feeling their emotions. When Thato rubs her eye with the tip of her trunk, it is a self-directed behavior because it is directed toward her own body. I've seen her do this in the field many times. It brought an automatic smile to my face, and the memory of this lovely gesture makes me smile still.

When it comes to elephant body language, understanding and reading it correctly is a matter of life and death. The guides in the field are vigilant, reading each elephant's behavior at all times. To start with, those large ears are the best first indicator of an elephant's emotions. When they are pricked, the elephant is tense about something. If Thato shakes her ears or head, she is expressing frustration or irritation. If she shakes her body, look out. She is upset! Elephants also show anxiety with a certain 't-twist' at the tip of the trunk. When Thato fidgets or scratches herself more vigorously than a passing itch, she is showing signs of stress. Primates scratch themselves when under stress the way we humans have a variety of behaviors exhibiting stress, including nail-biting, fidgeting, jaw clenching, fist tightening, and tightening facial and shoulder muscles. Fanwell chuckles heartily as he recalls, "Thato is walking in a line with the others and appears to be minding her own business. But, when she thinks I'm not looking, she darts her trunk to the side to grab a stray mushroom or wildflower." He is laughing out loud, so smitten with her is he.

Aggression and dominance behaviors are not always serious; some are done in play. Madiwa and Mashudu demonstrate this daily as a form of play and of flirting. It's a kerfuffle of the elephant variety. A mock charge is performed in order to intimidate. It starts with ears fully out and vocalizations and can lead to an elephant kicking, shoving another as Sally does at the barrier when she wants to displace another elephant to get more of the fruit, stealing a branch from an elephant higher up in the hierarchy, or placing a tusk to another elephant's butt are all aggressive behaviors. In a full-blown charge, the elephant's ears remain close to the head, and as they run, they are not kicking up dirt and making a spectacle but much more serious, streamlined body language. And believe it or not, even though they can't run, elephants cover a lot of ground quickly, so if you're out in the field and an elephant displays these behaviors, look out!

Knowing her place within the herd, Thato often exhibits submissive behavior. For example, when Sally puts her gently but firmly into her place at the barrier, she backs away from Sally or backs into another elephant with her butt, a more submissive pose than if she used her face. Other examples of submissive behavior include putting their rear end toward another elephant purposefully or walking away. Today I looked over toward Thato as she grazed on browse in the field near Sally and was stunned to see Thato and Sally, standing face to face, trunks entwined, a picture-perfect moment, their love for each other contagious.

When Thato touches her trunk to another elephant, she is showing affiliative or affectionate behavior, which strengthens the social bonds between individual elephants. Other affectionate behaviors include putting a trunk into another elephant's mouth, tangling trunks, placing a trunk on another's head or back. Self-soothing behaviors can include sucking the tip of the trunk as a human baby would suck on a pacifier, using the trunk to touch their own body or rub their eyes. Vigilant behaviors include head up, tail up (which enhance special proprioception or one's sense in space), swishing tail, ears out. Frustrated behaviors include shaking the head or a full body shake. Nervous behaviors include putting their trunk straight out or curling it, fidgeting, pacing, and shaking a foot. And beware: If an elephant flicks

Keisha and Mashudu showing affiliative behavior by the edge of the pond with elegantly entwined trunks. The water is muddy from recent rain, and these two went in for a swim right after this picture was taken.

its trunk on the head of another it is the equivalent of giving them the middle finger.

AERU is the foremost leader in researching emotions, particularly anxiety in elephants, and is continuing projects to understand these behaviors better. As they do, it will provide fascinating insights into understanding their personalities as individuals and as a herd.

The Striped Contingency at the Park

The dramatic mountain view from KEP is always a welcome sight. Note the two zebras near the lower left-hand corner.

I awoke from a deep sleep to trumpeting elephants on my first morning at KEP. Was I hearing things? I stepped outside my room, still half asleep and almost tripped over something large. I regained my footing and rubbed my eyes. Was a zebra in front of my door? The elephants were already out in the fields. I couldn't see them, but I heard them clearly. I really am finally here, I thought, in my foggy jet-lagged state. When I turned to go back inside, there were two more zebras grazing with no

Zebras often graze on elephant scraps out in the field. The zebra on the right is pregnant. Their coloring is a soft earthy brown between the black and white stripes; their noses look like they were caught in a bowl of chocolate.

barrier separating us. One was sniffing the open doorway to my room! They were three or four feet away. As I reached an arm out to touch one, they ran askance, skittish. I froze, not daring to move as they continued to graze, their heads bent toward the spring grass. I was surprised to notice they had a brown, shadowy stripe in between the black and white, an earthy, sable color, the elegant, unique trademark of Burchell's zebras. They have short manes down the back of the neck, tails trailing long, black hair. I would learn that males are slightly larger than females, a narrow, black stripe running vertically between their hind legs. The females have a wider stripe. The side stripes run down the body, joining under the belly. Like human fingerprints, the stripe pattern on each individual zebra is unique. Incidentally, South Africans and British pronounce "zebra" with a short e, rather than the American long e.

Every volunteer takes a turn hiking the park to identify and check on each of the zebras. I took this hike early in the morning with Clare, using picture postcards of each zebra to identify and take "attendance," making sure each zebra is accounted for. It was a fascinating hike; I learned that my zebra-identifying skills need considerable improvement.

Zebras can sound high-pitched alarms. They also snort and make barking and baying vocalizations. What I did not realize when I encountered several zebras outside my door that first morning at KEP was that zebras can and will kick if one gets too close, and they feel trapped. I've since seen them kick each other, and it looks painful. I count myself lucky they didn't kick me.

Zebras play an important role at KEP by feeding on the grassy areas the elephants don't reach. Burchell's zebras are named for the famous British explorer and naturalist William John Burchell. Grimly, Burchell's zebra is the only subspecies of zebra which may be legally farmed for human consumption, but these particular zebras are in a safe haven and are free to reproduce and live as they would in the wild, with no predators. The elephants mostly ignore them.

Clare explained on our zebra walk that there are approximately 30 zebras here at KEP, a fluctuating number with babies born throughout the year. They live in several types of family groups. A harem group consists of a stallion and one to six mares with their most recent foals. Bachelor groups consist of two to eight, sometimes up to 15 unattached stallions. These outcast males form bachelor herds of about 15, in which dominance is usually determined by age. When stallion herds meet, they sniff each other to decide whether or not they will get along. The males in these herds are often the younger or older stallions of the population. Stallion zebras are not territorial, each having a dominant stallion and a dominant mare who lead the pack and another four to eight mares with their young ones of both genders.

Like elephants, young male zebras are chased out of their herd by their mothers when they reach the age of 12–14 months. Like elephants, when the mating urge strikes, the males sniff the mare's urine to determine her readiness for breeding. A female is pregnant for 360 to 390 days and, like elephants, almost always gives birth to only one offspring. Twins have never been recorded in this variety of zebra.

In the wild, Burchell's zebras have the distinction of migrating the longest distance of any terrestrial animal in Africa, often traveling 160 miles one way. During the dry season, they dig out underground tubers and rhizomes to eat, and because they are dependent on water, they never stray more than a few miles from a good water source. They generally adapt easily to various terrains and are not deterred by mountainous areas. The zebras at KEP do not have to worry about sources of food and water, nor do they have to worry about predators. When sounding their alarm call, it is a sharp, high-pitched "kwa-ha," enough to stop you in your tracks. They also make snorting, barking and baying sounds that might fool you into thinking they are from outer space to one unaccustomed to hearing them. While walking back to my room one night, I was dreamily looking at the massive numbers of stars I could see and heard this otherworldly sound that scared me into running home!

Today, as I watched the color drain from the sky at day's end, zebras fight in the field. I hear one cry out before he bucks his hind legs into the enemy and saunters away victorious. Throughout my stays at the park, the zebras were a constant source of amazement and often amusement as they nudged and played with each other. Their exotic beauty never grows tiresome, and people really do learn to differentiate them from each other, myself being the exception. I found it much harder to differentiate the zebras than the elephants. The zebras were grazing outside my room, out in the field, picking up leftover food scraps missed by the elephants, and they were frolicking out in the field. But I could not tell one from the other. They were a constant presence of splendor and grace.

Mala: A Baby Zebra's Story

Mala was born in the summer of 2018 and immediately rejected by her mother. There was no time to figure out why. Clare Padfield immediately came to Mala's rescue, sleeping with her in a pen outside at nighttime for months, everyone at the park helping feed her around the clock until she was strong enough to be left alone for brief intervals. She came along quickly and within six months to a year appeared ready to be with a flock of other zebras. It was dangerous to put her with the KEP flock, as the mother who rejected her was still a vibrant part of their zebra herd, so arrangements were made for her to live at another park several hours away. It would be a fresh start for Mala. This meant Clare, her main caregiver, had to go with her to ease the transition of bonding with a completely new herd. So, Clare and Mala lived together at the new park until Clare felt comfortable that Mala was completely accepted by the new zebra herd. She returned to KEP with gratitude that Mala had been saved and relocated successfully and sadness as she did not know when she would see Mala again. It could be a long, long while.

Keisha: Nearly Everyone's Favorite

"I have spent hours and hours watching elephants, and to come to understand what emotional creatures they are ... it's not just a species facing extinction, its massive individual suffering."—Mike Bond, *The Last Savanna*

"Keisha" means "favorite" in Swahili.
Identifying Characteristics:

Very small tusks
Long tail and long tail hair that looks wavy
Tears in ear tissue of both ears and a hole in left ear
Born December 2003

On a balmy summer day three-month-old Keisha and her mother were loaded onto a truck for the long ride to their new home. When they arrived, her mother remained motionless. Keisha poked and prodded her massive mother with her trunk and made some rudimentary noises in an attempt to wake her but to no avail. Her mother had passed away during the ride, leaving a defenseless infant alone in a new place with elephants and people whom she didn't know. Keisha was profoundly traumatized. For her this was an urgent moment determining her survival. Elephants need to nurse for a full two years while they gradually introduce other foods into their diet. In the infant Keisha's frenzied attempts to find an "auntie" she could nurse from, she was pushed away repeatedly, utterly rejected. At times she was pushed so hard her ears tore and were pierced by the tusks of females who had no use for her, probably having all they could handle caring for their own calves.

Once Lisette Withers heard Keisha's story, she intervened without delay. Keisha was immediately brought to KEP. When she arrived at the park in January 2004, she was close to death. With a great deal of love and care, she made a full recovery. Once settled, Keisha sucked hungrily on the bottles of specially made formula and bonded with the guides who spent every day and night with her until she was old enough to fend for herself. Would the elephants at this new place accept her?

Keisha is quiet, gentle, an intriguing blend of nurturer and loner but the first to greet newcomers to the herd. It is as if she has taken her traumatic childhood experience and resiliently reframed it into empathy and compassion. Keisha is the favorite of many, who can't resist her gentle, kind spirit.

When elephants like Keisha are orphaned, they must find ways to eat or they will die. Calves begin to sample actual food items at one or two months old but are still dependent upon their mother's milk for a full two years. Sampling food items for calves consists of grasping an object with the fingers at the tip of the trunk, which they are just learning to control, rolling items in their trunk, or pulling an item from the mouth of an elder or allomother. According to Wemmer and Christin in *Elephants and Ethics*, it is estimated that through their first five years, elephant calves spend 15.8 percent of their social contact time exploring the food intake of other family members.[1] And so, in addition to receiving her specially prepared, bottled mother's milk substitute, Keisha was left to try these various ways of finding food. This formula is loosely based on a recipe created by the renowned Dame Daphne Sheldrick, which she developed by trial and error during her esteemed effort to save dozens of orphaned elephants under her care in Kenya.

Another danger to young, orphaned elephants is dying of "broken heart syndrome," which can happen when a young elephant is put in an enclosure alone, away from other elephants, so strong is the social element in elephants. It has been known to happen to adult elephants as well when they are suddenly separated from other elephants and left alone.

In addition to calves nursing for a full two years, they engage in what scientists refer to as coprophagy, eating the dung of their mother, which is rich in probacteria, just as rabbits eat their nighttime feces called cecotropes for the same reason.

Edison speaks softly but with big insights into these elephants that he clearly loves. "Keisha's infancy changed her a lot. She has a unique personality and different behaviors than the rest of the herd. Sometimes she just wants to be left alone, maybe because of the way she was treated by other elephants when she became an orphan. She is very comfortable being by herself. Recently, Mashudu pushed her away from her regular place at his end of the barrier, so she moved herself down to the other end next to Shungu, where she is more welcome. She's let Mashudu know she is angry with him by ignoring him, and as a result, has become closer to Shungu. These boys are always like that—they don't have an adult male as role model."

Translocating Elephants

South Africa has been at the forefront of translocating animals for the purpose of saving them. Harry and Sally were translocated to KEP in 1994. As you can imagine, translocating an elephant is no small feat. The process is divided into six stages: capture through darting if the elephant can't be persuaded to enter the crate, transport, wakeup, recover, release, and post-monitoring release. Most of the time translocations are successful, but in Keisha's case, tragedy ensued.

When Thato arrived as an infant in the park, Keisha was four or five years sold. It wasn't long before Keisha took it upon herself to allomother Thato. Allomothering is motherly nurturing performed by an individual other than the biological mother of an offspring. When I asked Edison what he thinks compelled Keisha to care for the infant Thato in spite of her own personal history, his reply was, "She knows how it feels to have no one to take care of you, no friends. She thinks, 'I don't want another elephant to have to go through that experience.' Keisha really lives the spirit of Ubuntu. She thinks, 'No one can stand on their own, so let's be together, and let's unite.' When the three newest girls were introduced in May 2017, she was the first one to make accepting overtures to them by walking slowly toward them when the others in Sally's herd stood their ground. She is such a good-hearted girl, a girl full of mercy. She doesn't want others to feel lonely, so she makes sure they feel accepted." Stay tuned for a close-up of the meeting of these two elephant groups.

There is a scientific reason for this. In their book, *A Path Appears*, Nicholas Kristof and Sheryl WuDunn write, "One key driver in altruism is oxytocin, the 'truest molecule.' ... It's almost like a social glue that promotes 'survival of the kindest.'... She calls it a compassion molecule that is like a 'chill pill.' It calms down our stress responses and makes us more interested in others; in particular, we look into their eyes more. When we look gently into someone's eyes, that person will probably release oxytocin and feel more compassion. When an owner makes eye contact with his or her dog, greater amounts of oxytocin are released in the human brain; researchers suspect that the dog may be releasing oxytocin as well. ... People who do have oxytocin sources in their lives tend to be less stressed and more prosocial. It can be pets, lovers, kids—just love in general."

Kristof and WuDunn continue

"Oxytocin works alongside two other neurotransmitters, dopamine and serotonin, to make us feel good when we do good. Serotonin interacts with Oxytocin and dopamine to drive the happy feeling we get as a result of an altruistic act. Dopamine helps trigger the rewarding feeling you get when you eat chocolate.... Oxytocin, which runs near the bottom of the brain and is thus harder to image clearly, helps give us a tingle like a warm bath. With the oxytocin system we're hardwired to get bodily rewards from being prosocial and altruistic. We kind of get those benefits very peripherally by calming down our heart and feeling warm and fuzzy."[2]

Keisha is often referred to as the calmest, most empathetic of the herd. Because she is not part of Sally's core group, she is low in the pecking order. Followed only by the boys, who are always considered lower in herd rank, Keisha knows her place is low in the pecking order but doesn't let that stop her from coming to the aid of another elephant or person who is sad or having a difficult time. Although Keisha has never had her own babies, she treats Thato as if she is her own child, keeping a close eye on her in the field and in the boma at night.

If you remember reading *Horton Hatches the Egg* by Dr. Seuss as a very young child, you will remember that Horton happened on Mayzie the Bird who was bored to tears with sitting on her egg. She convinces Horton to sit on the egg so she can take a short break, but she doesn't come back for many, many months. Horton persevered on the egg through storms, extreme heat, and all kinds of other dangers, all the while famously saying, "I meant what I said, and I said what I meant ... an elephant's faithful—one hundred percent!" When the egg finally hatches, the baby bird has a trunk and ears just like his.[3] This comic tale of allomothering describes Keisha to a T. She has an uncanny knack for providing the necessary nurturing for others she herself got only after experiencing titanic trauma and even then only from humans.

According to T. Vidya in a research study about allomothering, "In the absence of large sample sizes, logistic difficulties, and, more importantly, knowledge about appropriate hypotheses to test cognition in elephants, reliable anecdotal observations from field studies are increasingly being realized as valuable in this context. I report here a novel behavior shown by a sub-adult female in the context of allomothering." What Vidya observed was a young adult cow, who was not the mother of the infant, offer her trunk when the calf tried to suckle her. Vidya believes this to be a problem-solving behavior since the allomother was irritated by the calf trying to suckle her nipple and reacted by nudging and kicking the calf and attempting to walk away. Trunk-to-mouth behavior has been frequently observed in elephants, in which an elephant either places its own trunk in its mouth for self-soothing or in another elephant's mouth as a greeting. Some elephant researchers believe this behavior to be an elephant's version of human thumb-sucking. Vidya continues, "During a study on African savannah elephants in Amboseli, it was found that lactating females generally did not tolerate allosuckling [allowing an infant who is not theirs to suckle] and were aggressive in their rejections of the calves, while nulliparous females—those who have never given birth to an offspring—were tolerant of allosuckling, and such bouts were often terminated by the calves.... The function of allonursing, therefore, may be to pacify an infant rather than to supply milk."[4] More research needs to be done in this area, but clearly Keisha has allomothered several of the younger elephants at KEP. She gives freely of her heart knowing who is in need.

In human terms, we call childhood traumas ACES, or Adverse Childhood Experiences. Mental Health professionals use an ACES assessment with people of all ages to help ascertain whether or not certain treatment modalities would be more helpful than others. Left unchecked, ACES can cause disease, both physical and mental, later in life. We can only imagine it is no different for elephants because they are so similar to us emotionally.

Trauma

Human trauma victims have difficulty moderating emotions, particularly anger. Survivors often vacillate between uncontrolled rages, intolerance and aggression. Judith Herman writes in *Trauma and Recovery*, "The traumatized person therefore frequently alternates between isolation and anxious clinging to others.... In the immediate aftermath of the trauma, rebuilding of some minimal form of trust is the primary task. Assurances of safety and protection are of the greatest importance."[5] Like psychologist Abraham Maslow's Hierarchy of Needs, victims prioritize between immediate survival needs such as food, water and shelter and other less important needs, such as esteem and self-actualization.

Herman believes chronically traumatized people no longer have a baseline state of physical calm or comfort. Over time, they perceive their bodies as having turned against them. They begin to complain, not only of insomnia and agitation but also of numerous types of somatic symptoms. According to Herman, recovery unfolds in three stages. The central task of the first stage is the establishment of a sense of safety. The goal of the second state is remembrance and grieving. The third stage involves reconnection with ordinary life. She cautions that in the course of successful recovery from trauma, it should be possible to recognize a gradual shift from unpredictable danger to reliable safety, from dissociated trauma to acknowledged memory and from stigmatized isolation to restored social connection.[6] Since we are aware of the high intelligence and empathy levels in elephants, there is no reason to think their trauma process is any different.

It is a well-proven fact that elephants, like most animal species, experience a range of emotions just as we humans do. Anecdotal evidence lies in observations of elephants with tears streaming from their eyes when they are ill, when a close ally dies, and when an infant is displaced from its mother. Recent research has revealed that all vertebrates share the same underlying structures and mechanisms that dictate properties once considered unique to humans. Elephants have culture, strong family bonding, elaborate communication patterns, personality, language, the show of empathy, infamous long-term memories, remarkable playful natures in which they exude joy and happiness, and the way they mourn for their dead. In the elephant world, social structure and processes are key to their survival and way of life. This makes the emergence of post-traumatic stress disorder in elephants an alarming development, one that reinforces maladaptive behavior. Many are the reports of baby elephants who witnessed their family members murdered and dismembered, experiencing what appear to be night terrors, during which they awaken screaming, restless, and inconsolable.

It bears mentioning that a relatively new field of study is Trans-species psychology. This is the branch of psychology that investigates the commonalities in cognition and emotion that humans and animals share. This field was established by Gay A. Bradshaw, an American ecologist and psychologist. Trans-species psychology often points to a common model of brain, mind and behavior for human and nonhuman animals. Bradshaw made this claim based on information gathered from the fields of neuroscience, ethology (the study of animal behavior), and psychology, both currently and going back through the evolutionary research of Charles Darwin, which showed that evolution conserves brain and mind across species. What this forces us to realize is that of course other species can feel emotions, think and feel in complicated ways, experience joy and trauma. And following that thread of logic, this implies that some nonhumans are *not* conceptualized as being inferior to humans, and elephants definitely fill those shoes. Denying animals their earned status as psychological beings is understood as a belief that goes hand in hand with animal exploitation.[7]

In 2005, Bradshaw came to the conclusion that post-traumatic stress disorder (PTSD) does indeed exist in free-ranging elephant survivors of severely traumatic events, such as mass culls, poaching, translocation, and other human-inflicted situations. She observed that traumatized elephants displayed behavioral aberrations such as inter- and intra-species aggression, abnormal startle response, depression and infant neglect. Bradshaw integrated psychobiological and ethological principles, which led her to the understanding that maternal and community loss lead to pathogenic right hemispheric neurological development, which often results in hyperaggression and social-emotional dysfunction. Her Pulitzer-nominated book *Elephants on the Edge: What Animals Teach Us About Humanity* delves into the ways human interference leads to the breakdown of elephant culture and society and illustrates the ways Keisha's trauma may have affected her for life.[8]

Well renowned are the stories of elephants standing by the bodies of their deceased kin for hours, days and sometimes weeks. Also well known are the stories of elephants amassing bones of their dead into "monuments" to them. Amboseli ethologist Karen McComb found that playing back the contact call of a deceased elephant elicited significant attentive responses by her family almost a year after her death. McComb et al. established that elephants recognize and usually answer the individual voices of their own family and bond group, and they also distinguish between familiar and less familiar elephants on the basis of how often they are encountered.[9]

*   *   *

It is a sparkling, clear day at the park, the afternoon heat building to an unbearable level. I wonder if a thunderstorm could pop up at dusk. In the distance, I see Shepherd hiking down the slope from higher ground, a lumbering Keisha at his side. They amble toward the field shelter where the guides can escape from intense sun or rain. Shepherd lowers himself to sit on a log, his leg stretched out in front of him, a pained look on his face. He pulls up the leg of his pants, revealing a bleeding wound from a sharp branch piercing his skin. Keisha saunters off as the guides began to chatter among themselves. Several minutes later, Keisha returns with a mound of thick mud wrapped in her trunk. She strolls over to where Shepherd sits. Lo and behold, she began applying the mud to his wound as she would do for herself! Shepherd said it took his breath away. He knew it was a loving gift from Keisha.

Shepherd is a self-confessed elephant whisperer who is still learning about these humble elephants even after working among them for more than a decade. With a reticent smile, he recounts the way the elephants greet him after he returns from a vacation, sniffing him and touching him gently with their trunks. He considers these elephants

Several guides wait for rain to pass by under the shelter that was built around a huge tree. Note the elephant grazing behind the guide on the left. Others graze out of view.

part of his family, knowing that when you respect them, they pass on that respect, and it comes full circle.

The Keisha Project and Stereotypical Elephant Behaviors

Keisha displays some atypical body motions in the boma from time to time. She sometimes rocks from side to side in a twist, referred to by staff and volunteers as "weaving." Keisha always performs this behavior in the same way, in the same position, facing the same direction and only in the evenings. Initially, there appeared to be no consistent pattern to when she would perform it. Many weeks would pass with no occurrence of the behavior, and then suddenly Keisha experiences one or more nights with 20–30 minutes of repeated abnormal weaving. Partly because of the desire to study her atypical behavior, there is a remote camera and infrared light in the boma in order to track the motion of the elephants at night. These films contribute to the "Keisha Project," which is devoted to finding the root cause of this strange, self-directed behavior. The aim of this project is to look at Keisha and her stereotypical behavior patterns to pinpoint the triggers of this behavior. Not only will this allow AERU to identify and change factors contributing to Keisha's behavior; it has wider implications for other elephants in captivity worldwide.

Interestingly enough, Keisha does not stream when she weaves, but she is more likely than the other elephants to stream in many other situations. You'll recall, streaming is a wet patch of secretions on the side of the neck that are indicative of an elephant displaying intense emotion. It looks like a wet patch on the side of the neck, almost like a sweat spot. During my time as a volunteer at KEP, I spent many hours watching the tapes of Keisha's nighttime behavior and recording research data. It was a fascinating experience, one that was calming as well. I watched the tape of the next night in the film queue in fast forward. If I saw the weaving behavior, I stopped to record the time, length of the behavior and the date. Then on to the next night and the next. While I'm watching Keisha and her nighttime behaviors, I also am aware of the behaviors of all the others who gather in the boma on the fresh sawdust to sleep, most standing up but Thato and some others often lying down. It is one of the most peaceful marvels to witness, these massive creatures at rest, like watching a baby slumbering peacefully. I'm smiling ear to ear and filled with a deep tranquility. In an afternoon, I often went through weeks of tapes to help AERU catch up, never tiring of watching elephant night-time behaviors.

Weaving is what researchers refer to as a stereotypical behavior, one that is repetitive and lacks any function or goal. Stereotypies are sometimes coping mechanisms or adaptive behaviors resulting from anxiety, depression or some other unresolved emotional issue. Very often zoo animals in small confines develop stereotypies as maladaptive coping mechanisms from lack of space and often boredom. I once saw a polar bear at the Central Park Zoo who swam a repetitive loop for hours on end in a tiny pool, a sad state for such a regal animal. For elephants, some of these behaviors include head-bobbing, pacing, leg swinging, and body swaying along with trunk. Circus elephants tend to show an increase in stereotypic behavior before regularly scheduled performances.

The AERU research team hypothesized and predicted that Keisha would perform more stereotypical behavior during or in a pattern directly corresponding with the luteinizing hormone, a reproductive hormone which surges during her reproductive cycle. AERU also allowed for the possibility that factors extrinsic to Keisha were causing or exacerbating the effect and collected data on as many of these ideas as possible. Beginning in April 2015, the team collected dung samples twice a week from Keisha for 30 months. Their aim is to compare and evaluate any connection between fluctuations in reproductive or other hormones, Keisha's weaving behavior, and how the extrinsic variables play a role in these relationships. The results will not only help all understand Keisha's behavior but will have widespread implications for all elephants under the care of humans.

Understanding and reducing stereotypic behavior in captive animals is a complex task, especially for emotionally complex, intelligent animals such as elephants. Through this study, AERU hopes to give insights to other zoo curators and captive facilities into potential triggers of stereotypic behavior and offer advice on how to help reduce these behaviors in other animals as well. If their answers lead to them making changes to the management of their own elephants, then the welfare of all elephants worldwide could potentially be improved by a single elephant, Keisha.

To date, AERU has almost 300 dung samples which need to be measured for hormone levels through the process described earlier. The on-site laboratory, Fiela's Lab, named for Thandi's baby who passed away when still an infant, enables volunteers and staff to collect dung samples, freeze-dry the samples and process them to the point where extractions can be sent for hormone analysis to the Endocrine Research Laboratory at the University of Pretoria. Each dung sample costs over $12 to analyze. Volunteers are trained to prepare the dung samples for lab examination, which is a tedious process requiring precise measurements and deep concentration to get each sample primed exactly right. The more samples that are tested, the closer AERU will come to identifying and understanding Keisha's behavior and consequently be able to work toward developing methods of alleviating these stereotypical behaviors—both for Keisha and for others like her. Donations can be made to Fiela's Lab at: AERU (*www.aeru.co.za*).

A newer hypothesis from AERU is that Keisha experiences an imbalance between artificial and natural light and that if the infrared lights are turned down earlier, she might sleep better. Recently, newer technology has enabled AERU to see more detailed elephant activity

I am humbled to be having a special moment with Keisha. She exudes calm in her slow, deliberate movements and seems to like the attention from a human as evidenced by remaining near me while I stroke her.

during the night. Keisha is now known to occasionally touch her trunk to the ear of elephants sleeping on the thick bed of sawdust on the boma floor. This is yet another mystery in the endless quest to understand the complexities of elephant behavior in general and trauma in particular.

The mystery is: why is Keisha the only one to exhibit this unusual behavior? After regular observations and data collected by staff and volunteers over several years, there appeared to be a pattern that initially seemed to resemble the hormonal peaks in the estrus cycle of female African elephants. AERU researchers speculated that in Keisha's case the extrinsic factor of confinement and/or lack of choice were not the primary trigger but that there might be an internal hormonal trigger for stereotypy. Could it be a post-traumatic response caused by the trauma in her infancy? Could it be a response to not having been raised by her mother? What if it's a response to lighting? Only further research will answer those questions.

Meanwhile, Keisha is an integral part of Sally's herd. She is often off on her own but not unhappily so. She has an amazing presence. Empathy seems to ooze from her pores. When I stand close to her and gently stroke her skin, she is the embodiment of calm and unconditional acceptance. Her gift to me is time to look into her ochre eyes, especially when she blinks her long, wiry eyelashes, a feeling of profoundness overcomes me, and I am speechless.

11

Mashudu:
The Handsome One

"If anyone wants to know what elephants are like, they are like people only more so."—Peter Corneille

"Mashudu" means "lucky" in Venda.
Identifying Characteristics:

Long tail with lots of tail hair
Medium-sized tusks, longer than Shungu's
Tusks point downward and inward
Born July 2007

Mashudu was translocated from a hunting farm in the North West Province to Knysna Elephant Park in May 2008 along with Thato. His parents suffered the same fate as Thato's. He is a typical boy—full of zest and energy, a mischievous sparkle in his eye, and he can often be seen playing with Shungu and often flirting with Madiwa. Mashudu is almost textbook perfect physically, the male "model" of the herd. According to Dan Wylie, "Indeed there are sophisticated criteria for beauty amongst elephant handlers—proportions, head breadth and the shape of bumps, tusk symmetry and thickness, length of trunk, and overall height, all combine to produce subtle classifiable types of elephant elegance. For example, some are identified as 'deer-like' in physique, which is very different from 'royal.'"[1] Mashudu is indeed of the "royal" type, in case there was any doubt. Just looking at him tells you at a glance. Currently, he is in his early teens.

Shepherd worked with Mashudu when he was a young calf. "I would touch his ear and he would stop walking. Now if I touch his ear he turns. He likes to swing his back leg back and forth, and he is realizing his strength as he enters adolescence. At some point, when Sally gives us a signal that it's time, he may have to go live somewhere else, away from the females of the herd, which is just how it would be if they were a wild herd. Her signal might be to ignore him, push him around, or otherwise cause him to feel he's not wanted in the herd any longer. It will be interesting to see how it plays out. When compared to Shungu, Mashudu is the more mature, eligible bachelor who will soon go into musth, the state of hormonal readiness for males to mate."

Mashudu's characteristic nervous mannerism is moving one of his rear feet back and forth repeatedly in a self-soothing way. It appears he is deep in thought when he does it. Indeed I was almost the recipient of one of Mashudu's self-directed back leg swings when I foolishly walked behind him one day in the field, not realizing he was actively swinging his leg. He doesn't like people being behind him where he can't see, and fortunately, Ndyebo yelled urgently, telling me to change directions.

Puberty and Adolescence in Male Elephants

Puberty in bulls occurs between the ages of nine and 15, and sexual maturity is reached at age 17, although they often don't mate until they are in their 30s. Musth is a period of frenzied sexual activity in male elephants recognized by high testosterone levels, urine dribbling, green penis syndrome and swollen temporal glands and frequent streaming. The first musth a bull goes through usually lasts only a few days. But in a full-grown, healthy adult bull, it can last up to four months. Male elephants are physically unusual in the mammal kingdom for yet another reason—their testicles are located internally near their kidneys, as opposed to most other mammals whose testicles are located externally. They don't begin producing sperm until between the ages of ten and 15 years old.

According to Evans and Harris, only a few species of mammals undergo a period of adolescence, but for the species that do go through it, it is probably one of their most important life stages. Adolescence in elephants is considered to last from age ten until age 20, and in their research, they found that adolescent male elephants showed a tendency for higher levels of socialization. Bulls in the wild would normally hang around with older bulls in order to learn the social skills required to be a part of bull society. Wild bulls would normally leave the maternal herd late in adolescence to wander off and perhaps form a bachelor herd, spending part of their time alone. Matriarchs signal to these males when it's their time to leave.[2] Mashudu and Shungu have no older bull to teach them about the birds and the bees, a potential problem. There is an implicit understanding between bulls that the older elephants get to go first when it comes to mating. When young bulls observe courting and mating behavior, they are learning lessons valuable in preserving the species and in socializing successfully with matriarchal herds. Remember, they are still growing and will continue to grow until they are in their late 20s. These older bulls are role models to the adolescents, similar to the way a matriarch models behaviors for her girls but more sexual in nature.

Years ago, at Kruger National Park in South Africa, a group of young wild males were saved from a cull and sent to Pilanesburg National Park. It was there that rangers found the dead bodies of endangered white rhinos. When rangers realized that the rhinos had no gunshot or knife wounds, they concluded that the rogue bulls must have killed them, leaving deep puncture wounds. This kind of aggression is extremely rare among elephants. After wondering what had gone awry, they realized that this band of juvenile delinquents were "fatherless," not having experienced the benefit of having older mentor bulls to learn from. To test their hypothesis, they brought in several older bulls, and soon enough, the elders let the younger rogues know that their behavior was not acceptable. Eventually the youngsters followed their elders around, taking a crash course in how to be a proper elephant bull. This holds a strong parallel to human life in situations where troubled youth are raised with no suitable elders to learn from.

Adolescent male elephants exhibit high levels of socialization, sticking together in larger bachelor groups, and they preferred to be physically closer to their peers and elders. Evans and Harris concluded that associating with their peers enabled bulls to establish their individual position in the hierarchy.[3] In particular, greeting and sparring with peers plays a role in the establishment of social position and familiarization with social etiquette. Opportunities for males to learn the rules of bull society from older individuals may come through males who have closer relationships to older bulls. As we know in some captive situations, young bulls show a number of inappropriate behaviors due to the lack of an older bull mentor, including aggression, uncharacteristic antics and, at times, changed feeding habits. These issues are thought to arise because the young males come into musth prematurely, whereas nature would delay the onset of musth if older bulls were present regularly. Evans and Harris conclude that it is entirely possible that the older males might be the ones who are choosing to be closer to the younger bulls in order to suppress musth in them, thereby eliminating mating competition. In addition, they did not rule out the possibility of kin recognition and the fact that old bulls are providing protection to related males.[4]

As Mashudu gets into his teens and early 20s, he will start engaging in mock sexual activity referred to as play mounting. This practice activity takes place for a while, sometimes a few years, before a bull goes fully into musth. Elephant researcher Caitlin O'Connell studied the musth/mating phenomenon in bulls and concluded that these rogues might benefit from having older male role models to provide social guidance and behavioral boundaries that would help them be better members of their herds or societies. O'Connell believes further exploration of mentoring and mentorship could provide valuable lessons for captive and reintroduced elephant bulls. In addition, humans could benefit from understanding how nonhuman societies manage these significant interactions.[5]

Clare explains, "Elephants always put their trunks in their own and other elephants' mouths. A bull will smell a pool of urine left by one of the females in a group, then lift his trunk to the roof of his opened mouth where he blows the inhaled smell to the pits in the palate. The substance is called flemen, and is found in urine, feces, saliva, and the excretion of the temporal gland as well as in the genitals. Chemicals and hormones in the urine signal to a bull when a female is ready to mate. This specific trunk to mouth behavior is known as 'The Flehmen response.'"

The dating game proceeds when musth bulls approach a herd of females nonchalantly, lowering their heads, maybe even resting their trunks on a tusk. They move from one female to the next and the next, testing with their trunks for signs of estrus by probing between their hind legs, taking urine samples with the tips of their trunks which they place in their mouths for taste and smell. If nothing smacks of the perfume of estrus, they move on until they find it, so intent are they on mating, so full of hormones coursing through their bodies.

When a bull does find a suitable female to mate with, the mating itself happens very quickly. A male in pursuit will find the cow in estrus walking away from them with her head askance, looking back over her shoulder. The bull takes after her, releases its penis from its sheath, which is almost the size of its trunk, and he catches up to her with his trunk stretched out, reaching for her. As he places his trunk along her back, she stops. He rears up, placing his front feet behind her shoulders, but leaning back so that his weight, which can be as much as three times the weight of the cow, falls on his own hind legs. The bull's penis is three to four feet long when fully extended and weighs about 60 pounds. It curves into an "s" shape. He searches for the cow's vulva opening, which is facing the ground. Once his penis is inserted, the act takes less than a minute, and he dismounts. But now comes the excitement. The cow lifts her head, lets out a loud, deep, long rumble, while her family members rush toward the couple, rumbling, bowing and touching the couple with their trunks. Elephant researcher Cynthia Moss calls this behavior "mating pandemonium."[6] It is reminiscent of the way we humans shower newlyweds by tossing rice at them just after they are married.

The concept of a sanctuary just for elephant bulls derives from the disruption in behavior caused by musth hormones. Many bulls in musth are punished for their behavior in circus and zoo situations, sometimes tethered in small spaces for months until the musth passes, all in the name of safety. This causes severe psychological damage to the bull, not to mention physical damage due to the lack of movement allowed. In a bull sanctuary, the idea is to allow bulls in musth to socialize, roam, and reestablish social ties and a feeling of belonging. Real healing begins when humans and elephants establish loving, trusting relationships, which happens only over time.

Mashudu and Madiwa spar in the field, a flirtatious festival of fun, he approaching adolescence, she in the throes of it. She beats him every time, outlasting his youthful vigor. It only succeeds in making him try harder to win her over, and to win, *period*. They put on quite a show with their give and take, trunks reaching out, enjoined, and then reaching out again. Wind blows the banana branches, but the taproot holds steady. The periwinkle mountainous horizon dwarfs these two, who stop sparring momentarily to browse in the valley. Slanted spring sunlight highlights them pulling tufts of grass from the ground with their trunks, dusting them off on the ground and putting them into their mouths. Before long the sparring starts all over again. Dark clouds gather, blown by easterly winds, bringing much-needed rain.

Zenzo Moyo, one of KEP's longtime guides, has a close relationship with Mashudu. Hannah Needle, a long-term volunteer from the UK tells this story:

"The other day I witnessed Zenzo protecting Mash (as volunteers and staff affectionately call him) while eating his straw pile for almost a half hour. By this I mean he was literally running at elephants that came anywhere near Mash to stop them from displacing his 'boy' from his straw pile. At one stage of these antics, Shanti and Thandi (a strange

Mashudu and Madiwa often mock spar in the field. She beats him every time, but he keeps coming back for more. Mash, as he is affectionately called, is "model beautiful" physically and beautiful on the inside as well.

alliance to begin with), were working together each of them coming at Mash from different sides, with Zenzo and Mashudu in the middle. One of them would start walking toward the boys, so Zenzo would approach them to move them on and then while his back was turned the other would start creeping toward Mash. Zenzo did not stop chasing elephants away until the next tractor came all the while, Mash was munching carefree on his straw. I'm not sure if he was completely unaware of what was going on or completely chilled out because he knew his human had his back—either way he didn't seem overly rushed with eating but he did get a good fill, and I … I got a good hard laugh!"

The sky blushes with vibrant hues as the sun sets over the South African coastline. The petal pinks, raspberry streaks, bands of orange and white accents are breathtaking as they hang over the jagged amethyst mountaintops in the distance. How I love sitting at the picnic table, looking out over the brick patio outside my room to see those mountains that dwarf the elephants who graze in the foreground. I eat my dinner at the picnic table in the twilight, hearing only cricket frenzy. The sky grows dark more quickly than when I'm home in the northern hemisphere. It's interesting to experience, leaving me to the stars, denser here than anywhere else I have ever seen. It is an astounding sight. I am left

One of my favorite places on earth is the patio outside my room at the park. Here I started my days watching the sun rise on the right and ended my day watching the sun set on the left. Here I wrote many of the pages of this book and let the soul of South Africa seep deeper into me.

speechless, staring, for just how long I have no idea. There is something about Africa that enters one's blood and takes hold of your soul, never to let go. Like an exquisite dessert, it embraces you, haunting and compelling you to return and experience more of it. What is it about this orange soil, this sparkling air and southernmost slant of sunlight that envelopes me, changing me forever? As hard as I search, I cannot find the words.

As the moon rises, I grow sleepy. The morning dung walk and field data sessions seem like long ago. So much happens here in a day. I am left feeling grateful for the opportunity to be here, of being able to help the elephants in some way and so appreciative that I can wake up tomorrow and do it all over again.

12

Shungu :
Poor Boy... Or Is He?

"Elephants love reunions. They recognize one another after years and years of separation and greet each other with wild, boisterous joy. There's bellowing and trumpeting, ear flapping and rubbing. Trunks entwine."—Jennifer Richard Jacobson

"But perhaps the most important lesson I learned is that there are no walls between humans and the elephants except those that we put up ourselves, and that until we allow not only elephants, but all living creatures their place in the sun, we can never be whole ourselves."
—Lawrence Anthony, *The Elephant Whisperer*

"Shungu" means "patience" in Shona.
Identifying Characteristics:

"N" shaped tail hair, more on right side
Distinct kink in the tail itself
Medium-sized tusks, shorter than Mashudu's
Tusks are pointed outward from the front view
Born January 1, 2007

Born right at KEP, Shungu was given his Shona name, which means "patience," because no one knew his mother's exact due date, so all patiently awaited his arrival. The legendary Harry is his father. His mother, Thambile, lives in the Eastern Cape. He is a naughty, playful elephant with a great sense of humor. As a baby, he loved chasing guinea fowl and was often heard trumpeting out in the fields as flocks of birds flew for their lives! Shungu is easily identified by the kink in his tail, with more hair on one side than the other, and is slightly smaller than the elephants older than he. Poor Shungu has the lowest social standing in the herd. But is he really "poor Shungu?"

Part Two

Of the many of Shungu's unique talents, according to Nikki Mila-chowski, one of AERU's former research assistants, is that he is the only one of the elephants who appears to stick his tongue out! She explains, "Elephants are not able to stick their tongue out because of the way it is attached to the bottom of their mouths. Shungu likes to bulge his tongue outward as much as possible, so it looks like he is sticking it out. ... I've seen him do this and it is hysterically funny and cute as all get-out. I have the feeling he knows we think it's adorable and does it to please us."

Taryn Tainton, KEP's former volunteer coordinator, tells this story: "Shungu lifted his head and perked his ears out as he looked in the direction of the tractor entering the field, discreetly, he raised his trunk to give a quick sniff asking himself, 'Are there buckets of fruit with these tourists?' With an excited strut he quietly ambled toward the barrier, looked around, and mysteriously, none of the other ellies noticed that the tractor was on its way! 'Silly ellies,' he thought to himself, 'who would turn down a bucket of juicy fruit?'"

"Just in time to meet the tractor and its tourists, Shungu decided to be brave and stand in the middle of the barrier—where Sally would nor-mally be! He then spotted not one, not two or even three, but four over-flowing buckets of fruit! 'For me! All for me!' he thought with delight. One by one he munched and crunched his way through the buckets, starting off a little nervous but gaining confidence with every mouthful as it became clear that no one was going to join him. Once the last fruit was chewed, swallowed and savored, Shungu spun around and took off leaving nothing but dust as a thank you to the tourists. He trotted back to the others, ears out, head up and tail straight, trumpeting a tune of smug victory, making it known to all that he, Shungu, had four buckets of fruit all to himself! ... He figured out how to hoodwink the others!"

One day, while taking data in the field, I saw a gleam in Shungu's eyes. I wondered what he was thinking about as he chewed on one stick before spitting it out in favor of another. Just then, the tractor climbed the hill past the big pond, clamoring and rumbling. Out in the distance elephant heads pop up one by one, hearing and feeling the vibrations on the ground, drop what they're eating and make for the barricade, know-ing buckets of fruit await them. Shungu, fearing he won't get any, tries to sidle up to the tractor and its passengers before it stops. But the guides are a step ahead of poor Shungu.

Sally's herd lines up, each one knowing their place at the barricade. Sally did her anticipatory back and forth swaying with bated breath as the passengers disembark with their fruit baskets. She was restless. They

12. Shungu : Poor Boy... Or Is He?

Shungu, giving his "Poor me" look, stands alone at the barrier. He is the lowest in the herd's pecking order and knows it. Perhaps this explains his affinity for being more friendly toward people than many of the others.

On an average morning at the barrier, Shungu (left) stands alone on a far end, while (left to right) Nandi, Thandi and Sally are at the center, with Sally taking most of the fruit for herself! Most tourists stand in the center, so those three girls get the lion's share of the treats.

took too long. She shoved Thato aside, who sauntered to the far end of the barrier, head hanging down, and tail swishing like a windshield wiper. As the guides gave their introductory talk, there was such excitement in the air with ten trunks waving in keenness, accompanied by low rumbles of readiness for fruit buckets, and flapping ears. Shungu is often at the far end of the barrier by himself since he has the lowest standing in the pecking order. He often gives a look of "poor me" with his eyes wide and innocent looking

The distant mountains appear to change color from purple to golden as the sun travels, bouncing its light off the clouds. It has been a beautiful spring day, one full of all kinds of activities and discoveries.

Bonds of Steel: Human-Animal Ties

Of the ten elephants at KEP, Shungu is by far the most social with humans. A landmark study by Zoe Rossman, Clare Padfield, Debbie Young, Lynette Hart (2018), investigated the ways individual elephants choose to initiate interactions with humans. They began by examining whether interaction types and frequencies vary both between elephants and with regards to the category of human involved in the interaction.

12. Shungu : Poor Boy... Or Is He?

Measured by the seven elephants who resided at KEP at that time, the study provides evidence for elephant-handler bonds as well as information on the extent of interactions between humans and African elephants managed in free range.[1]

Clare explains,

"The human-animal relationship (HAR) and its subset, the human-animal bond (HAB), are two additional concepts that are gaining importance in the field of animal behavior. HABs have been defined as 'reciprocal and persistent' relationships that benefit both parties involved. The potential for animals to develop HABs has been evidenced in multiple species, including dogs, horses, farm animals, and some zoo animals. A positive relationship has been shown between the frequency of HARs and the subsequent development of a HAB. The implications of the HAB in a captive facility include increased ease of management and potential increased quality of life for the animals. Personality and temperament play a role in HARs, since the extent to which an animal is willing to interact with humans varies depending on the individual.

Elephants, specifically, have been shown to differ individually in temperament and personality related to leadership, aggression, social integration, and exploratory behaviors. Individual personalities and temperaments play a large part in determining how animals will interact with humans. Individual behavioral observations in response to the presence of a stranger, more specifically exploratory behavior vs. fearful behavior have been documented in pet cats and deer. The personality of the human(s) involved also has an effect on HARs, with chimpanzees shown to differ in their response to humans whether the experimenter acted shy or bold.

These elephants differed in the frequencies with which they initiated interactions with different categories of humans, such as tourists, volunteers, and the guides and staff. They also differed in the types of behaviors they used to initiate interactions. All of the elephants were highly familiar with the guides because they spend the most time together. Certain individual elephants, however, showed preferences in interacting with specific guides, indicating particular elephant-guide bonds. This study provides evidence for elephant-handler bonds as well as information on the extent of interactions between humans and African elephants managed in free contact."

There is a highly evident degree of mutual respect between the guides and the elephants. When a guide tells an elephant to back up, he or she obeys. From the elephants, guides are touched gently by an

119

elephant's trunk as if they are saying good morning or it's nice to see you. Some elephants will walk toward a guide as if to ask for attention.

For the purpose of this study, only interactions initiated by elephants that were not motivated by food or a command were counted. In the study, the time, the identity of the elephant, and the behavior were recorded, as well as the category of human involved (i.e., volunteer, guide, or tourist). Thirty individual behaviors were used by the elephants to initiate interactions with humans; these behaviors were grouped into the following six categories: trunk out, trunk to human, trunk to object on human-animal, seeking out, prolonged contact, and other, where the intent of the elephant is not clear. Keep in mind that this study was done when there were only seven elephants living at the park, the three "new girls" hadn't arrived yet.[2]

Using statistical software, it was determined that Shungu sought interaction with humans most frequently, initiating an average of 1.4 interactions per hour. Not surprisingly, Nandi initiated the fewest interactions, at an average of 0.51 per hour. The most common interactions were trunk to human and trunk out with guides, volunteers and tourists, yet seeking behaviors varied greatly in frequency depending on the elephant. Individual elephants varied in the types of humans with whom they chose to initiate interactions. The majority interacted almost exclusively with guides, while others interacted more with volunteers or tourists compared to other herd members. Shungu, Mashudu and Thandi preferred to interact with certain specific guides rather than others. These were special bonds that were clearly reciprocated by those specific guides.[3]

Shungu, the lowest elephant in the herd's pecking order, interacted with guides and volunteers far more than any other elephant. As a male he is not considered part of the core group in the herd, and he is lower in status than the only other male, Mashudu. Keisha and Mashudu, the other two elephants who are not part of the "in crowd" of Sally's original seven, initiated the next most frequent numbers of interactions. The combined number of elephant-initiated interactions by the core group of Sally, Nandi, Thandi, and Thato was less than the combined number of interactions initiated by the other three. One hypothesis is that there is an exploratory component to the trunk-to-human and trunk-out behaviors, which might explain the high percentages when tourists and volunteers are within sight. Since African elephants are extremely social animals, another potential hypothesis is that some elephants may seek out human interaction in order to acquire the social interactions that they lack from their peers. The study raised the question of the "safe haven," where an animal views a human as a source of safety rather than facing the bullying of other herd members, especially the high-ranking females. This thought-provoking issue is ripe for more research. Seeking behaviors indicate a higher level of commitment from the initiating elephant since they are prolonged interactions. They are the third most frequent behaviors shown toward the guides and volunteers but the fourth most common behavior displayed toward tourists. This phenomenon might be explained as bonding behaviors since seeking behaviors require the human and the elephant to be in close proximity. Only Thato performed seeking behaviors more frequently than trunk-to-object behaviors toward tourists.[4]

Seeking behaviors indicate a higher level of commitment from the initiating elephant since they are prolonged interactions. They are the third most frequent behaviors shown toward the guides and volunteers but the fourth most common behavior displayed toward tourists. This phenomenon might be explained as bonding behaviors since seeking behaviors require the human and the elephant to be in close proximity. Only Thato performed seeking behaviors more frequently than trunk-to-object behaviors toward tourists.

Evidence of individual personalities within the herd can be supported by the ranges in frequencies of behavior groups exhibited by each individual animal. Interestingly, Nandi and Thandi, the only elephants who are blood relatives in the herd, rarely interact with tourists or volunteers. Their efforts and energies, it would appear, are spent on the close bond they have with each other, as well as with Sally and Thato, and may account for their disinclination to interact with volunteers and tourists.

The four lowest-ranking elephants interacted more with volunteers than the three higher-ranking elephants. Shungu and Mashudu interacted the most with volunteers. Since volunteers do not usually feed the elephants, and there is no long-term relationship as with the guides, there is a lack of food-based motivation to interact with volunteers. Therefore, the data showing that lower-ranked elephants interact more often with volunteers potentially supports the safe haven hypothesis. The volunteers wear green shirts and jackets with neutral-colored pants, the same shade of green that the guides wear, and perhaps this contributes to the safe haven theory.

In addition to looking at elephant-guide bonds through data collection, guides' perspectives of the elephants were used to determine the reciprocity of these bonds. AERU conducted surveys on the guides' feelings about the elephants, including their individual preferences for specific elephants and information on elephant personality traits. The three guides who identified stronger bonds with a specific elephant all ranked their respective bonded elephant as either their first or second favorite. They also described that particular elephant as responding to their commands either best or second best. Each of these guides ranked his bonded elephant in the top three out of seven for confidence, curiosity and activity. In addition to feeling their bonded elephant to be more responsive to their commands, they also viewed that elephant as a bolder, more exploratory animal.[5]

There is little more thrilling than to be out in the field with the guides and ellies and an elephant allows you to get close enough to touch, stroke its rubbery skin, touch the wiry hair spikes and look into those amber eyes that shine with an unmistakable ancient wisdom.

* * *

Sweet Dreams Inside the Boma

The boma is a night shelter to protect the elephants from the elements. At KEP it stands as a large metal building with a high, pointed, metal roof. It has garage-like doors that remain open to the adjoining field, so the elephants can alternate between being inside and outside as they please. The floor is a cushiony depth of wood chips which are replaced at regular intervals. Every morning I was at the park all the volunteers would start the day shoveling the dung from overnight and collecting the sticks scattered about the floor. Then we would move out to the adjacent field and do the same thing. By the time of our breakfast break, usually around 9 a.m., we had already put in something of a workout.

A smattering of beautiful hotel rooms are on the side of the boma where guests can sit in a common overlook and watch the elephants sleeping under the infrared light. I can tell you from experience that this is not only interesting but soothing, calming, and addictive.

The boma projects peacefulness in the darkness of the African night. Outside the number of stars is astounding to one accustomed to North American skies. Birds fly to the ceiling beams of the boma and tuck themselves into nests. They croon their last song notes for the day. Several times I had boma duty at night. There I sat alone or with

12. Shungu : Poor Boy... Or Is He?

The daily morning cleanup in the boma is a workout to start the day. When the volunteers do the daily boma cleaning, the dung is carted away to Dung Mountain, a self-explanatory monument to the elephants behind the boma area. We clear away partially eaten branches, sprinkle fresh sawdust and the boma will be clean for another night's use.

another volunteer in the loft, taking nighttime data. Every five minutes I recorded which elephants entered or exited the boma. This is done every few weeks straight through the night, volunteers covering two-hour shifts from dusk until dawn. Darkness descends slowly over the boma; cool air sinks onto layers of fresh wood chips. I saw in the soft, infrared lighting the gleam of ivory tusks against the darkness. Shungu enters the boma before the others on this night, trunk moving, tail swishing, teeth grinding, silently walking. Far behind him, Sally is heading inside. He grabs a large Port Jackson branch (a personal favorite), steals away to a quiet corner, savoring it like cookies and milk before bedtime. Sally wakes from a dream with a start but still standing. Thato lies on her side on the downy bed of sawdust. Not a sound can be heard but crickets chirping. One by one the others enter in search of the acacia, Port Jackson, and wattle branches that await them in a heap. The infrared lights cast shadows that, at times, seem to take on a life of their own.

The boma at night is quiet but for the snap, crackle and pop of elephants chewing branches, snapping sticks, which echoes against the metal walls. There is the occasional sound of the elephants expelling air, and I was grateful for the steady breezes that blew through the boma. Most of the elephants sleep while standing with trunks on the ground, legs locked. Needing only half the amount of deep sleep as humans, they average about four hours of sleep per night. Giraffes sleep a similar amount, while lions and tigers sleep more like 15 hours per night. Mathew Walker writes in *Why We Sleep*, "So what does explain the difference in sleep time (and perhaps need) from species to species, or even within a genetically similar order? We're not entirely sure. The relationship between the size of the nervous system, the complexity of the nervous system, and total body mass appears to be a somewhat meaningful predictor, with increasing brain complexity relative to body size resulting in greater sleep amounts.... There was a moment in research history when scientists wondered if the measure of choice—total minutes of sleep—was the wrong way of looking at the question of why sleep varies so considerably across species. Instead, they suspected that assessing sleep quality, rather than quantity (time) would shed some light on the mystery."[6] Sleep amounts in various species differ because of a complex blend of factors, such as dietary type, predator/prey balance within a habitat, the presence and nature of a social network, metabolic rate, and complexity of the nervous system. Walker believes that sleep has likely been shaped by numerous forces along the evolutionary path and involves a delicate balance between meeting the demands of survival while awake, such as obtaining food, minimizing energy outlay and threat risk, and participating in the animal's herd or group. Sleep restores the physiological needs of an organism. The higher the species' metabolic rate, the greater the requirement for restorative sleep. As in humans, elephants dream in the rapid eye movement (REM) stage of sleep. During REM sleep, the body is temporarily paralyzed so that the dreamer will not act on their dreams (think: sleepwalking), and the eyes move around under the eyelids. The subject of sleep, its length, types: REM vs. Non-REM remains an area rich for discovery in future research. All mammals have both REM as well as Non-REM sleep, and it is in the balance of the two that each species reaches its ultimate best functioning.

When the volunteers do the daily boma cleaning, the dung is carted away to Dung Mountain, a self-explanatory monument to the elephants behind the boma area. We will sprinkle fresh sawdust and the boma will be clean for another night's use. The aroma of fresh sawdust is a refreshingly clean scent. There is a great deal of human activity in the boma during the day with several offices on the side of the building on the first floor.

Toward the end of my two-hour evening shift in the boma, darkness grows deeper; the infrared light seems brighter. Sleep overcomes these gentle creatures, ushering them into dreams. Rain pounds the metal roof like the roar of a subway car. Tonight Sally, Keisha and Nandi stand dreaming with the occasional twitch of an ear or a leg, trunk resting on the ground, the telltale signs of REM sleep.

The boma in the middle of the night. Notice that most of the elephants sleep standing, while Thato sleeps lying on her side. The infrared light allows a camera on a corner to film activity within the boma through the night as part of the Keisha Project.

Shungu has a special bond with Ndyebo Momsemge, who is also called Welcome. He was raised in the Eastern Cape region of South Africa. As a young adult, he was unsure of what he wanted to do for a living, so he learned building trade skills such as tiling, woodworking, waterproofing, and some electrical work. Through an elder at his church who worked at KEP, he found out about the park and its elephants. With Dr. Debbie's help, he began work at KEP as an apprentice and was quickly shocked to realize, "Something tells me this is what I want to do for a living. I worked on building bonds with the elephants. They can tell who you are, how you're feeling. At first, my family was not happy about me working with elephants. It was not something most people from my area decide to do. But now they are fine with it. I want to help the youth in my village, I want them to come visit here and see this place and these creatures and learn about them. I learned to speak English in my mid-twenties, and never had white friends until I came here."

Ndyebo's sense of humor is contagious. Here he stands in the field with Keisha, the holes in her ear visible. He has an excellent relationship with all the elephants but has an especially strong bond with Shungu.

126

12. Shungu : Poor Boy... Or Is He?

Ndyebo has been a guide at KEP for eight years. "Every day is different here. We guides have to bring understanding about these amazing animals to volunteers and tourists and be sure there is mutual respect and trust between us and the elephants. Not everyone can work with them. It is not about perfection. Really loving them is to really understand them."

He and Shungu have an especially strong bond. Ndyebo says Shungu comes to him for comfort. "Being on the bottom of the pecking order, Shungu is often bullied by the others, even Mashudu. Once when the boys were fighting, Thandi got upset and ran to them to try to break it up. Then Shungu followed me and tried to steal pellets from my bag. I gave him some to spoil him. Some days he doesn't listen, but he is still young. He knows I love him and he trusts me."

Shepherd has a different viewpoint about Shungu. "If he's alone when you approach, he can act wild and seem like he might charge you. But if I talk to him calmly and firmly, give him time and space, he's fine."

Sunday Afternoon with Shungu

Volunteers are not allowed to feed the elephants on weekdays because we are busy taking data for various research projects whenever we are out in the field. On the weekends, however, we can go out on the tractor with buckets of fruit and spend extra time with the elephants, feeding and observing them closer up with tourists. I grabbed every chance I could to be in the field with them wanting to be near them as much as I could. Because Sally, Nandi and Thandi are more assertive in getting the attention of tourists with fruit buckets, I wanted to come up with a strategy to be able to feed the entire bucket to Shungu. I tiptoed over to Ndyebo, who was standing at Shungu's end of the barrier and whispered that I intended for Shungu to get my entire bucket. He obliged and whispered that I should stand back and wait for the girls in the middle of the barricade to start eating their fruit first and then approach Shungu to feed him. Meanwhile, he told me to keep the fruit bucket behind my back so the other elephants wouldn't see it yet. As Sally and her attendants began feeding on fruit, Shungu rested his chin on the horizontal metal pole giving his typical forlorn look. He tugged on my heartstrings. I was instantly in love.

I followed Ndyebo's wise instructions and Shungu ate piece after piece of fruit so quickly I could hardly believe it. I offered an orange slice

These special moments with Shungu are what I waited for. On the weekends volunteers are able to go out to the field as tourists to hand feed and touch the elephants. On weekdays we were too busy taking data to allow any individual interactions. Most of the time, Shungu would stand still as long as I wanted him to.

to him by holding my palm out and letting him use the fingers on his trunk to grasp it and fling it into his mouth. The tip of his trunk was wet and rubbery and the hair on it bristly. I wished he'd slow down so I could savor the experience of feeding him. I loved every second of feeding him by hand and at that moment, the world felt balanced and right. He was in elephant nirvana and I was in a parallel bliss.

I rode the tractor back to the main building, returning with more fruit buckets for Shungu. When the last piece of sweet fruit was swallowed, his mouth dripping with fruit juice, Shungu victoriously strolled back out to the field, his bent tail swishing back and forth behind him, leaving a trail of dust in the Sunday afternoon spring light. I was elated, smiling from ear to ear. "That's my boy," I thought as I gripped the railing during the bumpy tractor ride back from the field. My Sunday afternoon with Shungu was amazing.

13

Madiwa: The Cheeky One

"No one in the world needs an elephant tusk but an elephant."—Thomas Schmidt

"Madiwa" means "darling" or "dear one" in Shona.
Identifying Characteristics:

Long tail with thin tail hair
Small elephant, about the same size as Thato
Thandi-like face and ears without the wrinkles
Medium-length tusks that curve up like a mammoth
High shoulder bones
Born May 2005

Madiwa, or Maddie as the staff and guides affectionately call her, is the youngest and smallest of the new girls. She is clearly the bravest of the three, always the first to try something new and bold. Madiwa was originally from the same hunting farm as Thato and Mashudu, near Botswana, and she may in fact be related to Mashudu. There is no record of what actually happened to her mother. According to Fanwell, "Madiwa likes to touch people with her trunk. I have to tell tourists to be extra alert around her so they don't get scared and then scare the elephants!" he says with a big grin. He adds, "When I see people enjoying being out with the elephants, it makes me so happy, it makes me want to share more information about these elephants with them." And he does that daily in his friendly, eloquent style.

From the hunting farm, the new girls were relocated to Elephants of Eden. The farm was ideal for a "halfway sanctuary" for elephants that could not be housed at KEP due to regulation and permit conditions with nature conservation bodies. (Only a maximum of ten elephants could be housed at a time.) Finally, after much planning, a bonded group of six elephants were relocated to an over 3,000-acre game farm outside Mossel Bay. As we've seen, Sias Van Rooyen, who is currently the general manager at KEP, worked with the three new girls there before they were brought to KEP. Sias followed the girls here and has known them for most of their lives. Having grown up on a horse farm in South Africa, Sias knew he was destined to work with animals as an adult.

He explains,

"Madiwa arrived in the Eastern Cape in 2008 along with 2 young males. They came all the way from the northwest close to Botswana, where they were rescued from a culling operation. Madiwa was probably close to 3–4 years old and very small. She was quick to accept the attention of the new handlers and being the curious girl she is, she explored 'every corner' of her new home. When she saw through a fence in their outdoor enclosure, Madiwa was very interested in her new play mates. Being a relatively small elephant, she was very playful and never missed the chance of a mud bath with the 2 young males. She was a fast learner and was the first elephant to follow us on our morning walks to the outside camps of the farm. Amari and Shanti followed soon after and the 2 males and 3 females made a beautiful juvenile group of elephants reintroduced to each other."

It must indeed be very comforting to Madiwa to have Sias around, whom she's known for most of her life as well as Shanti and Amari.

During my stay at KEP, I continued to watch Madiwa sparring with Mashudu in the field. He acts as if he is trying to win her over. When they both trumpet, look out! You can feel the excitement in the air.

An orange and black butterfly touches down on golden buttercups and periwinkle wildflowers fed by fresh dung. Ndyebo and I get closer to the pair as they settle in for a grazing break. Their skin feels like rubbery leather with wrinkles as deep as gorges, thick black hair accenting at intervals. The eyelashes on these two are amazingly long and luscious. Standing near each other they chew silently and walk noiselessly through the field together when they need more browse. They are a handsome couple, and who knows what's in store for them as Mashudu reaches puberty. Plenty of the staff and volunteers daydream about these two mating and having offspring together. Time will tell!

Volunteers from All Corners of the Globe

After a week at the park, I am deepening into the routine. Each day is totally different than the day before, and I am rarely with the same people for a whole day. It is getting a bit easier to tell the elephants apart in the field, and collecting data is more routine. The research we are assisting with is necessarily a very regimented program, and we are all happy to oblige. It's why we've gone to great lengths, literally, to be here.

One of the most compelling ways to experience a very deep connection with elephants is through an immersive experience. Since 2010, AERU researchers have been assisted by a team of volunteers from all corners of the world. AERU trains volunteers on site to collect data in the field relating to the biological, behavioral, anatomical, veterinary, physiological, behavioral and dietary requirements for their research records. They collect this data not only to establish baseline values for all elephants but to coordinate and assimilate research investigating the complex dynamic between behavior, biology, ecology, anatomy and physiology of these mammoth creatures and how these factors play a role in their collective welfare. By the way, there is an intricate system of field etiquette at the park that everyone has to obey. No one, not even the researchers, is allowed to go into the field without a guide.

Volunteers from all corners of the globe pay their own travel expenses and a housing fee, purchase food at the local supermarket weekly, and cook their own meals in kitchens on the premises. Each volunteer is given an individualized schedule, but all volunteers end up participating in everything. The volunteers are required to wear their green shirts and jackets, which the park provides, while in the field on weekdays to differentiate them from tourists and show that they are part of the staff. Volunteers have the privilege of being treated as locals, a sign we are being welcomed into the wider community. Volunteers are then taught the complex arrangement of social relationships among the elephants in this, Sally's herd. Volunteers are trained to collect data in the field which includes monitoring social interactions, grazing and feeding habits and frequency, as well as the movement of the elephants. Other research duties volunteers assist with include botanical surveys relating plant diversity to grazing patterns, data input and analysis. The overall aim of the research is to map the behavior of captive elephants, as there is more and more need to safeguard elephants in sanctuaries. Ultimately, research results from AERU are disseminated to other facilities and influence captive elephants worldwide.

One of the research projects, Nearest Neighbor, involves volunteers going out into the field with a clipboard, stopwatch and chart on which they record which elephant is standing closest to whom and for how long. If Madiwa is the "elephant of the day" in this project, every five minutes I record any changes in which elephant is standing closest to her, who is walking near whom, and which elephants are out of sight. Volunteers then feed this information into the computer to be analyzed by Dr. Debbie and Clare. In order to complete this project, one has to be able to identify all ten elephants and judge the approximate distance between them. Clare says, "The very first thing a volunteer learns is how to differentiate each of the ten elephants by sight in order to collect data on each correctly. This is not as easy as one might think, as at first sight, each outsized grey shape looks very similar to the others."

Another research project, Herd Activity, holds volunteers to task by requiring that they record the code for each activity each elephant does every five minutes. Choices include feeding, grazing, walking, standing, swimming, streaming and a dozen more. When taking data in the field, the hours fly by since it is not easy to record data for ten elephants every five minutes. There are many subtle interactions between the elephants that would go unnoticed to the untrained eye. These include body language mannerisms, like the position of the trunk, the tail, the head and even the ears. Between elephant body language, scenery and other wildlife, there is always much going on in the field even when the scene appears to be quiet.

Aside from research duties, other elephant care duties volunteers engage with are preparing food for the elephants, mucking out the boma every morning, clearing used branches from the night pasture, growing food in the garden for the elephants, weekly visits to a local fourth-grade class to volunteer, visiting a local animal shelter to assist them, and making handcrafted items for sale at the park shop as fundraising for the elephants. Those activities might include making dung paper or organic pots from the dung as a recycling project or helping craft any of the many items sold at the shop. I often engaged in these activities at the end of my day, and it was a satisfying, relaxing way to reflect on all I'd learned and experienced each day as well as create saleable items to benefit the elephants.

The Ever-Present Guides

Everything that happens at the Knysna Elephant Park depends on the guides. They number about 20 and are as different from each other as the elephants are, landing here from many different countries, cultures, and experiences. Some left their families behind in their country of origin because of economic hardship and see them only once a year. One guide was about to go on leave for three weeks to see his wife and children in his native Zimbabwe. The bus ride would take three days each way, cutting his family time by almost a week, round trip. Some of the guides live at the park, and still others commute by common van from a township nearby.

Although most of the guides don't say this, I have it in the strictest of confidence from a reliable source that each of them has a song of gratitude in their hearts when volunteers come to the park to help with the elephants. They appreciate the lengths people from all over the world have gone to and the expense to come help the elephants. Their love for this herd is immense. In fact, the guides have a bit of the elephants in their blood. I'll swear to that. They are very soulful people, each of them. I hope they know how grateful volunteers as well as staff are to them!

Day after day they stand with the elephants out in the fields in their tan and green uniforms in wind, rain, cold, and scorching heat,

After breakfast, part of the training session includes walking out to the field in single file. Shungu leads the way by default, but he doesn't mind. I've walked next to him to the field, and it is marvelous to feel his rhythm and stance as he lumbers toward the fields. Shepherd walks next to me, periodically telling Shungu to slow down or turn right, and he silently obeys.

all for the love of elephants. Their uniforms are natural colors by plan, causing them to almost blend into the tree line with the dark lavender mountains rising sharply behind them. Today the gray of the elephants mirrors the sky, overcast and dark. The emerald grass is the only brightness as I watch them far out in the field. Although they appear calm, they are always anticipating the next moves of all ten elephants and the interactions between them. Their attention is engaged at all times. They know each elephant's personality, rank, typical body language. Each guide has a bond, invisible and strong, with every herd member. The feeling of safety is mutual, almost tangible between man and beast.

Golden butterflies glide in the cool breeze as if whispering messages; doves and finches fly overhead, land on a pile of dung, picking out seeds. Sally, Amari and Keisha put their trunks out, sensing a change in the weather. The distant mountains dwarf the elephants who are browsing in the valley. From the hilltop, the guides appear small as crickets. Dark clouds gather, blown by easterly winds bringing much-needed rain.

When I exited the tractor in the field, I heard several elephants trumpeting. I turned to the barrier and saw Nandi smell a pile of yesterday's dung and became upset by the stale pile. As others followed her actions, she threw her trunk into the air as if in disgust. A half hour later the tractor rattles in the distance. It is full of passengers, young and old. When it clamors to a stop, the passengers walk with their fruit buckets to a guide who awaits their arrival. This time it is Dumisani, who speaks engagingly with the crowd about elephant life. Sally sways in her place, throwing her weight from side to side in anticipation. Like a kid in a candy store, she knows the scrumptious fruit is moments away. The guides are carefully orchestrating the movement of the visitors, the volunteers and the elephants themselves, making it look easy; however, it is anything but easy. We entrust our lives to these guides.

During the park's open hours, the elephants are regularly exposed to an assortment of humans, some familiar, others not. Tourists arrive every half hour with buckets of fruit and vegetables to feed the elephants as their trunks reach across the steel barrier. The fruit buckets include a variety of fruits but especially citrus fruits, which have a lot of vitamin C, and the sweet potatoes which have antioxidant properties. Afterward tourists feed the elephants hand to trunk, guides bring tourists close to the elephants while tossing pellets on the ground for the elephants to munch on as a distraction so tourists can touch the elephants and interact closely with them. The pellets are a blend of lucerne, molasses and other nutrients.

As a whole, the guides agree that elephants don't attack unless they are provoked. Sias explains, "It is just not in their nature. They are peaceful creatures in their giant hearts. They want wellness for all. They have Ubuntu in their hearts—that means things are for the benefit of all. They walk so quietly, it's amazing that a creature that big can sneak up behind you and you wouldn't know until they wrap their trunk around you; startling you with their version of a hug."

As today is Sunday, we volunteers are allowed to be in the field in street clothes and feed fruit to the elephants along with tourists. I am surprised to see Ndyebo in street clothes as well. He is visiting the elephants on his day off for the same reason: to interact with them in a much more leisurely way. "I wanted to just enjoy them on this lovely Sunday afternoon," he says with his contagious grin. The sun is shining brightly today, pouring itself over the whole lot like some visible spirit. Ndyebo spends extra time with his good friend Shungu, whose trunk moves like a vacuum across the ground seeking leftover pellets. Shungu flaps his ears to cool himself from the afternoon heat. Doves sing their hearts out, their song repeating nonstop. Zebras dart in and out of the elephants, gathering, scavenging for food scraps. When the rattle of the tractor loaded with people bearing fruit buckets clangs its way over the ruts in the dirt-packed road toward the field, zebras dart to safety while elephants trot toward the barricade.

Born to be an elephant whisperer, Davidson Mbaura grew up in the Mas Vingo Province of Zimbabwe, largely a farming area. His brothers and extended family are still there. He explains in his shy but firm way, "It's almost as if I started working with ellies when I was still in my mother's belly. The experience was already in my bone marrow. My father used to shepherd sheep while other relatives worked with cattle. I am the first born of 4 brothers and one sister. My brother, Garrison, also works as a guide at KEP. God gave me something internal. I believe I was born to work with elephants and God will protect me," he says thoughtfully, looking out at the ellies grazing nearby.

"Growing up I was worried because I didn't go to school. We had family problems and I worried about how I'd support myself. It's a family thing to be an elephant whisperer. The ellies in Zimbabwe are not wild, but they are not trained either. There the people are fenced in and the ellies ran free. When they culled elephants in Zimbabwe, they kept the babies not realizing they would grow big. At one point I helped train ellies to herd cattle from paddock to paddock. As a young boy I stuck around the guys who worked with elephants just to be near them. I used to ride on their back. The boss asked, 'Who is this little boy?' I had no birth certificate and no ID. When I was 15 and they called me to fill in, that was my first real job. The boss had a project in mind which required me to have 6 months of training, including learning to speak English. In 1998 we moved to Victoria Falls, but then a land reform program in which blacks were taking land from whites affected tourism negatively, so we all moved to Zambia in around 2000. After that I came to South Africa. I met Sias in Limpopo Province where he worked at an elephant park. He liked my hand and offered me a job. It's because of Sias that I'm here at KEP with my brother Garrison."

Davidson continues, "The ellies know that we can disagree. They find it easy to forgive but they don't forget. They teach me love—they greet each other after being away even just for a short time. I'm short tempered by nature but through them, I've learned to forgive. I've realized that I can't work with them when I'm angry. I don't concentrate well then, and we need to read their body language constantly. Like in football when you stop the ball dead in its tracks and the fans cheer and give you the energy you need to read the environment. Without the ellies in my life, I wouldn't even know how to speak English, which I am enjoying. I get to meet many interesting and caring people through my job. I love each of the ellies and feel like a parent to them all."

When asked about a favorite moment he shared with an elephant, Davidson did not miss a beat. "An elephant I knew in Zimbabwe named Madina loved to play football. If someone kicked the ball to her and asked her to throw it back, she did it! Then she got a reward. She would throw the ball by sucking on it with her trunk, creating a vacuum, and then used her trunk to throw it. I'll never forget these moments of joy!"

*   *   *

The Wildfires Arrive

It was a typical Wednesday in May at KEP, and I was out in the field taking data for the Nearest Neighbor project. Autumn is a time for winding down, for preparing for winter, the rainy season here in the Garden Route. As I stood with a few other volunteers and guides, I noticed a strange-looking curl of smoke drift by in the sky. With the need to take data every five minutes, I was distracted for quite some time before I began to notice more smoky wisps. Was it fog rolling in? It was midday, and that would be highly unusual. It didn't appear to be a cloud because the rest of the vast sky was clear, although the sun was not strong. We puzzled over it in between taking data, and within a few hours it became clear: It was the smoke from a series of rapidly growing wildfires. The wind began to billow, the smoke growing darker by the hour. By sunset, ashes began to fall like sinister snow. The stench of smoke began to descend on the park. This was downright frightening.

When the guides walked with the elephants back to the boma at dusk, they seemed to linger in the field long after. The sky was dark with smoke; the wind caused shadows to flicker.

At dusk, tiny pieces of ash drifted onto the patio outside my room. It looked as if the sky was falling. Those of us who stayed at the Main House brought our dinners out to the picnic table in the courtyard and ate under the canopy of smoke and ash, fearful that if we stayed indoors we might miss determining whether or not the fires were creeping closer to the park. For the moment, they remained distant enough that we were not in immediate danger. The wind was ominous.

We sat outside until almost midnight, and saw distant tree plantations go up in flames, with what must have inevitably been houses and grasslands. The flames grew so tall we had no trouble seeing them from many miles away. We checked cell phones continuously for any changes in weather reports and for messages the staff might get from friends in the surrounding area. None of the news was good. The fires appeared to burn closer with each passing hour. We had been told to pack an emergency bag in case we needed to evacuate the park, complete with passports and any other valuables. We worried about the safety of the elephants if the fires came any closer to the park and were told that the park had an evacuation plan for them if needed.

Unexpectedly, just before midnight, the wind shifted, nudging the fires away from the park. Relieved and reeking of smoke and ash, we retreated to our rooms, knowing that if anything changed, the staff would wake us up to evacuate. It was an ironically beautiful sight if you were unaware of the fires' destructive powers.

By morning, the fires had drifted farther from us but left a heavy

Part Two

The flames grew so tall I had no trouble seeing them from many miles away. I checked my cell phone continuously for any changes in weather reports; others checked for messages from friends in the surrounding area. None of the news was good. The fires appeared to burn closer with each passing hour.

smoke-filled sky with ashes raining steadily down like snow. Management decided to have the guides take the ellies deep into a valley area where they liked to graze so that they would not be breathing in the thick, sooty smoke. The air was thick with dark smoke and ash, and it smelled of fire. As for AERU staff and volunteers, we stayed indoors all day, catching up on data entry and other necessary chores. We were lost in the chaos of the fires which still burned in the distance. Volunteers received calls and text messages of concern from family and friends who saw the wildfires on television from other countries.

Reports drifted in from staff who ventured out of the park to offer help. Hundreds of houses were burned beyond recognition, this being the largest wildfires ever to devastate the area. Very slowly, as the day progressed, the air began to clear, and we knew the park would be spared and that we and the animals were safe ... at least for now. Because the weather had been dry for many months, there was always the chance of a spark riding the breeze and landing on park grounds. Helicopters regularly crisscrossed overhead with water and flame retardant, attempting to eradicate what was left of the fires.

In the end, not only were hundreds of homes destroyed, but several people died. Thankfully the park was spared, ostensibly by some mammoth miracle.

14

Amari:
The Observant One

"If elephants didn't exist, you couldn't invent one. They belong to a small group of living things so unlikely they challenge credulity and common sense."—Lyall Watson

Identifying Characteristics:

Long tail with short tail hair
Large-sized elephant, about the same size as Keisha
Medium-length tusks that point down and out like an "A"
Top of head is rounded
Born April 2000

Originally from a reserve near Hoedspruit, Amari arrived at KEP with Shanti and Madiwa in May 2017. She is thought to have been born in April 2000, making her 18 years old. She is the matriarch to Shanti and Madiwa, the other "new girls," and is highly observant, always keeping an eye on her girls. Like Keisha, she is a quiet, gentle elephant, often keeping to herself.

Sias Van Rooyen, general manager for KEP, has known these three new girls longer than anyone else at the park. He tells this story about them: "Amari, Madiwa and Shanti arrived at an almost 1500 acre farm owned and managed by KEP at the time I was working there, and was located along the Eastern Cape. Amari and Shanti came from a Mpumalanga relocation due to overpopulation. They were part of a group of 4 elephants (2 bulls and 2 cows) that arrived at our farm in 2008. They were slightly bigger elephants than we expected. The first night Amari and Shanti got into a brawl and Shanti received a bad cut from Amari's tusk below her left eye. This left Shanti with a swollen eye which needed veterinary treatment. Soon enough they settled down very well and in time became better friends. Shanti was the shyer one. Being very nervous and very vocal, she can easily put up a scream or trumpet for the smallest things. Amari was the fighter, always charging the fence and throwing sticks, a good sign of her dominant behavior and the leadership she shows today."

"When I started to know them better," Sias continues, "Shanti was a fast learner and was quicker to accept comfort from us than the others. The handlers enjoyed working with her very much. Amari had to be handled with more caution as she was always fast in her actions. She took longer to accept us."

"One morning, we decided to take the first walk with all the elephants and handlers to the back of the farm to explore the area of the farm they were to live in. Madiwa led the way, followed by the bigger girls. Suddenly, she saw a bush buck running out of the scrubs—she panicked and started running. Amari and Shanti followed her, Shanti trumpeting and running faster. They disappeared into the lush bush. So there we were, standing without any elephants, laughing and surprised by what had happened as the farm was big and we could not see them. Still new to us and their environment they chose to stay in the bush and refused to come to us when we called them. The bush was so thick it was difficult for them to move and basically impossible to do so safely."

Sias continues, "We were not sure how to get them back and spent 2 days following the sound of the elephants braking branches and moving even higher into the hills. Soon after our efforts we realized we had only one safe option left, which was to use Clyde, an ex-circus elephant who was also living on the farm to go in to the area where the girls were hiding and hope they would follow him back."

"The girls had 'met' Clyde through the fence and knew him well," recalled Sias. "We stuck to our strategy and walked with Clyde to the top of the hill where we had last seen the three girls. The plan worked very well. Sooner than we thought the 3 girls were close to Clyde. But only Madiwa actually followed. Shanti and Amari had other plans to stay out longer. Upon returning, all the elephants were happy to see each other and clearly had lots to talk about as they rumbled and touched trunks all around. Amari and Shanti eventually came back into the camp later that night and finally we had all the elephants back in their holding camps."

"As time passed, our relationships with all the elephants became so good we were able to go everywhere with them," Sias recalls with a proud smile on his face. "When it was time for them to 'come home' for the night, they would run to great us! The elephants had a lot of free-range time and swam regularly in nearby dams while we sat on the side watching them playing and mock charging us as they got out of the muddy water. Today 11 years onwards they are still together and are now the part of the Knysna Elephant park resident herd with Sally."

Fast forward to 2017. Sias hadn't seen these new girls in about six years. "When they arrived at KEP and saw me, Sias recalls, I called them each by name and they walked up to me in a most welcoming way. I was able to help with the integration of these three girls with Sally's herd by being a familiar person."

Weeks later, however, it was Thandi who befriended Madiwa and gradually Shanti and Amari. It was as if she reconsidered and realized that they are peers of similar age and didn't mean any harm.

While grazing in the fields, Amari keeps a close eye on her girls, Shanti and Madiwa. She feels most comfortable when they are near her or at least within sight. They graze on grass, digging a divot by kicking the back of a front foot to gauge the grass from the ground, grabbing it with their trunks and shaking it or wiping it on their chins to clean dirt off. Amari's trunk brings it to her mouth for chewing. She looks so serene grazing, the towering mountains in the distance, billowing white clouds overhead. A gentle breeze is most welcome under the warm African sun.

* * *

Breakfast for Champions and Elephant Enrichments

Early each morning the elephants and guides participate in a training session to review commands. In addition to each elephant knowing his/her name, they all understand almost 20 commands, including back up, move up, pick up, kick, give, flap ear, turn left, turn right, get over, lift, foot, stretch down, put them out (ears), ear out, head shake, trunk up, come here, and steady (don't move).

After their training session, each elephant is given a giant bowl of breakfast. Served in huge rubber tubs, each bearing the name of its owner, it is served in an open area outside the boma field. As herbivores, elephants need a wide range of variety in their diet in order to get the many nutrients they require. They need to feed for at least half of their waking hours. Feeding time is monitored closely through the data taken in the field as part of the Herd Activity program. Put another way, in order to be in optimal health, they must eat for about 18 hours a day. The pellets used for training are made of plant matter, molasses, and extra nutrients with some rock salt thrown in for good measure. From time

Swimming is a time of frolicking and putting hierarchy aside. Often Sally and Keisha can be seen swimming together, as well as Sally and Shungu. Surprisingly adept at swimming, elephants are able to wield their weight through the water with remarkable ease. Standing on the shore watching them, it is impossible for staff and volunteers not to smile, laugh, and point in awe of the forward rolls, near cartwheels and other acrobatic performances.

to time deworming powder and vitamins are mixed into the breakfast bowls for preventative health. Branches are brought in from outside the park for the elephants to browse on, such as their favorite—the succulent Port Jackson tree branches. They eat the branch, bark and leaves of these delectables. Other types of branches brought into the park include wattles, black wattles, and lucerne, which is like alfalfa and other grains such as oats and hay which are high in selenium and aid with digestion. When elephants eat branches, they use their teeth, trunk action and tusks to remove the bark. It is a form of stimulation. They also love to eat rooikrans branches, another species native to the Garden Route. Black wattle, one of the Acacia species, is another favorite, but bringing it to the park has some unique challenges. For one thing it turns sour when cut too soon before eating. Aside from that, it can't be cut in the same place for more than a day in order to prevent an anti-herbivore response. Elephants also love gum tree bark, which is plentiful in the area. And of course, the fruit buckets are a large part of their diet, which they munch on as if it's candy. The fruit buckets include sweet potatoes, oranges, bananas, apples, and sometimes berries and watermelon when available. In the summer, the fields are a virtual salad bar for the ellies.

Since elephants are exceptionally smart and therefore can grow bored quickly, they are given treats in such a way that they have to solve a problem in order to get to the food reward. "Enrichments combat boredom," says Nicki Milachowski, who was in charge of enrichments for these elephants. These enrichments are provided to the ellies three to five times a week.

Nicki continues, "Staff and volunteers brainstorm and construct all sorts of things in order to hide food and challenge the elephants to figure out how to access it. One of their creations is a puzzle box, which is loaded with food and then given to the ellies in the night pasture for their entertainment and eating pleasure. It mimics the idea of a board game before bedtime. Developed by a volunteer, it's a delight to sit on the elevated benches outside the boma at night and watch the elephants try to decode the solution. The key to the puzzle box was to keep turning it over and over again so the food slips closer to the edge and they can grab it easily. Other kinds of enrichments volunteers help assemble include a tractor tire which is loaded with hay. Pieces of fruit are hidden in various spots underneath the hay. This toy is also fun to watch them puzzle over, but they've gradually become masters at the tire enrichments."

Nicki goes on, "We need to think outside the box when we create elephant enrichments. One day some volunteers and I made elephant burritos, using strips of thin bark to tie large banana leaves over pieces of fruit. It was good fun to watch them puzzle over a new brainteaser, the fruit aroma enticing them all the while. We also use enrichments for celebrating birthdays or holidays. It is especially fun to see them figure out how to eat a pellet cake off a tray. They usually try to grab the whole tray," she explains with a wide grin on her face. She exudes confidence when it comes to animal welfare and clearly understands these elephants inside and out. Other enrichments include tires hanging from chains, a sort of tether ball for elephants, setting up a treasure hunt in the night camp field, or providing treats frozen into an ice block on a hot day. "You should see Sally when she senses something delicious is hiding under the ground. It's a very humorous sight," Nicki says, laughing. "One Christmas I had the idea to get Christmas trees and tie fruit to them, and after it took us six hours to get the tree to stay in the ground, Sally walked over to it and pulled it right out with a yank of her trunk. Her 4-ton body no match for a mere tree!"

Nicki explains, "Fruit is an essential part of the elephant's diet. In the winter, when there are less tourists to hand feed fruit to the ellies, we supplement their breakfast buckets with extra fruit. This way their diet is even across the seasons. There is something called Lucerne, which is a kind of hay that is dried and baled and contains a multitude of nutrients. Lucerne grows all over Africa. The Lucerne also provides a good source of fiber and the ellies just love it."

Sometimes Nicki and some volunteers weave tree branches between the metal poles in the boma, which the elephants enjoy. She clearly loves creating challenges for these elephants that she is so fond of, and providing enrichments on a regular basis is a best practice for elephant welfare. In addition to cognitive stimulation, providing enrichments can decrease stereotypical behaviors such as those that arise from boredom, decrease aggressiveness, allow the elephants to make choices about how they interact with their environment, and increase the general activity level in a positive way. New tastes and textures can be added for a variation in stimulation, and handlers watch for signs of the elephants not liking something or becoming too frustrated at retrieval. Other techniques used include hay nets suspended above their pens in the boma, huge frozen ice blocks containing water, fruit and fruit juice. "One of the most successful ideas was large buckets, suspended above each elephant and filled with fruit, pellets and popcorn. The idea is that they will figure out how to nudge the bucket with their trunks so pellets and popcorn would dislodge from small holes in the bottom, and fall to the ground for them to savor. It was fascinating to watch them master this in one night. Sally, food loving matriarch that she is, just pulled her entire bucket down. No one realized she could stretch quite that far, and there was much glee from all of us as we watched the look of sheer elephant delight on her face as she feasted on the popcorn."

According to *The Elephant Husbandry Resource Guide*, enrichments should, "allow opportunities for appropriate social interaction. Few captive herds replicate the complexity of herds of wild elephants in terms of age structure, sex ratio, and history of past interactions. In particular, herds lacking young by reproduction are missing an important source of interaction and associated activity. Increasing social complexity through the careful consideration of appropriate social group size and composition, breeding and maintaining a male elephant, is considered to be an important aspect of enrichment."[1]

Once, the KEP staff was approached by a Canadian school whose second-grade students wanted to learn more about elephants. The school made a donation to the park, and after a brainstorming huddle decided to purchase supplies to build some new enrichments for the ellies. The plan was to videotape how the elephants interacted with the enrichments so these second graders could see their donation in action. In this way, they could actively contribute to elephant welfare and learn more about these animals in an original way. KEP staff members made and tested new enrichment prototypes, which were a popcorn blower, a rolling barrel and box to hide fruit in. Much fun was had by all, not the least of which was the elephants themselves.

Shanti was elected elephant enrichment contestant for the day. She tested the enrichments for three key strengths: elephant durability—does it stand the full assault of a three-ton elephant; is the enrichment challenging enough to keep the ellies entertained; and the final safety check. The winning device was the rolling barrel, which had many holes that were stuffed with yummy popcorn and pellets. In order to get the goodies to fall out, the ellies had to roll the barrel around a horizontal central bar, and with each spin treats would drop to the ground. Shanti had to do some quick thinking but figured it out swiftly and was quite proud of herself. With a belly full of yummies, she appeared to be smiling. The video was shown to the second graders in Vancouver, who were proud of themselves as well as the ellies.

Enrichments occasionally float in on the breeze in the form of music which the elephants enjoy. Music has been proven to reduce stress in a variety of human and nonhuman animals. For her dissertation project at England's University of Hull, Hannah Hurt explored the stereotypic behaviors of elephants, which can be a sign of boredom and stress and the ways these behaviors may be affected by music. This is the first study to look at whether the type of music influences nonhuman animal behavior, in particular that of elephants.

For the purpose of this study, Hannah provided questionnaires to 229 people who were asked to help categorize the music into four final playlists: Calm, Playful, Sad, and Triumphant. For a total of 105 hours, Hannah observed the elephants listening to each playlist as well as during a control condition, during which there was no music. The elephants were observed from the balcony inside the boma during the evenings, and each playlist was repeated seven times. I had the pleasure of spending several evenings with Hannah, helping her take data. The behaviors, which were recorded at two-minute intervals, included feeding, foraging, standing, sleeping, as well as time spent outside the boma.

Hannah's research concludes that the frequency of feeding behaviors was influenced by the Calm, Playful, and Sad music in comparison with the control situation of silence. She also found significant differences in the frequency of standing behavior when listening to the Sad and Calm playlists compared to the quiet. This study supports previous research suggesting elephants are indeed affected by music. There were no differences in the frequency of behaviors between the playlists, suggesting that the mood of the music does not influence elephants.

Hannah suggests that much more research be carried out in order to better understand elephant behavior when listening to music and ways music might benefit the elephants. She suggests that future research investigate the effects of tempo, volume, pitch, instruments, and human voices. She explains, "Since music has many components, these different factors may influence elephant's behavior in ways that could improve welfare, especially when measured against stereotypic behavior. Further research would benefit from a larger sample size, and field work conducted over a longer period of time. A longitudinal study would allow for more repetitions of playlists and the potential to identify long-term effects of music on the behavior of elephants."[2]

Getting Along Swimmingly

When rain arrives, elephants swim. They grow excited when it rains, the same way I anticipate a snowstorm by running to the door to catch the first flake. Renowned elephant researcher Cynthia Moss jokes of their tangible state of vibrancy when it rains, "How can one do a serious study on animals that behave this way!" The cooler air causes their energy level to soar, and they become restless. They begin to look for someplace to warm up. The water is usually warmer than the outside air, so in they plunge. They paddle their massive bodies around, head often under water, trunk poking the water's surface like a snorkel, and are truly comical. Their delight is contagious. All sense of hierarchy dissipates while they are swimming, splashing around and spraying water at each other with wild abandon. It is as if the water is a safe zone, a place where they don't have to worry about being bullied or bossed around. Sally might be seen carousing with Shungu, or Thandi might be seen frolicking with Shanti in unexpected combinations of personality and rank. Surprisingly adept at swimming, elephants are able to wield their weight through the water with remarkable ease. Standing on the shore watching them, it is impossible for staff and volunteers not to smile, laugh, and point in awe of the forward rolls, near cartwheels and other acrobatic performances. A large crowd of people gathered today, everyone smiling, laughing and cheering the ellies on. With water splattering and elephants creating waves in the water, it's an elepalooza of an event! We all walked away with wet shoes and clothes from the elephants splashing and spraying.

After a refreshing swim, the elephants roll themselves in the mud, which acts as a sunscreen to protect their skin from drying out under the unrelenting sunshine. It's hard to say which is more entertaining, watching the elephants swimming or watching as they mud themselves.

Shungu mudding after a leisurely swim. He rolls onto his back, all four feet up in the air and wiggles to pack the mud into the crevasses of his skin as protection from the sun.

When finished mudding, Shungu is a coppery caramel color that shimmers in the sunlight.

If you are fortunate enough to see it all, cherish the memories. They roll their bulky bodies by sensuously tossing themselves in the slippery mud and perhaps stand for a brief moment before wiggling and dancing themselves through another round of mudding. When they walk away, their bodies appear various shades of copper, bronze, dark chocolate, and caramel. Sometimes they move on to dry grass where they roll themselves vigorously, packing the mud into the crevasses of their wrinkled skin. At other times they suck up dry dirt with their trunks and spray it onto the wet mud, a comical activity referred to as dusting themselves. If the ellies are dusting themselves on a windy morning, stand with the wind to your back or you will be mud dusted too!

* * *

I heard a rumor that Sally wandered away at the end of the day yesterday. Edison tells me that she tends to get mischievous when the weather changes. He's not sure why, but it seems to hold true. She walked over toward the restaurant where she would normally not be allowed for safety reasons. "Several of us ran around to the other side to stop her," he explained excitedly, "and when she heard the tractor which was just returning from the field, she equated it with food so it was easy to get her to turn around and walk back to the field."

Edison also said, "The new girls like to separate themselves from the rest of the herd. We don't know as much about their early lives, so we need to give them time to gain confidence, and give Sally space to be able to get to know them better, to build trust between them. Elephants build relationships slowly, but I believe that if we give them enough time they will get used to each other. I believe that as long as Sally is taken care of it will work itself out."

Dung Walk

It is just after dawn in Knysna. The sky is streaked with bold pinks, tangerine and lavender. The distant, plum-colored mountains are enchanting as Christina and I walk the path to the field. We are bringing up the rear of a long parade of ten lumbering elephants and their guides as they set out on their daily trek from breakfast to the fields. I'm holding a thermal lunch box packed with rubber gloves, a small precision scale, small ziplock bags, a black marker and several other sundry items. The dew is thick on the grass, and the air is moist. We zip our field jackets and tie the hoods to keep out the chill as we walk.

The task this morning seems daunting. We are to collect a fresh dung sample from each elephant. Each dung sample is a unique time machine, enabling us to unlock the secrets that paint a moment in the life of an elephant. Each sample will undergo a long, precise laboratory process in order to provide research information on hormones, which will, in turn, help paint a picture toward understanding these complicated creatures. Sally, the matriarch and largest elephant in this herd, drops a fresh dung sample right on cue. She is about ten yards away from where I stand. When she continues walking and the guides give me the nod that no other elephants are heading toward her fresh dung, I walk over and take the sample. Donning rubber gloves, I crack it open like an egg, make sure that it's still warm, and extract a small amount of organic material about the size of

In the still of early morning, the ellies and guides walk to the fields and stop by the pond for a drink. Shungu likes to walk in front, Sally preferring to walk in the middle of the group. Their reflection in the water is picture-perfect against the jagged mountaintops, early morning fog lifting to reveal clear sky.

a tablespoon. We then weigh it on the scale, taking care to be sure it weighs close to 14 kg. I place the sample in a plastic bag, seal and mark it with the

elephant's name, date and sample weight. We save it in the lunch box, which houses a cooling element. When all ten samples have been collected, they are placed in a freezer in Fiela's Laboratory awaiting preparation for analysis. Later they will be freeze-dried, put through a centrifuge and undergo a dozen other steps before they reveal their mysteries.

As I soon find out, it is not easy to get a dung sample on demand from each elephant. The guides have small flags the size of a cupcake decoration, one for each elephant with their name printed on the front, which they use to mark fresh dung samples as they continue up the road ahead of us. From a distance they look like small, decorated cakes, the tiny

On the morning dung walk the object is to obtain a core sample from each of the ten elephants. The guides walk ahead of us with the ellies and help by marking dung samples with flags as if they are cupcakes with decorations. On this morning, Mashudu left a dung sample which was marked by a guide for us to take a sample from.

flags flapping in the breeze. We were able to get a dung sample from Sally and then Keisha, Shungu, Mashudu and Thandi, but after waiting over an hour, we needed to get back to the office to address the myriad of other tasks begging our attention. We left the lunch box with Fanwell, who was assigned the task of filling in the remaining dung samples, adding to his responsibilities for the day.

Dung pellets are rounded and shockingly large. Each bolus is the size of a cannonball and is held together by the plant fibers from grazing material. Since they are vegetarians and take in more than 300 pounds of plant life daily, elephant dung is quite fibrous. A dung bolus can often fill a pie pan. The brown of mud and amber of straw make them appear like mud pies. Mostly dry when they hit the ground with a soft thud, they have passed through more than 120 feet of intestine over several days, losing about half their water weight as they go along.

The digestive system of an elephant is highly inadequate for its size. Food generally travels quickly through the elephant's digestive tract, within about 24 hours. Digestion is usually incomplete because of a lack of symbiotic bacteria in the elephant's gut. About 60 percent of an elephant's meals, or 180 pounds of vegetable matter, ends up on the ground, including the undamaged seeds of bushes, trees and grasses. The elephants inadvertently carried this assortment of seeds miles away from their source and deposited them to flourish, continuing the ecosystem for other animal species. Filled with up to 300 different kinds of undigested seeds, elephant dung is a vital link in the African ecosystem. Interestingly, a few of the seeds will not germinate until they have passed through the intestines of an elephant. Fruit and vegetable sprouts spring from dung piles in the fields. I recognize pumpkin leaves on several seedlings sprouting from dung. The seeds thrive in the richness of dung bacteria.

In the cool weather, steam rises from the dung bolus as it lands in the damp grass. Their contents are rich with the secrets of mating hormones, cortisol stress levels and other valuable data that enables us to understand them. Surprisingly, there is no apparent odor until it is piled up into Dung Mountain on the far side of the park. It makes incredible fertilizer for flowers, vegetables and fruit trees, which, if sold, can contribute financial support toward the elephant's upkeep.

* * *

What Do Elephant Dung, Paper and Coffee Have in Common?

Elephant dung is a rich, versatile byproduct used for many things, including papermaking. Shocking as it sounds and as reluctant as some are to touch it or even use it, elephant dung paper is very strong and well suited to countless applications. Dung paper can be made to be soft to the touch or coarse, depending on how it is processed and the makeup of the dung itself. Dung paper can be embellished with glitter or sparkles, plant matter such as grasses and can easily be made in various shapes, embossed, die cut, and printed on. Elephants pass enough dung in one day to make over 110 sheets of paper. Making and selling elephant dung paper is a win/win for both elephants and humans, which can bring in proceeds with which to provide food and veterinary care as well as raise awareness about elephant conservation worldwide.

In order to make dung paper, dried dung is placed in a pot and boiled for 15 minutes. Small bits of newspaper or other scraps of paper are soaked overnight in water. Both are drained and mixed together. The dung is processed through a screen filter with water, the pulp pressed through the filter's holes and the water removed by pressing down repeatedly with a sponge. The screens are put aside in the sun and wind to dry and can be dyed with natural materials to make colored paper at this stage. The natural shades are richest to me, ranging from creamy whites and beiges to earthy browns and grays, depending on what the dung and scrap paper consists of. The paper has the texture of subtle peaks and valleys, adding to its allure. When dried, the paper is sturdy and absorbent for inks and paints.

I had several opportunities to make dung paper at KEP, which was a fun and interesting process. We added shredded old newspapers to the dung and water mix. There was no foul odor, and we mixed in nontoxic organic food coloring or vegetable dyes to shade the paper and added several kinds of glitter to the mixture for a shimmery effect.

There are many other uses for this vast supply of dung that accumulates from elephants. Since there are still many dirt roads in much of Africa, many villages use it to fill in roadway holes caused by erosion. The long, undigested fibers in the dung provide a filter of sorts to keep sand and soil that would otherwise wash away. Another popular and practical use for elephant dung is as fertilizer. The undigested bark, plant fiber, fruit and grass that make up a ball of dung is an excellent, nutrient-rich, organic supplement for most gardens, both as a fertilizer and as a mulch. An emergent use for elephant dung is as fuel, a much more renewable and sustainable fuel than trees. In much of Africa there is a high need for fuel sources for cooking and keeping warm. The methane and carbon dioxide released during the decomposition process is harvested and converted into energy. In America, the Rosamund Gifford Zoo in Syracuse, New York, uses the elephant dung it accumulates to power the zoo. The Munich zoo also uses its elephant dung for what they call "poo power" to power their entire facility. And elephant dung is considered a natural insect repellant because the smoke from burning dung kills mosquitoes. Fortunately, there is no need to apply it directly to skin! And although I've never tried it myself, word has it that the smoke from burning elephant dung can cure a headache fairly quickly! I've been told that if you are stranded in the woods and in survival mode, the water squeezed from a ball of dung is safe to drink with surprisingly little bacteria in it.

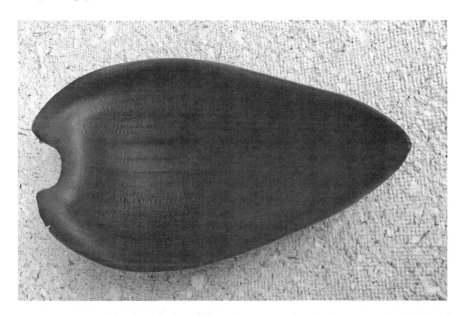

This photograph shows a flower petal of the banana plant which appears like miniature burgundy boats or dippers and rests on top of a piece of dung paper. Banana plants grow within KEP. Dung paper is very durable due to the high ratio of fiber in elephant dung. This paper, made by the author, is decorated with glitter and food coloring. One elephant passes enough dung in one day to make over 110 sheets of paper.

* * *

Trumpeted as earthy in flavor with a rich dark-roast flavor, a high-end (or in this case, low-end) kind of coffee is making its way to a coffee shop near you in the near future. Elephant dung coffee—coffee processed from beans that have been fed to elephants, passed through their intestinal tracts and picked from their dung, once excreted. A unique intestinal reaction to the coffee beans within the elephant's intestinal tract is responsible for its distinctive taste. At about $500 per pound, it rates as the world's costliest cup of coffee! And we can rest assured no elephants were harmed or even aware that their dung was collected from the ground and used for human consumption!

But the story doesn't end there. Now beer is brewed from those same coffee beans which have passed through an elephant's digestive system and, when gathered, are fermented into alcohol. Elephant dung beer is the rage in Japan where it is called Un Kono Kuru. It sold out completely within minutes of initially hitting the shelves!

And just in case you were wondering whether elephants can handle their liquor, an article by Rachel Nuwer in the *New York Times* states, blatantly, "NO. You've no doubt heard of birds gorging on fermented berries and falling out of trees, Moose wasted on fermented crab apples crashing around in the woods in a drunken stupor. How

This is a regular latte decorated with spices to be served at the café at KEP. It is not made from elephant dung and is far more reasonably priced! It makes a lovely ending to a day spent out in the field with the elephants, along with any of the pies, tarts, and other confections or meals baked in their kitchen.

many liters would it take for a 4–6 ton elephant to become inebriated? Based on the amount of alcohol it takes to get a human drunk, it would take 27 liters of 7 percent ethanol. There is a caveat to all this rough and tumble, though. Elephants, it seems, lack the enzyme that is responsible for quickly metabolizing ethanol. Humans, chimpanzees, bonobos and gorillas have an unusually high tolerance for alcohol because of a shared genetic mutation that allows them to metabolize ethanol 40 times faster than other primates." The article concludes that the myth of drunken elephants remains an open and tantalizing question, one that will undoubtedly be studied by someone, somewhere going forward.[3]

Lastly, a surprising use of elephant dung is in the form of artwork. British painter Chris Ofili has been using elephant dung in his paintings since he first visited Africa in 1993. He uses clumps or streaks in his multimedia work to add an animalistic and arguably controversial effect.

Villagers whose crops have been raided by elephants and are left with depleted or with no incomes at all could be trained to convert elephant dung into saleable items, with cottage industries springing to life to supplement the farms. Any new uses we can come up with for elephant dung can help eliminate both illegal poaching and illegal deforestation, enlighten people about elephant conservation and bring in much-needed income for elephant care. The ultimate goal is to unite efforts in the areas of job creation, elephant conservation, ecology, and rural empowerment so that elephants and humans may coexist more peacefully.

15

Shanti:
The Cautious One

"We admire elephants in part because they demonstrate what we consider the finest human traits: empathy, self-awareness, and social intelligence. But the way
we treat them puts on display the very worst of human
behavior."—Graydon Carter

"Shanti" means "peace" in Sanskrit.
Identifying Characteristics:
　Very short tail like Thato
　Large-size elephant, similar to Keisha
　Medium-sized tusks point straight down and look like pincers
　Piece of lower right ear missing
　Born April 2002

Shanti arrived at KEP along with Amari and Madiwa in May 2017
from another facility. She is from the same reserve as Amari and is
thought to be about two years younger. Shanti is quite a rebel, often
taking charge and doing her own thing. She can be very greedy, often
gobbling away when she finds something delectable to eat, keeping the
others at bay, and is always happy when treats come her way.

Charles Moyo has worked with elephants since 1996. He worked
at KEP before transferring to Plett Game Reserve to work with Harry
and his herd because of his special talent for working with large bulls.
He is both firm and gentle with them simultaneously, a tightrope act
if there ever was one. Underneath his quiet gentleness is a vast wealth
of knowledge and insight about elephants, nature, and many species of
other animals.

I saw a strong mutual respect between Harry, who is shockingly
large, and Charles, no fear from either side. Charles's average height
places him at just about Harry's front hip joint. I had the pleasure of

talking with him on several occasions. Charles refers to Shanti as "shy and sensitive. The bonds between the new herd and Sally's herd will grow in time in a natural way. All the elephants in both of these parks know what we humans are doing for them. I truly believe that."

Dr. Debbie explains wistfully, "For us here at AERU, one of the biggest occasions of 2017 was the transfer of Clyde and Shaka from KEP into a reserve with more land and less structure. Shaka had been at KEP since 2004 when he was about 3 years old. He had been saved from a cull on a game reserve in the Mpumalanga area. Clyde arrived toward the end of 2009 as a teenager with some emotional baggage—he had been in captivity for most of his life, including the circus, and it took time for KEP handlers to earn his trust. Both of these boys were initially part of the Sally's herd, but as they grew older, they were pushed out by matriarch Sally, a natural process for young males who would separate from the matriarchal herd automatically at that age, and formed their own little bachelor herd. KEP made the decision to start looking for a new home for them, with more land so they could live more independently."

"On the 5th of May 2017, Clyde and Shaka were relocated to their new home in Botlierskop Game Reserve. They were first placed in a release camp to enable them to settle in and where an AERU observation team spent a week watching them learn the meaning of 'wild.' Clyde seemed confused at first, still waiting for humans to take him to his stable at night. Two weeks later they were released into a vast 2200 acre piece of land where they met the other elephants living on the reserve—Sam, age 40, his daughter Thambile and Sam's teenage son Chima. AERU staff and volunteers continued their presence until they were satisfied that the boys were well settled in and thriving." Of one visit, Dr. Debbie says, "We spotted them deep in the valleys munching on all the food they could find. On another visit we arrived to see a very respectful elephant greeting between Clyde and Sam, while Shaka amused himself chasing waterbuck! It is great to see that elephants that come from a captive environment can be released back into the wild with so much success—especially Clyde with his circus background. AERU staff and volunteers continue to keep an eye on these boys as they establish deeper bonds with their new herd."

*　*　*

15. Shanti: The Cautious One

The New Girls Arrive at KEP

Transferring Clyde and Shaka to their new home set the stage for the new girls, as they are affectionately called, to move in to KEP. The very same day the boys left the park, Shanti, Amari and Madiwa arrived, translocated from another facility. For the first few weeks after their arrival, AERU staff and volunteers kept a watchful eye on them in an area on the side of the park called "The Orchard Camp" as they settled into their new home. The Orchard Camp is a huge fenced in area with a boma large enough to shelter several elephants comfortably. The new girls, as they will be referred to for years, were kept here so that Sally and her herd could familiarize themselves through smelling each other in the breeze for a month before meeting face to face. Amari as the dominant of the three girls, was their unofficial matriarch. How would she and Sally work things out?

Toward the end of their first month, the girls were introduced to the rest of the herd. I was at the park at that time and was privileged to witness such an unusual event. I felt like I was watching a world renowned history-making event. When we heard the news that the introduction would take place after breakfast, everyone at the park was nervous and excited. Would the herds be aggressive toward each other? Who would be the first to make a move and from which of the herds? If this were happening in the wild, each of the herds would be able to choose not to engage in the situation by leaving. Seconds felt like minutes, and minutes like hours while we waited to see how the elephants would receive each other.

Several volunteers stood on the far side of the pond so we could have a good view of the herds meeting on the opposite side. We were nervous when Shepherd, Mac and Geoff ushered the new girls along a back pathway from the Orchard to the side of the pond where Sally's herd was grazing. Everyone was practically holding their breath as the guides slowly brought the new girls to within 40 yards of Sally's herd. Sally, trunk up and sniffing, looked as if she didn't know what to think, and appeared frozen in place. All remained this way for about 15 minutes, which seemed like an eternity of wondering and worrying. And suddenly, Madiwa inched slowly forward, and, receiving no response one way or the other, continued to creep forward. As Madiwa slowly wandered closer to Sally and her girls, Thandi roared, lashing out at her. Madiwa let out a squeal. Thandi's unexpected trumpet sent Madiwa trotting back to the comfort of Shanti and Amari. Both groups continued to graze quietly while all who watched continued to practically hold our breath, for what seemed like hours. In reality it was probably a half hour. Clicking cameras, a few bird calls, and a brisk breeze were the only sounds to be heard. It was Keisha who broke the silence by strolling slowly over toward the new girls, trunk out in greeting. Of course Keisha would be the ice breaker, Keisha who knows what it's like to feel unwelcomed and unsure. She stopped about 30 yards short of the new girls and continued grazing. After another long silence that felt like hours, Geoff, Mac and Shepherd walked the new girls back to the Orchard and all of us let out a palpable chorus of relief. The initial introduction was deemed a success and there was much more time ahead for the two herds to meet and mingle with each other.

Through a slow process the two groups met briefly in the mornings. As the months passed, they began to spend longer periods of time together, and now, several years later, the two groups spend whole days grazing and roaming around the Park blended as one herd. Sally, as the oldest elephant in the park with more matriarchal experience than Amari, remains in her position. It has taken a lot of time and patience for the two groups to learn to trust one another, but now it is very exciting to see friendships growing between the elephants. By the time I returned to the park a year and a half later, I saw Keisha and Thato socialize with Amari, Shanti and Madiwa. I witnessed Madiwa flirt and fence with Mashudu out in the field. Keisha and Thato, always the first to embrace new elephants to the herd, of course reacted openly to the new girls from the start. Keisha and Madiwa have developed a close bond and it is always thrilling to see new relationships forming between herd members as they blend into one family. I often see electronic postings from the park that Shungu and Madiwa have become thick as thieves. Now that years have passed since their introduction, the park is researching the ways in which the new girls have changed herd dynamics. This is still Sally's herd, and always will be, but the new girls are becoming more and more an integral part of Sally's unified family. This most likely stems from the relationship they formed initially with Keisha, the first to welcome them.

The new girls have finally started to join the others at the barrier for fruit treats. It took well over a year for them to feel welcome there. Sally displaced them with a nudge or a shove every so often when she felt they were eating too much of the food that she believes to be hers. The staff have witnessed a change in how Shanti and Madiwa react to Sally's displacements, now only taking a few steps away from the barrier or browse pile, moving on to another pile of browse rather than leaving the area entirely, as they did when they all first met. Amari strays every so often to spend time alone, always returning to see what the others are up to. The guides continue to encourage all to have positive interactions with each other, respect each other's space and helping them be comfortable in each other's company. They do this with verbal praise, affectionate pats and strokes, and with pellet treats. This blending of herds could be a model for other parks and reserves as a way to bring groups together to merge. The more elephants there are in the world who need a safe home, the more the possibility of merging herds exists. More and more frequently the new girls join Sally's herd when browse is brought into the field. This encourages them to spend the day together as one herd, integrating and developing their hierarchy within the herd.

* * *

Hormone Levels in Cow Elephants

According to elephant researcher and author Caitlin O'Connell, "As for hormone levels, a pattern of higher amounts of stress during wet years, when the hierarchy was less linear, was reconfirmed owing to having had two dry years, and a stable, linear hierarchy, to compare with our wet year. I had wondered whether stress levels were higher due to the lack of linearity to the dominance hierarchy and the resulting social uncertainty, as well as whether the abundance of food and water would counter such effects. Greg—one of the elephants—definitely seemed more stressed, showing more signs of vigilance behaviors, particularly considering the amount of time he spent deciding in which direction to leave, if for no other reason than to avoid Smokey, another of the elephants. He displayed much more confidence in 2005 and 2007 when he had his posse in his pocket ... a structured society is a stabilizing influence on males."[1]

As we've seen, both genders of the African elephant have a gland located at the temple on each side of their head. When the elephant feels intense emotion, the gland secretes hormones, resulting in a dark stain. It almost looks like the elephant is sweating on the sides of their temples. Interestingly, male Indian elephants show a similar glandular response, especially when in musth, but the females do not show this when in estrus. This hormonal phenomenon is referred to as "streaming." Keisha streams the most frequently in Sally's herd. AERU researchers are working to determine whether or not this activity is due to negative emotions or to any intense emotion, including joy.

* * *

A cone-shaped shelter in the field made of weather slats of wood and held up by tree trunks provides protection from sun and storms for guides and sometimes elephants. A pine tree protrudes in the center through the top, which can be seen from quite a distance. Wilfred Nyamazunza, who has worked with elephants for the past 15 years, grew up with elephants and considers himself lucky to be taught by family members the ways of working with them. He took meticulous notes about all he was learning and put them into a book. Through moving and traveling from his native Zimbabwe, he lost the book and remains very sad about it. The thought of it pains me. But he likes his work and says he loves the idea that people will only know that this is an artificial herd if we tell them. They act completely the same as an elephant family in the wild.

When he was working in Zimbabwe, he worked with two bulls: Jumbo and Border. One day Border started going for a guide and Jumbo came to the rescue. He knows what humans are doing for them. He realized afterward that he can't outrun an elephant, so if one charges him, he will stand still, close his eyes and die peacefully. He says in his own quiet but firm way, "We must learn from elephants. They live Ubuntu, but we don't. I'm not afraid of them because I respect them. And they respect me in return. Those of us who see them every day have become part of their family. They have invited us into their herd."

Wilfred adds that he has a particularly strong bond with Shanti. He winks and says she's shy and sensitive and reminds him of his wife, who has a soft voice and moves slowly and deliberately. He is working to make that special bond even stronger as Shanti continues to settle into life at KEP.

An Elephant's Superpower: All About the Zombie Gene

Considering their enormous body size, elephants have surprisingly low rates of cancer. According to Athena Aktipis in *The Cheating Cell*, susceptibility to cancer differs across life forms due to some trade-offs, such as the cost of being large, growing fast, healing wounds, and being a viable reproductive candidate. Shockingly, some species have developed cancer suppression mechanisms through evolution.[2]

As cells routinely die and are replaced by new cells, common sense dictates that the larger the body, the more chance there is for error to occur, for cells to multiply incorrectly, activating genetic errors and causing cancer. In elephants, by line of reasoning, since they have trillions more, or 100 times the number of cells as humans, logic dictates that they should suffer from genetic, cancer-causing errors much more frequently than we do. However, elephants have an evolutionary trick up their trunks. They were endowed with an extra copy of a gene called TP53, which acts like a gallows or a nuclear bomb to obliterate cells that proliferate too quickly or incorrectly. When the TP53 gene is activated, it produces p53 protein, the mechanism that hands down death sentences to the abnormal cells. One of many tumor-suppressing genes, p53, can recognize damage to DNA, and if it determines that the damaged cells cannot be repaired, it tightens the noose, killing them. Elephants are surprisingly cancer resistant considering their girth. Mice and some other small animals, and certainly humans, get cancer far more frequently than elephants do.[3]

Looking at this cancer inequity through the lens of evolutionary biology, Aktipis argues in favor of an evolutionary approach called Petro's Paradox. The paradox explains the conundrum of why some organisms invest a lot in cancer suppression mechanisms and others don't. Larger dogs are more susceptible to cancer than smaller dogs, and likewise along that stream of logic, taller people are more susceptible to cancer than short people since the more cells that need to proliferate to keep the organism in working order, the greater the chance for a cellular mistake known as a mutation.[4]

Yet this theory does not correlate with cancer rates across species. Petro's Paradox explains that in a cell-by-cell comparison, humans must be more cancer resistant than mice or we would succumb to cancer at earlier ages. Research by Aktipis and her associates confirms Petro's Paradox: that larger species with longer lifespans indeed do not experience higher cancer rates. She also points out the interesting fact that too much cellular freedom can lead to cell mutations and cancer, while too much control and we risk evolutionary failure and lack of adaptation. Elephants and humans reproduce at later ages than smaller species. Elephants don't have any predators except humans, so they focus on cancer suppression in order to live long enough for that strategy to work in their favor as a species.[5]

Recently, scientists have identified another genetic difference in elephants as compared to smaller mammals. Leukemia Inhibitory Factor, or LIF, also known for its role in fertility, may be the second hand at the electric chair. Researchers are currently thinking that it also slays damaged cells. And where most mammals have just one copy of LIF, elephants have 20 of them. One subcategory of LIF, LIF6 has to date only been found in elephants. Scientists have traced LIF6 back to 59 million years ago when the prehistoric proboscidean ancestors of the elephant, the mastodons, were alive and thriving. Researchers believe that initially, LIF6 was a useless, broken gene that evolved, as elephants did from their ancestors, and eventually reawakened as a working "zombie" gene, a change that may have helped elephants reach such momentous sizes unrestricted by cancer. "If p53 is the doctor in charge of genetic triage, LIF6 is in charge of carrying out its orders to eliminate damaged cells," writes Joshua Schiffman, a pediatric oncologist. Schiffman's team published a paper in 2015 detailing this exciting discovery and the paradox between the mismatch of organism size and cancer rates.[6] The discovery could have profound effects in cancer research for humans. If scientists can decipher how elephants fight cancer, it may provide inspiration for new strategies, new drug discoveries and new understandings about this most dreaded, harsh and expensive disease.

* * *

I arrived home from my time at KEP to a trunkful of my own woes. Spending time with the elephants is so all-encompassing; it is a culture shock to return home. I found myself thinking I needed to wake up in time for the morning meeting in the boma at 7 a.m. and expected to see the elephants and clean the boma before realizing I'm back home in my own bed. I miss the people I befriended, the rhythm of their Khosa conversations, their smiles, unconditional passion for the elephants, and the cadence of their mammoth hearts. I returned different from when I left. The elephants, the African people, and the land itself changed me in ways that continue to reveal themselves to me and will for a long time.

My brother-in-law died unexpectedly after I was home for a week. That shocked me into the reality of being home. The same week, after going for a routine mammogram, I was told that I needed a biopsy on a mass that was spotted. It turned out to be cancerous, although discovered early. That diagnosis unleashed months of constant tests, doctor appointments, surgeries and daily treatments. This was my second time dealing with breast cancer. The previous episode was 14 years prior.

15. Shanti: The Cautious One

In realizing what lay ahead after diagnosis, I found myself marveling at what prevents elephants from developing cancer and was fascinated to read about why this is so. Could it be that these magnificent creatures, whom I'd come to know on a personal level and am so smitten with, could help shed some light on my own situation? Time will tell, but here is yet another potentially significant solution that benefits both humans and elephants.

16

AERU into the Future

"It is absurd for a man to kill an elephant. It is not brutal, it is not heroic, and certainly it is not easy; it is just
one of those preposterous things that men do like putting
a dam across a great river, one tenth of whose volume
could engulf the whole of mankind without disturbing
the domestic life of a single catfish."—Beryl Markham,
West with the Night

AERU consults with over eight other elephant facilities in South
Africa alone. These include zoos, small private reserves, sanctuaries and elephant-back safaris. As AERU grows and matures, their aim
is to expand operations and influence beyond KEP by providing other
elephant facilities with research-based guidance for their operations.
Research initiatives will include the collection and assessment of baseline data for each individual elephant, the herd as a whole, as well as the
park in general.

Some long-term research goals include studies on seasonal influences, trends in behavior between specific elephants, between elephants
and guides, and between elephants, volunteers and tourists. The results
of these studies will influence management, help predict future animal
behavior, and correlate activity and behavior to medical, reproductive
and other biological and environmental factors.

Other areas of study for the future include diet and nutrition in
which the age and gender of herd members will provide information
on how diet changes and reproductive conditions alter with age and
reproductive condition. Still other areas ripe for research involve anatomy and physiology. One such study will monitor growth and development; nutrition and the overall health of our herd, the height, length,
girth, foot diameter, as well as tusk development will be carefully monitored. The physiological well-being of the elephants will be monitored
through blood tests, urine and dung samples. AERU will obtain regular

samples for as many elephants as possible. Standard blood tests are vital for investigating the overall health of the animal as well as the relationship between physiology and diet, age, sex and reproductive condition. Blood can be taken fairly easily from an elephant's ear. Hormonal analysis will offer an indication of reproductive activity and how it develops with age in their elephants and how it compares to other populations. Data related to endocrinology will also be assessed in terms of behavior and social records in order to investigate further behavioral shifts associated with reproductive changes.

Also included will be studies monitoring stress, a vital part of any animal management program, captive or otherwise. Concentrations of stress metabolites will be monitored in the blood, urine and dung. Regular samples will assess stress levels in this herd, but in correlation with all other data collected will also facilitate the identification of potential stressors, both natural and artificial. Regular monitoring of heart rates in relation to age, sex, activity levels and environmental factors will also play an important role in assessing levels of stress in KEP's elephants as well as their physiological well-being.

Studies will also be conducted on the influence of tourism and the well-being of the elephants. Due to the nature of activities at KEP, the elephants are exposed to thousands of visitors each month. AERU will continue to identify any influences these people-elephant interactions may have on the elephants, both positive and negative. By guiding management through science, AERU hopes to continue to optimize the relationships between elephants and tourists for their mutual benefit.

And of course environmental impact studies will be performed. Any baseline data collected cannot be assessed accurately without taking the environment into consideration. Environmental data will be recorded daily, including temperature, rainfall, wind speed and direction and cloud cover. In order to assess the dietary and distribution data, a botanical survey of KEP will be conducted to identify plant species within the park, their distribution and abundance, and will provide insight into the reasons for preferred grazing areas. Since KEP is located in the Garden Route, the area is home to thousands of plant species unique to this biome.

Over the last several years, the park, in conjunction with AERU, has recognized the need for changes to be made to traditional elephant management protocols used in South Africa. These changes have been vital to prioritizing elephant welfare and to balancing the needs of elephants with the tourism activities conducted at the park.

16. AERU into the Future

More emphasis will be placed on responsible, educational interactions as opposed to only touch and feel. The park will try to get guests to become part of the herd by just being with them and watching the natural behaviors from a distance. They will keep feeding and tactile interactions to a minimum to give the elephants as much choice and freedom as possible. Changes will be made to the boma which will allow the elephants more interaction, space and movement overnight. The park will continue to formulate and produce feed on site, ensuring the elephants get the best possible nutrition all year round. And the park will enhance the enrichment program, which is aimed at keeping elephants stimulated, both physically and cognitively. The traditional bull hook has been redesigned to eliminate the metal hook. Bull hooks, which were used in the field during times past, have been replaced by a simple fiberglass walking stick. The research unit and its volunteers contribute on a daily basis to the welfare and management of our elephants. There is no other facility in the world that has that capability.

Long-term goals and objectives for the park include building a 5000-acre free-range habitat so that elephants may be released into a reserve sanctuary-type environment. This would create South Africa's first real elephant sanctuary and be open to elephants in need throughout the country. In order to accomplish this, fundraising needs to reach approximately $2,000,000 to get enough land to start the pilot project as well as make the long-term project viable.

After that exhaustive list, what do we still need to understand about African elephants? Any and all areas of research into elephants, including the human groups that advocate for saving them, the ecosystems that they live in and anything to do with their behavior is always needed. Understanding their behavior is critical in manipulating situations in order to help reduce human-elephant conflict. Understanding human behavior and providing disincentives for poaching are just as critical.

There are, however, some specific areas of research that are more urgent for elephant survival. These include understanding human value systems that lie beneath the conflicts surrounding elephant management and better ways of managing issues that occur within a context of conflicting value systems and political and ecological systems. Also, the economics of elephants in South Africa, specifically ways of ensuring that the potential benefits of elephants reach those with the greatest need for them must be looked into. And we must thoroughly understand poverty, its underlying causes, and the causes of its perpetuation and eradicate them so that poaching is less desirable. Caitlyn O'Connell writes in *Wild Rituals*, "Having witnessed the poaching crisis in Africa firsthand, I can't help imagining that if humans could understand the inner lives of elephants, we might better understand our impact on their lives and, ultimately, on their well-being.... We are connected to elephants, whales, wolves, and all other sentient beings in ways that may not seem obvious, although it's perhaps more obvious than the fact that we share 50 percent of our genes with the banana. We have the power to protect or destroy our surrounding habitat and all the other citizens that share this extremely unique planet with us. This is particularly important as the impacts of climate change increase.... Whether disasters are natural or unnatural, everyone is affected. And if we make a conscious decision to save other species and habitats we also save ourselves."[1]

With elephant population in mind, it is critical that we understand the importance of the long-term physiological and behavioral consequences of contraception and the practical implications of contraception in large elephant populations. It is also highly important that we understand the effects of stress in elephants, which can be induced by exposure to culling, hunting, capture, translocation, or separation from other members of their herd. By examining stress behavior and demographics in elephant populations living at various densities, we can better understand the effects of living in high density areas as well as the biodiversity consequences.

As humans who care about the future of elephants, we would do well to research the potential to control elephant distribution through the use of behavior modification and the manipulation of water locations. We ought to be moving toward granting institutions permits to keep elephants only if the captive situations provide ample space for adequate exercise, food and water, stimulation, and allow the elephants to choose among social partners. Elephants that live in zoos and other facilities in colder climates should not be allowed to house these elephants since outside temperatures below 40 degrees F usually mean they are restricted to indoor barns.

Other critical issues for optimal elephant welfare include the fact that no elephant should be kept in isolation unless it is for reasons of medical quarantine. They are social animals by nature, and keeping them solitary is cruel. Males should be allowed to remain with their herd until the age of natural dispersal, while females should be allowed to remain together for life. Females should remain unchained during and after childbirth if family members are nearby. Infants and calves should not be removed or separated from the care of their mothers and the other females in the herd. The movement of an elephant from its well-established, bonded social group for the purpose of sending it away—whether to a circus or zoo—should stop entirely. All forms of punishment, chaining and physical discipline must be discontinued immediately. Elephants have proven that they, without a doubt, respond very well to positive reinforcement, love and respect. Chaining should only be allowed in the case of types of medical care and even then only when absolutely necessary.

The act of culling must cease. Period. According to Wemmer and Christen in *Elephants and Ethics*, "In the wild, the practice of abducting young elephants from their families should end. The culling of elephants should be avoided except where all other options have been exhausted. When culling is deemed essential it should include whole families; infants and calves should not be spared for export to zoos, circuses, safari parks, or private reserves. The parallel practice of introducing traumatized youngsters to new areas without adult role models should stop. Alternative practices to culling such as translocation and birth control also have welfare implications, and these must be carefully evaluated. Human-elephant conflict is cause for increasing ethical dilemmas, and in cases where it is deemed that an elephant must be euthanized, it should be done efficiently and humanely." Clearly, the benefits must far outweigh the risks in all the above situations.[2]

Writer Douglas Chadwick comments on this matter in his book, *The Fate of the Elephant*, saying, "If a continuum exists between us and such beings in terms of anatomy, physiology, social behavior, and intelligence, it follows that there should be some continuum of moral standards."[3]

17

The Future
of Elephants in Africa

"It's war now. We are losing our national heritage; we are
losing our elephants. We have to act now."—Dr. Paula
Kahumbu, WildlifeDirect

Despite every poacher's desire to make a quick buck, elephants are
far more valuable alive than dead. That statement bears repeating: Elephants are worth more alive than dead. According to the David Sheldrick Wildlife Trust, an elephant is worth 76 times more alive than
dead—$1,600,000 vs. $21,000. The conservation tourism industry in
Africa provides 7,700,000 jobs, according to the United Nations and the
World Tourism Organization. Every dollar spent on eco-travel and tourism can yield upwards of $10 in benefits to local communities, according
to the World Bank. Aside from valuing the life of these amazing creatures, these numbers speak for themselves.[1]

The Wildlife Conservation Society, based out of New York City's
Bronx Zoo, is credited with doing the most effective work to save African elephants. WCS protects approximately 3,000 elephants at several
African national parks. They estimate that 65 percent of forest elephants
have been lost to poaching since 2002 and believe that fewer than
100,000 remain. Over 400,000 have been lost over a 20-year period, a
totally mind-blowing statistic.[2] In 2012 WCS gained respect for entering a territory where few NGOs (non-government organizations) will
venture. It is one filled with massive levels of corruption, according to
the Niassa National Reserve in northern Mozambique. This is an area
the size of Denmark with one of the most threatened elephant populations in Africa.

Another NGO, Elephants Without Borders, touts the return of elephants from Botswana into Angola since the end of its civil war. Elephant numbers in southern Angola have grown from 36 in 2001 to

more than 8,000 today. Providing safe passage across political and geographic boundaries is key to the future of wild elephants. Microsoft's Cofounder Paul Allan helped initiate The Great Elephant Census, which involved 50 scientists responsible for collecting these census numbers. And while elephant censuses are notoriously difficult to execute, ultimately the combination of aerial identification and boots on the ground census-taking has proven to be the most effective.

Big Life, yet another NGO, is a dedicated anti-poaching initiative between Kenya's Amboseli-Tsavo region and Tanzania, which was thwarted by the inability to pursue poachers across the border into Tanzania.

An NGO called African Parks is known for its direct approach and donors. For example, almost all incoming funds go toward their efforts on the ground, while proceeds from an endowment fund cover most of the overhead costs. Many other NGOs do valuable research and conservation work in Africa. Potential donors are encouraged to research those organizations before donating to ensure that their contributions are maximized in saving the elephants. Responsible conservation should present considered facts and opinion, genuine action and accountability. With the lives of African elephants at stake, donors and NGOs need to be held firmly accountable. So do parks, sanctuaries, refuges and anyplace housing *Loxodonta africana.*

Only recently, in the summer of 2018 to be exact, the largest number of elephant carcasses was found in Botswana. Home of the largest elephant population, which equals more than a third of all of Africa's elephants, 87 dead bodies were found, some fully decayed and others freshly killed, partly covered in bushes in an attempt to camouflage them from aerial view. Their tusks were hacked off in gruesome ways. It appears to have been a slaughterhouse frenzy, signaling a large escalation in poaching. According to Simon de Greef in the *New York Times,* "This slaughter shows that despite all the time, energy and money poured into anti-poaching operations in recent years, organized poaching gangs can still wipe out large herds with impunity."[3] How utterly sad.

Some nations like Kenya, who was the first to opt to destroy its ivory stockpiles, do so to sway public opinion as well as to educate people about the plight of the elephants as well as to demonstrate the government's commitment to putting the kibosh on poaching and illegal black market trade. In an interesting development, in 1989, Kenya elected to have a mass burn of its ivory stockpiles, which were doused with gasoline and set on fire. And while some countries equate burning ivory with burning money, those countries see trading ivory as their ultimate right. Kenya had its largest white gold burn in 2016, with 105 tons or 210,000 pounds of ivory going up in flames. Since then more than 20 other countries have followed suit with tusk pyres.

Some countries have the burns partly because keeping the stockpiles safe is costly and often dangerous, so by burning it, they make a political statement and rid themselves of the inventory. Unfortunately, there is no way to know the effect, if any, these huge burns have on poaching. Hopefully, they help educate people and sway public opinion.

Until recently, Botswana was considered a safe haven for wildlife, with militarized patrols in protected areas and a shoot-to-kill policy to deter poachers. Annette Hübschle, a criminology researcher at the University of Cape Town, explained, "This tough stance on poaching had made Botswana 'the darling of the conservation world.'" So how did this enormous slaughter happen, you ask? The policies did not address the issues underlying the illegal ivory trade. Hübschle continues, "Rural communities are likely to support poachers and poaching economies because there are no benefits to these conservation areas for them." If local communities experience no direct benefit from conservation areas, "They may not turn to poaching, but they won't support policing either. You need to reach out to communities for conservation to work."[4]

So you ask what the solution is. Hübschle explains, "Rather than shooting poachers to kill them, we should be focusing on who's controlling the trade. Follow the money and target the intermediaries, and the organizers behind them." Not long before the incident, Botswana welcomed a new government which demilitarized the anti-poaching unit soon after taking office, with no explanation. They then went a step further to dispute the findings of the aerial surveys, calling them false and misleading. To Americans, this type of statement has come to be called "fake news." The nonprofit organization, Elephants Without Borders, discovered the Holocaust in Botswana by aerial view and reported the bodies to the government right away but received no response. The organization sent two more reports. The government of Botswana responded that the elephants died of natural causes, with some being killed in "retaliatory killings as a result of human and wildlife conflicts." Elephants Without Borders then repeated that the poached animals had their tusks pried off gruesomely and that poachers appeared to have been targeting large old bulls that tend to have the largest tusks. Most poachers shoot with automatic weapons and hack off the tusks in horrifying ways, sometimes before the animal has died. They often use chainsaws and axes to chop the tusks off. In formerly war-torn countries, some poachers use grenades and mortars found lying around from the war in order to kill elephants. Unfortunately for elephants, many poachers in Angola and other countries use poison-tipped spears, spiked traps and snares or poison water holes, causing slow, agonizing deaths to the elephant victims.[5]

In 2020 a mysterious illness took the lives of hundreds of elephants in Botswana. Researchers discovered that a naturally occurring bacteria became toxically concentrated during drought conditions, underscoring the importance of maintaining a healthy balance of gut microbes for all living creatures. Climate change alters the makeup of grasses, which alters the gut makeup of rodents and other small creatures, which, through the food chain filters up to larger animals. Scientists have found increasing evidence that rising temperatures around the globe impact the symbiotic relationship many species have with their gut flora. Also in 2020 hundreds of antelope deaths in Zimbabwe were thought to have been caused by natural respiratory bacteria.

We must take a long, slow look at the root cause of the poaching industry: poverty. Some of the best deterrents to poaching include improving the economic opportunities for local people, building broad-based law enforcement capacity, using roads and rivers to facilitate patrolling, increasing operational management budgets and decreasing the number of hunting camps. According to Zafra-Calvo, "The success of anti-poaching actions are likely to depend on context-specific circumstances, thus more information about what determines the spatial distribution of elephant carcasses in known poaching hotspots is therefore urgently needed."[6]

They conclude, "Our analysis suggests that the warmest sites with lower rainfall are where the likelihood of finding elephant carcasses is highest. These sites are normally the lowest elevation areas.... Our results also indicate that fewer elephant carcasses are observed in areas at higher elevations, which are less accessible...[In] lowland areas that are drier and hotter areas with seasonal rivers that dry up during the dry season, forcing elephants to aggregate at the few remaining available sources of water, where they are more easily hunted. In addition, the drying of seasonal rivers allows increased accessibility to poachers and facilitates transporting tusks from remote regions."[7]

According to Dr. Debbie, "There has been a 30 percent increase in the number of captive elephants in South Africa in the past decade. Captive elephants are maintained in parks and zoos where management techniques range from protected contact to free contact, a method where elephant handlers work alongside elephants with no physical barrier. The control of elephant populations by culling was made illegal in South Africa in the 1990s, but the conversation is far from over. Interactions between elephants and humans are likely to become an increasingly important political issue in South Africa, and likely the rest of Africa and Asia. The expansion of conservation areas, growing elephant populations, a thriving tourism industry and greater participation by communities in managing resources all compete for the same resources, namely land and flora. And like most things in life, there are positives and negatives to our shared existence. On the one hand, man's constant expansion to develop unused land leaves less land for elephants to live on, and is what has forced elephants to raid crops for food. On the wonderful side, it is the elephant that helped eliminate the deadly tsetse fly, which causes sleeping sickness, by opening up thickets and forests. Elephants are smart enough to raid crops only in the dark in order to minimize the chances of being caught, which would explain why crop raiding drops significantly during a full moon."

The reduction in elephant density through culling ends up having the opposite effect—in the long run it inflates population growth rates by releasing fundamental rates (age at first calving and inter-calving interval) from limitations set by density dependence. Put simply, culling can only be effective to reduce numbers in the medium term if it is maintained indefinitely and at a rate above the population's growth rate. Density dependence becomes apparent when the population reaches about 0.37 elephants per km or .62 miles, and it is highly suggested that culling is unnecessary unless populations remained at densities higher than that for two or more years. Ironically, inappropriate culling may effectively increase the population's growth rate.

According to Graeme Shannon et al. "African elephants ... that had experienced separation from family members and translocation during culling operations decades previously performed poorly on systematic tests of their social knowledge, failing to distinguish others on the basis of social familiarity. Moreover, elephants from the disrupted population showed no evidence of discriminating between callers when age-related cues simulated individuals on an increasing scale of social dominance, in sharp contrast to the undisturbed population where this core social ability was well-developed.... These findings highlight the potential long-term negative consequences of acute social disruption in cognitively advanced species that live in close-knit kin-based societies, and alter our perspective on the health and functioning of populations that have been subjected to anthropogenic disturbance."[8]

Since poachers usually target the oldest elephants touting the largest tusks, their elimination from the herd often causes not only the trauma of losing a family member but the additional trauma of losing a wise leader or matriarch. These murders cause disruption right down the social structure of the herd. Researchers are finding that many families dissolve because of poaching, or they join forces with each other for the sake of survival. This is a positive response to the warfare being waged on them. We need to pay for their expenses, which tourism and education programs do beautifully.

According to Noleen, "Tourism and eco-travel bring far more money into the country than poaching does, provides many jobs and in the case of KEP/AERU, gives back research data which benefits the elephants. It's a win/win scenario." Noleen adds, "Because of man's actions so many years ago regarding the killing of elephants, facilities like ours are necessary for their survival, not for the purpose of taking elephants from the wild and placing them in captivity, but in order to provide homes for those orphans, injured, and other elephants in need of a safe and nurturing home. Sanctuaries definitely have their place when there is a need to step in because the alternative would be for them to die." Through Ian's vision of conservation through education, we help people understand elephants, bond with them and hopefully become advocates, just as these elephants are stewards for their species. "We basically have to farm wildlife like we've always farmed cattle and sheep in order to save them from extinction," Noleen concludes.

The consequences of culling for individual elephants, especially in selective culling, are poorly understood and badly need to be reassessed. Initially, culling episodes were not thought to traumatize the young calves. In Kruger National Park, initial culling was carried out with "military precision," with ground crews rounding up the elephants, a hovering helicopter with armed rangers, and enough noise to warn other elephants of the danger for many miles around. The trauma endured by orphans and those raised by inexperienced mothers puts calves at risk for developing symptoms of post-traumatic stress disorder (PTSD). As in humans, symptoms of this range from an abnormal startle response, depression, unpredictable asocial behavior to hyperaggression, lack of adequate sleep and high levels of anxiety. Adolescent males require older bull role models to ensure proper social development, a factor often neglected by the humans in charge, as in the case of Shungu and Mashudu, who were left with no role models.

A continuum of environmental orientations exists in human society. There is the traditional African worldview whose culture includes hunting game for food, which considers humans and their needs. Then there is the pro-ecology model, which considers the needs of humans as no more important than those of any other species. In talking with people at KEP, I am amazed that there are such diverse opinions on culling and the future of elephants in Africa, the common denominator being a deep love for elephants. An individual's environment and background influence which side of the coin they take on this hot-button issue.

Scholes and Mennell explain why two people who are equally passionate about elephants' orientation can have opposite beliefs, attitudes and opinions on topics such as culling. They claim that there are several orientations people have about these sensitive issues. One is what they call the biocentric orientation, which they describe as broad and underpins both the perspective of animal rights groups, who place great importance on the existence value and rights of individual elephants, as well as the perspective of people who believe that the control of elephant populations may be necessary for the greater good of ecosystems and other species who depend on them. This second view is anthropocentric and underlies the perspectives of those who support sustainable utilization of elephants as a valuable resource for consumption.[9]

Elephant death is the currency of the illegal wildlife trade. Believing that culling results in a loss of cultural information and experience from the population, especially if older individuals are targeted, Scholes and Mennell explain that it also results in trauma associated with the culling since calves witness culls. This trauma can result in the inability to self-regulate aggressive and stress-related feelings, sleep and eating disturbances and other abnormal behaviors. In South Africa, the Norms and Standards Act DEAT was created in 2008 and took the brave stance that it will no longer allow the capture of young elephants during culls. They now consider it inhumane. Juveniles should not witness the culling of their family members. While elephants have evolved to be able to deal with a certain degree of stress, this kind of stress is over the top. Horribly, to my way of thinking, some believe that the young elephants should be killed along with their parents and grandparents.[10]

Culling automatically boosts the potential population growth rate. Scholes and Mennell continue by proving that once a population is released from culling, even if the culling is age and gender neutral, it enters a growth phase that inevitably leads to an age distribution skewed toward younger individuals. There are several reasons for this. The reduction in density leaves the underlying resources on which the population depends intact, thereby increasing the amount of resources available to each individual, which then aids breeding at a maximum rate. This effect continues for at least one generation, after which a new stable age structure will gradually establish itself. The consequences of culling red deer included demographic and spatial effects that persisted for 30 years, which translates to four generations after the culling stopped. Although the long-term consequences of culling have only been modeled in elephants, given their very long intergeneration times of about five years, the possibility exists that such effects may at least in theory persist up to a century.[11]

Other complications that arise from culls include daughters who must prematurely step into their matriarch mother's shoes, very suddenly and without being fully prepared. Researchers worry that the loss of elders, who were most likely killed for their larger tusks, severely impairs the younger herd members to survive and thrive. They aren't up to speed in the vast amount of knowledge a matriarch needs in order to ensure the survival of herself and her herd. Things like migratory routes, water and food locations throughout various seasons are necessary to know, as well as spatially, a matriarch needs to know routes of travel. Some researchers have observed elements of resilience exhibited by survivors, such as wrapping trunks, rubbing against one another as if for comfort and reassurance, smelling each other's mouths, and other gestures known to be affiliative for elephants.

From an ethics perspective, a huge cancer of corruption keeps poachers killing. It's Africa's version of organized crime. Many can't afford to live off the land, can't afford to put food on their table for their family so poaching becomes a matter of survival for the poacher and a matter of death for the elephants and rhinos. One rhino farmer had the idea of removing horns from some rhinos to sell on the open market. He claimed that the horn grew back within two years and the animal could continue to live a normal life meanwhile. Another idea is to sell ivory from elephants that have died natural deaths on the open market. Granted, it would be difficult to keep the demand to a minimum, and there would be no deterrent for poaching.

Noleen says of this phenomenon, "When you see anti-poaching information on Facebook and other social media, they are targeting the educated while not educating the un-educated. Does the actual poacher realize his impact on the elephants and the environment? No, because he lives in the bush, and he's been paid a few thousand rand to cut off a handle around a rhino horn. While the millions are being made somewhere else, he thinks there are lots of rhinos in the world. That poacher is not being educated on the impact his actions have, and as a result has no idea." Noleen added, "When I lived in Mozambique, I was flying out of an airport and officials seized an entire truckload of three tons of rhino horns. The truck had gotten through the border of South Africa, so someone got a payoff somewhere. I got on the plane. Worse, yet, the truckload was confiscated, and the people who were driving the truck were Chinese. They were thrown in jail one minute and the next minute they were out of jail on bail. And worse still, was that the next day the whole truck disappeared. It disappeared and the people were let off the hook. So there you had the truck, you had the guys, so who released them? Where did the missing truck go? It was various governments involved, South African, Botswana, and others. These are inside jobs, inside crimes."

When it comes to humans and elephants coexisting peacefully while humans continue to take over more and more land, there are some interesting solutions on the horizon. According to the advocacy organization Save the Elephants, a Kenyan conservation and research nonprofit, the average elephant living in and around Samburu National Reserve in northern Kenya ranges over 580 square miles during the course of a year and may travel as much as 37 miles a day. Much more research is needed so we understand the traditional migratory routes and work to gain international cooperation for these elephants to roam across borders without repercussion.

A large part of the future survival of elephants rests with CITES, or the Convention on International Trade in Endangered Species of Wild Fauna and Flora. CITES is a binding treaty among governments created in 1975 "for the protection of certain species of wild fauna and flora against over-exploitation through international trade." The treaty has now been signed by some 183 countries, and it claims to protect over 35,000 species, its power resting in the fact that it is now binding international law.

African elephants in Botswana, Namibia and South Africa are listed as threatened species classified under Appendix II with the Convention for International Trade of Endangered Species (CITES). Appendix II species are those deemed not threatened by extinction but with a slight change could result in being in the extreme danger zone of extinction.

17. The Future of Elephants in Africa

The remaining elephants in Africa are listed as endangered species classified under Appendix 1 with CITES. Appendix 1 is to account for plants and animals threatened with extinction. Regardless of which category they embody on paper, elephants are an endangered species, let there be no doubt. It may seem strange that the United States gives any legal status to animals in other countries, but the truth is that American protection of "foreign" animals or plants under the powerful Endangered Species Act can bring tangible benefits to those species, including preventing the animals' parts from being sold in the United States and preventing our government from sanctioning or paying for actions that hurt the animals. It can also provide funds for research and public education.

The *New York Times* reported in 2015 that in Tanzania alone, which is home to one of the largest elephant populations, the census plummeted from 109,000 animals to about 43,000 in the five years between 2009 and 2014. Research now shows two distinct species of African elephants—forest elephants, which are much smaller, with rounder ears and straighter tusks, and the savanna elephants, whose ears are more triangular and whose tusks are thicker and curved. In purely genetic terms, the two species are as distinct from each other as monkeys are from rhinos. The article concludes that there is a growing acceptance of two separate species, which are currently both protected under the Endangered Species Act under the category of "threatened." If separate censuses were taken for each of the species, the populations would register as significantly smaller and therefore place them both in the truly "endangered" arena. That status, as heartbreaking as it is, could mean more urgent help for these high-risk elephant populations. If the United States were to recognize and protect the two species separately, the International Union for Conservation of Nature and CITES, the treaty that regulates global trade in endangered wildlife, could follow suit, which would tighten restrictions on the import, export and sale of ivory products to and from and within the country. Following China, the United States is the world's second-largest market for ivory with the legal trade in old ivory being used as a cover for illegal trade in new ivory.[12]

This translates to the Unites States having the potential to take the lead in banning the import and sale of all ivory and helping sway the Chinese government to follow suit, the result being that the two largest economies in our world who are also the two largest ivory consumers are handling the crisis—and it IS a crisis—of the systematic slaughter and conceivable extinction of the largest mammals on the planet. Tragically, the Trump administration wavered and even reversed decisions affecting the lives of elephants; his grown sons boast of being proud elephant hunters.

Tuskless Elephants?

Addo, one of South Africa's largest wildlife refuges, is home to an astounding percentage of tuskless female elephants. Addo is not the only reserve in which elephants are born tuskless, but it is the most dramatic example. Born this way, they beg the question of whether this was caused by natural selection or by genetic drift, a phenomenon attributed to inbreeding among the small number of surviving elephants. Or is it evolution in play? This phenomenon can cause a "tuskless gene" to become more prevalent in the population. Of the 300 cows residing at Addo, the rate of tuskless females is between 90 and 95 percent! Here's how it happened.

In the early part of the 20th century, the legendary Major PJ Pretorius, also known as "the great white hunter," had nearly wiped out the elephant population there. He spared the life of 11 elephants, who continued to live there and reproduce. Today all of the elephants at Addo descend from those original 11 survivors. Some scientists attribute tusklessness at Addo at least in part to what they call "genetic drift," a randomly initiated shift in gene pools which often affects smaller or isolated populations. So, the unnatural selection caused by massive poaching has not affected bull elephants much, although their tusks tend to be smaller than those of bulls elsewhere. A 50-year-old bull can grow tusks weighing 108 pounds each. With a world ivory price in the range of $1,000 per kilogram (two pounds and three ounces), it translates to nearly $100,000 (USD) payday for poachers. Not bad for a day's work. Scientists are not only seeing an increase in tuskless elephants, but they are also seeing an increase in elephants with smaller tusks, both males and females.

Although tusks are tools for gathering food, digging for water, and fending off predators and aggressive peers, tuskless elephants can indeed thrive using their cognitive problem-solving skills to find other ways of accomplishing these functions. The case in point is Sally, who was born with only one tusk. The good news is that poachers don't want tuskless elephants and would have no reason to harm them ... or would they? In a new twist of elephant enemies, it turns out that some poachers are targeting elephant hides for consumption in China as elephant leather and traditional remedies made from elephant hides as well as elephant livers. Is there no end to the whims of man when it comes to these peaceful, magnificent creatures?

In order to keep elephants from raiding crops and villages in search of food, several promising and surprisingly nontechnical solutions are being tried. One is a fence of bees, given that elephants are petrified of bees. Luckily for elephants, their skin is for the most part so thick a bee can't penetrate it. However, the skin near the eyes, ears, and the tip of the trunk is thinner, allowing a bee to sting effectively in these vulnerable areas. The elephants are so afraid of these pollinating creatures they will avoid an area in which there are many bees. This solution brings with it a bonus—honey from the bees, which can create another valuable income stream. Experiments are being tried in at least a dozen African countries with the use of bee fences, preliminary results showing a fifth as many elephant raids in areas where there are bee fences. The downside to utilizing beehives as a deterrent to elephants is that wire fencing is far cheaper and requires much less maintenance. Wire fencing is also used to wrap around select prized trees to deter elephants. This practice has proven to work in many parks and reserves and boasts prolonged survival of many large, old trees. Unfortunately, these wire fences aren't able to prevent branches snapping off, leaving the trees vulnerable to destructive insects such as borers, termites, and other pests. Often if there are only a few large trees that need to be saved, beehives are the preferred deterrents. Otherwise, unless the honey is an additional stream of funding that could offset some of the cost, beehives are the more ecological method but require higher up-front financing.

Elephants detest spicy food. Another method of deterring elephants from destroying crops is planting a variety of chili plants around the perimeter of the field. Sometimes referred to as "Chili Bombs," they are a mixture of dried elephant dung and hot chili. When they are placed around the circumference of the fields, elephants tend to stay away.

Organizations such as the World Wildlife Foundation (WWF) monitor the interactions between humans and elephants and work with local communities throughout Africa to develop sustainable practices in minimizing conflict with elephants. In case you were wondering, the formal term for studying human-animal interactions is anthrozoology. They are highly scientific and dedicated researchers who travel the world for the benefit of all wildlife.

On my first trip to KEP, two researchers from the World Wildlife Foundation (WWF) were present to do research on whether or not specific elephant sounds can forecast whether a poacher is near. They have been walking around in the fields with a microphone that looks like a sculpture several feet wide and several feet tall. They tried to strap a radio device on Keisha, but she wasn't having any of it!

In another study by Anni and Sangaiah, they utilized several types of wireless sensor networks as an early warning system that elephants were on their way to intrude. The sensors included acoustic and vibration sensors which enable elephant detection even when they are out of sight with visual identification enabled by a camera. Acoustic monitoring provides data on elephant behavior; visual monitoring records elephant motion patterns. Overall, these researchers highlight efficiency in the detection of elephant presence based on the integration of three sensors and the respective ranking scores.[13]

Wadey et al. did a study regarding human-elephant conflict entitled, "Why did the Elephant Cross the Road: The Complex response of wild elephants to a major road in peninsular Malaysia." Their objectives were to describe patterns of road crossing, quantify road effects on movement patterns and habitat preferences, and quantify individual variation in elephant responses to the road. They found that elephants crossed the road on average 3.9 times, and 81 percent of the time they crossed at night. Given that the risk of mortality from poaching and vehicle collisions increases near roads, and to minimize the impact of this, they recommend avoiding further road expansion, reducing and enforcing speed limits, limiting traffic at night, managing habitat near the road, and enhancing patrolling and other anti-poaching efforts. They believe their results are relevant for landscapes through Asia and Africa where existing or planned roads fragment elephant habitats.[14]

Other researchers are experimenting with satellite neck collars to see if they can proactively detect elephants approaching an agricultural or village area. Such collars can aid rangers in guarding remaining elephants in areas known for heavy poaching. A satellite collar takes a half hour to implement. The elephants are lightly sedated and then collared, and additional health data is collected while the elephant is sleeping. These collars allow rangers to identify and respond to threats in real time through the use of mobile devices and help predict the movement of herds as well as individual animals in order to alert settlements ahead of the elephants' approach. Farmers can then go outside banging pots and pans or drums as a further deterrent to the approaching elephants. This strategy has been very successful and has saved many a human/elephant conflict.

Yet another approach to deterring crop-raiding elephants uses playbacks of threatening vocalizations such as tiger, leopard and lion growls and human shouts. The elephants have become numb to some sounds, so they have lost their effectiveness, but tiger growls remain effective. Used in conjunction with other deterrents such as fencing, chili plantings, bee fences, or elephant-proof trenches, it can contribute to the elimination of crop raiding by elephants and promote peaceful relationships between elephants and humans.

18

The Poaching Crisis

"Elephants can sense danger. They're able to detect
an approaching tsunami or earthquake before it hits."
—Jennifer Richard Jacobson

Elephants are the international poster children for the illegal wildlife trade. Throughout the centuries man and elephant have shared land; hundreds of thousands of elephants have been killed for nothing more than their tusks. If these numbers symbolized human murders, we would call it genocide ... a gruesome Holocaust. We would be out in the streets protesting, banner-slinging and chanting anti-poaching slogans all the way to Congress, begging for laws to protect elephants. But for most of us on planet Earth, it is an armchair war that we are aware of but do almost nothing about. Sometimes we just don't know what to do. If that's the case, see "What Can You Do to Help" at the end of this book. Ivory is the white gold of corruption, fraud and black market capitalism.

Throughout human history there has been a collective cognitive dissonance regarding the slaughter of animals, whether for food, skins, tusks, or just killing for sport. Man has always collectively had inconsistent thoughts about raising and then slaughtering animals. And we have not always cared whether or not this was done humanely. Elephants are no exceptions to the rule, even though they are rarely eaten as food.

According to Rachel Love Nuwer, author of *Poached*, "The 1970s and 1980s saw elephant killings reach such skyrocketing proportions as to threaten the continued existence of Africa's two species. It was virtually speciacide, or the intentional elimination of a specific species. By the mid–1970s, seven hundred tons of ivory on average—roughly equivalent to 70,000 dead elephants—were leaving Africa each year, much of it stopping in Hong Kong for carving before being sold in other countries. As sales abroad grew, the price a poacher in Africa could expect to fetch for ivory jumped from around $2.50 per pound in 1969, to $34 per pound in 1978, to more than $90 per pound in 1989...In just 10 short years, over half of Africa's elephants had disappeared—from 1.3 million in 1979, to just 600,000 in 1989. Put another way, total losses over a two-decade period topped 80 percent."[1]

Nuwer points out that it's a misconception that all Chinese citizens want ivory. Those who purchase it are a small fraction of the population. The problem lies in the overwhelmingly huge population residing in China, so much so that even a small minority can cause such a significant impact on elephant populations.

2002: Zakouma National Park, Chad, was home to 4,000 elephants, but by 2010 there was a 90 percent decline, leaving only 450 elephants.

2010–2015: Mozambique lost half its elephants to poachers, while Tanzania's population declined by 10 percent. In Zambia dead elephants outnumbered living ones six to one. Chad's herds were reduced by horseback raiders.

2007–2014: 140,000 elephants died, a 30 percent reduction in population. An estimated 415,000 savanna elephants remain today.

2008–2013: 750 poachers are arrested, but 70 percent of the arrest records were missing, either destroyed intentionally or just lost from incompetence and carelessness. Of those who did go to court, only 4 percent received jail sentences. The rest were let off the hook. In 2015 just 6 percent of cases had missing files and convictions involving jail increased to 6 percent. We have a long way to go in this armchair war.

More than three-quarters of Africa's elephants are caught in regions that involve international border crossings. They are refugees, unaware of these invisible boundaries. Therefore, it is critical that we implement unifying policies for elephant protection between countries that will minimize threats to highly mobile elephants whose numbers are already endangered. According to Lindsay, Chase, Landen and Nowak, there is an acute need for "approaches to conservation that transcend geopolitical frontiers.... Isolationist policies and politically motivated compromises will help neither the elephants nor people in an interdependent world facing common environmental challenges needful of harmonized agendas and scaled-up cooperation.... A key threat to their survival in the longer term is habitat fragmentation and blockage of dispersal routes by human activities and solutions lie in maintaining and protecting connections between populations within, and inevitably, between countries through coordinated trans-national approaches to their conservation.... The primary mechanism that governs international trade in endangered species is the Convention on International Trade in Endangered Species of Wild Fauna and Flora, or CITES, and it is in CITES that some of the solutions to illegal elephant killing and international ivory trading must be sought.... If elephants are to be saved, a policy shift toward greater trans-national cooperation must be promoted and consolidated. Agreed to in 1973, CITES is the only multilateral environmental agreement to bring biodiversity conservation to bear on international wildlife commerce."[2]

Killing elephants is perhaps considered understandable when human life is in imminent danger. But we must remember that elephants only attack when they feel threatened. Otherwise they are peaceful creatures. Given the politics and ethical positions on killing elephants, it is a practical necessity in a participatory democracy like South Africa for nonlethal options to be seriously considered and found lacking before the lethal option is selected, according to Scholes and Mennell.[3] Large populations of elephants impacting the environment result from the concentration of animals in specific habitats at particular times of the year rather than the absolute numbers of elephants, they explain. Therefore, creating methods of altering the distribution of elephants are an important way of managing their impact on the land. Fencing is the main option currently, though behavioral modification holds some promise. Fences can be used to keep elephants inside protected areas, or conversely, to keep them out of undesirable areas within the protected area. Another way of encouraging the distribution of elephants is the manipulation of available water. Maud Bonato, the current Head of Research at AERU, said the water holes at Kruger National Park were relocated so that tourists could have a better chance of seeing the elephants. This in turn completely destroyed that specific area because of extensive grazing and browsing that took place there after the water holes were relocated.

Elephants: Beware the full moon, otherwise known as a Poacher's Moon. When elephants perceive poaching danger, they alter their speed of travel. The elephants believe that poaching is a daytime risk, so they reason that if they increase movement during the night, it will help keep them safe. Using elephant GPS tracking and mortality data, researchers verified this hypothesis. Conversely, elephants in low poaching areas travel more during daylight.

18. The Poaching Crisis

Conservation biologist Sam Wasser of the University of Washington began to map elephant genetics several decades ago using DNA extracted from their dung. Since populations from different regions have differing gene mutations, Wasser was able to create a map of where each mutation was found. When he analyzes a piece of ivory confiscated from a poaching operation, he is able to pinpoint the DNA and trace it to its origin. From this work, he has been able to show that most illegal ivory is coming from two "hotspots" of poaching activity. This knowledge in turn has provided a powerful tool for law enforcement officials. One discovery in particular stuck with him: a pair of teeth, one tiny, the other enormous. He figured that poachers had shot a baby elephant, waited for its mother to come to its rescue and then shot her. "That was a turning point for me," Wasser said. From that moment on, "I was on a mission," he stated.[4]

Pulitzer Prize-winning author Elizabeth Kolbert puts Wasser's work in perspective. "In the mid–1970s, when Wasser first started working in Africa, 1.5 million elephants roamed the continent. Over the next decade and a half, the value of ivory, which at that point still could be legally traded, skyrocketed. During the 1980s, the price of ivory more than quintupled, from about $25 to $135 a pound. The elephant population, meanwhile, plummeted; by 1989, it had fallen to around 600,000, and experts warned that Africa's elephants were headed toward extinction."

Kolbert continues, "To reverse this gruesome trend, parties to CITES, enacted what amounted to a ban on international sales of African ivory. The ban went into effect in 1990, and for several years it seemed to be working. Poaching eased, and in some parts of Africa, elephant populations started to recover. But in 2006, just after Wasser began putting his map to use, the killing started up again. Growing demand in Asia elevated prices to new levels. By 2012, black market ivory was fetching $1,000 a pound in Beijing. That year alone, an estimated 22,000 African elephants were poached. Clearly deaths were outpacing births, and, once again, experts warned of a crisis."[5]

Humankind has never been known for altruism toward nature. In the United States, the attitude toward protecting elephants has varied greatly. President Obama banned elephant trophy imports. President Trump's sons are trophy hunters. His son Donald Jr. posted photos online in 2012 of himself standing next to several bloody, dead elephants during a safari in Zimbabwe; one shows Trump Jr. holding a knife in one hand and a severed elephant tail in the other. He told reporters that the hunt was legal and that it is his belief that safaris like the one he experienced actually help preserve wildlife by providing financial incentives to local residents to maintain their game populations. He told *Forbes* magazine that he and his brother picked up hunting from their maternal grandfather. Late in 2017 Trump uncharacteristically put a stop to these trophy hunts, calling big-game hunting a "horror show" that he did not believe helped conservation, according to the *New York Times*. He has since done a head-turning reversal of his decision, making trophy hunting legal again. Given the illogical Trump family line of thinking, elephants are more endangered than ever.

The African Wildlife Foundation takes a three-pronged approach to elephant protection in Africa: Stop the killing, stop the trafficking, and stop the demand for ivory. They train rangers in best practices for anti-poaching and provide tools and equipment needed to succeed in these dangerous and challenging jobs. To help deter trafficking, they have a canine program which places highly trained detection dogs and handlers at strategic points such as airports, seaports, and border crossings. These dogs have proven to be successful in finding confiscated ivory and the like, which is fine evidence in court but doesn't restore life to an elephant.

Most of us don't stop to realize that most rangers in Africa are almost as poor as the poachers themselves. According to Rachel Love Nuwer in *Poached*, "A 2016 survey of rangers in forty countries found that about 50 percent of those in Africa and Asia did not have life insurance. Many also lacked health insurance or long-term disability, meaning they would receive no support should they be seriously injured on the job," or, as happens all too often, killed on the job. And yet this is one of the most dangerous occupations on the planet. Nuwer continues, "Yet anti-poaching is one of the most dangerous enforcement roles, as it typically occurs in remote areas far from reinforcements and criminals are usually armed.... Around the world, more than a thousand rangers have been killed in the line of duty over the past decade," thus leaving their families with virtually no government aid to surviving children and families. Widows often lose their homes, children often have to be pulled from schools, and life is even harder than it was prior to losing their loved one. Complicating an already complex job, whistleblowers put themselves in an even more dangerous position by exposing themselves to the wrath of the poachers themselves, receiving death threats, or worse, assassinations with no warning.

Nuwer adds, "Post Traumatic Stress Disorder is a growing issue among rangers, some of which have been involved in twenty or more firefights.... The four hundred-odd Kruger (national park in South Africa) rangers tasked with defending against the poaching threat works out to be about one man per twenty miles (of park land)."

Newer says of South Africa's stance on poachers, "South African authorities avoid publicizing the number of poachers shot down by rangers and police. As of 2016, at least two hundred poachers have been killed across South Africa since 2011. In 2015, Mozambique's former president, Joaquin Chissano, claimed that at least five hundred poachers—most of them his citizens—have been killed in Kruger Park alone since 2010. Each of these dead poachers means more poverty for his family, because they can no longer count on him for better living conditions. Even then, South African authorities did not release their figures. Although South Africa is a democratic country, and all deaths here are a matter of public record, the silence is deafening. Shoot to kill orders are not only morally reprehensible, they are ineffective according to many."[6]

Although guns are the weapons of choice for most poachers, there are other, more cruel ways of poaching. Some leave out cyanide-laced buckets of salt or poison water holes with cyanide or Temik, another poisonous chemical compound. Temik is often referred to as the two-step killer because after ingesting it, the animal takes two steps and dies. These chemicals do not only kill elephants; let's be clear, they kill all the birds and small creatures that drink its contents. Other techniques include poisoned arrows, poisoned vegetables and fruits and worse.

So, what of the future for elephants in our world? Writes Wylie, "In some ways, the prospect for the elephant isn't wholly gloomy. In some places, populations are healthy, albeit only in relation to the resources within severely restricted ranges. Scientific knowledge of elephants and their needs has expanded exponentially. Hence better legislation is gradually being implemented world-wide. Public pressure worldwide is forcing zoos and circuses to clean up their treatment of all animals, but has especially improved the welfare of elephants radically. Thankfully, there are more organizations dedicated to elephant welfare than one can wave a trunk at. Raising awareness of alternatives to ivory involves educating people about the plight of elephants, rhinos and the plight of Africa's poverty victims. Domestication of African elephants for touristic purposes, though itself controversial, is at least making the electrifying touch of an elephant available to more people, with some positive conservation and eco-tourism spin-offs. In West and Central Africa, some progress is being made in establishing and improving anti-poaching policing. More and more effort is being devoted to finding workable ways of allowing elephants and rural communities to coexist."[7]

As humans, our own selfish interests often compel us to disregard the needs of other species we share this planet with. Why should humans be generous to elephants and allow them large tracts of land where people could have made productive livelihoods? Why not use elephants as resources to combat poverty and create jobs? Why should some elephants sacrifice their lives to ensure the long-term survival of their species? Why don't we judge elephants as part of the natural resources of Africa that will help us provide a better life for every human involved? How can we justify safeguarding elephant lives and caring for elephant well-being if human lives are wasted through devastating poverty? There are far more questions than answers. Many would argue that our generosity toward higher mammalian species only goes as far as taking care of ourselves first allows us. Such is the complex web of ethical questions we find ourselves tangled in.

Of late, the South African government has accepted full responsibility as trustee to ensure that the management and conservation of biodiversity and the sustainable use of natural resources lies within the black and white of the country's laws. When an issue such as elephant management causes so much emotion and generates such a high level of controversy, wildlife managers of public conservation must demonstrate their accountability to the public for all decisions made. In such cases they ought to consult thoroughly with all stakeholders, as has become standard practice in modern democracies like South Africa. Not all protected areas are managed by the government, however. Private institutions, social organizations and individual citizens manage the majority of protected areas in SA and are obliged to also take responsibility on behalf of the public when they deal with natural heritage and resource management. They should be equally accountable to the public.

There arises now an urgent and unprecedented outcry of global concern for the welfare and safety of elephants. The most common action people take is to donate money toward the protection of these majestic creatures. A list of NGO organizations which advocate for elephants can be found at the end of this book. New policies create an enabling environment for wildlife conservation, which includes elephants. They can and should be designed so that both conservation and the development of economic opportunities are successful, satisfying the needs of both humans and elephants. Perhaps the answer is just that simple: that compassion for the fate of an extraordinary species of creatures will ultimately swing the pendulum to the side of safety for them. That would be a best-case scenario, an outcome that benefits us and them.

Dan Wylie has this to say about the present-day situation for the wild elephant in *Elephant,* "Like almost any other 'charismatic mega-fauna' that you could name—the situation is generally dire. The recent efforts to reverse the trend by zoos and national parks, international conservation agencies and government legislation, are rearguard actions; they are all but overwhelmed by human population growth, which now additionally unfolds against the backdrop of deleterious climate change. The reasons are simple: people have killed too many elephants for their ivory; and too many people have robbed the elephants of their historical habitat. As we have seen, elephants have always been hunted and used by humans in a multiplicity of ways, some uncaring, some worshipful. But the number of elephants captured alive for warfare, for circuses and zoos, for food, logging and religion, while widespread, pales into insignificance against the numbers killed for their tusks.... Human lust for ivory is the elephant's curse."[8]

Garstang adds, "Evidence that there is a link between abhorrent elephant behavior and traumatic dislocation of an elephant's early development is a valid hypothesis. Whatever the nature and magnitude of the cause and effect is, the question of why and how it is possible that the human species can inflict such trauma upon another species remains unanswered.... In confronting this tragic relationship between humans and other species, there are at last two rays of hope: Sanctuaries that have worked and an evolutionary history that ultimately may prevail. Poaching must be viewed by the world's community in the identical light as we would a crime against humanity. We must see the slaughter of elephants and other wildlife with the same horror that we view ethnic cleansing." Indeed, there is no difference between the two.[9]

Wylie continues, "CITES...had no legal teeth, even amongst its 113 signatory nations. There were too many loopholes in its regulations, and little chance of finally distinguishing on the ground between 'legal' and 'illegal,' 'worked' and 'unworked' ivory. A recent report estimated that 94 percent of ivory merchandise sold on eBay, the world's largest online auctioneer, was in fact illegal; eBay has now banned it. More damaging still, CITES was at times partly funded by and therefore reluctant to alienate ivory traders themselves. Douglas Chadwick discovered, as he related in his excellent, frightening book, *The Fate of the Elephant,* that in the late nineteen eighties Japanese ivory merchants were feeding a kind of self-imposed tax on their products into CITES coffers.... CITES director Eugene LaPointe had for years been exploiting legal loopholes to release tons of 'stock piled' African ivory to Far Eastern entrepreneurs. To this day, CITES is, rightly or wrongly, regularly accused by its detractors of actively abetting the trade rather than suppressing it. In July 2008 CITES succumbed to pressure from southern African nations and permitted them to release large stockpiles of ivory onto the open market, in face of East African protests that this is likely to reinvigorate poaching. As it is, recent estimates are that in Africa the elephant death rate from poaching is already eight percent higher than it was twenty years ago."

Wylie argues yet another point worth considering. "There is ongoing argument, then, about the extent to which an international ban merely drives the trade underground, and to what extent the open economization of elephant products as has been practiced to some local benefit in Zimbabwe and South Africa, is a better option.... The Douglas-Hamilton vs. Parker dispute also highlighted a third problem; determining the extent to which other factors—international prices, waves of fashion, local politics, cultural inhibitions, modes of land use, poverty and both short and longer-term ecological changes might also play a role in reducing elephant populations. Since elephant distribution is not perforce fragmented, each population suffers and enjoys a unique mix of influences, threats and benefits, so a blanket policy forged by international organizations is unlikely to cater adequately for all situations. This underlies, on a broad scale, the southern African/East African split."[10]

Asian elephant guru Raman Sukumar, in his memoir *Elephant Days and Nights*, captures these complexities succinctly. "We live in a world of contradictions, where there is an obscene disparity between rich and poor, and where there are tugs and pulls in every direction, where there is a need for the have-nots to catch up with the haves, and a need for both modernization and conservation. As we recklessly continue to assault the earth's living systems, our hearts are sometimes moved by the plight of the more charismatic creatures—the whooping crane, the tiger, the elephant. Often the plethora of issues, political, social, economic and biological, involved in the effort to save a species, makes us throw up our hands in despair.... Hence in many areas, a new emphasis in conservation is on trying to manage human-elephant conflict, and to find ways in which preserving wildlife that is otherwise dangerous can benefit rural communities. As Kenya's Richard Leakey wisely realized, the welfare of human and natural populations are mutually reliant; Giving up natural spaces and killing animal species will not bring prosperity.... Clean air, clean water, plentiful forests, and a human population that is well fed, educated, and reasonably affluent is our goal in Kenya. Saving the elephant is symbolic—a means to achieve these greater objectives."[11]

The Campfire Project, which stands for Communal Areas Management Program for Indigenous Resources in Zimbabwe, was one pioneering effort that poured all its hunting and tourism revenue directly back into local schools and clinics. Despite the corrupt rule and collapse of law and order under former leader Robert Mugabe's regime, the project was successful in several instances. Other efforts are being directed toward deterrence—using walls, trenches, electrified fencing or "fences" of repellent chili plants or bee hives. The newest experiment is broadcasting audio recordings of bee swarms, since we know that elephants are terrified of bees. Elephants are also victims of other kinds of territorial conflict. Some inadvertently step on landmines in war or former war zones and are injured or killed. In addition, the devastating civil war in the Democratic Republic of the Congo and in nearby Rwanda resulted in extensive loss of habitat for elephants, poverty-driven meat consumption, and a constant supply of illegal ivory fleeing these war-torn countries.

In the end, maybe it does not matter why one gets caught up with elephants; they are bound to mean different things to different people. Central to the reasons these animals have captured our mind is, of course, their sheer size, their incredible minds and gentle spirits. The elephant dwarfs us, humbles us, and reminds us that we are fragile, even as we encroach upon its numbers and its dignity. We have barely begun to comprehend the opportunities that elephants represent. The elephant today symbolizes Africa and ecology as never before.

* * *

In *Elephant Sense and Sensibility*, Michael Garstang writes about the similarities between elephants and humans: "What have we learned about an elephant mind and what separates them from us? Despite taking different but parallel evolutionary pathways, elephant and human cognitive systems are more similar than they are different. We each have 5 senses, humans responding more to sight and sound and elephants more to sound and smell. While humans have progressively lost their dependence upon smell, touch and taste, we have not abandoned these senses. Elephants on the other hand, depend on all 5 senses and may do much better than humans at integrating and assimilating input from multiple sensors, extracting information critical to survival, and storing that information in long-term but accessible memory. The evolution of both the human and the elephant brain has resulted in substantial storage within the unconscious. Much of the complex functioning of our respective bodies is carried out by the unconscious and both humans and elephants are capable of involved motor skills directed entirely by the unconscious. Memory is vital to the well-being of both species, and memory played a key role in the social systems of both species. Both species depend on and are part of a highly complex social system. Prolonged care of the young and comparable long life within stable societies meant the evolution of rules of behavior or morality and the emergence of empathy, altruism, and emotions. Elephants recognize self and others, form long-term bonds and interdependent relationship, and participate in cooperative living. They display a wide range of communication skills that includes all of their sensory systems, resulting in measurable intelligence, strong communication skills, and perhaps even rudimentary language and the ability to teach others."[12]

Garstang notes that in the presence of elephants, humans almost universally experience a deeply felt awakening of their connection to nature. He believes strongly that it may very well be possible that with even the smallest sign of tolerance extended by humans for the well-being of elephants, it will be the elephants that meet us more than halfway.

Humans and elephants have much in common and have walked a long, tangled trail of history together. We can both be traced through fossils to our African roots. We each took a different fork in the road about 10,000,000 years ago that caused evolutionary changes which remain in each species today. Of this, Watson says, "Our ancestors went through similar adaptive changes. [They] became more omnivorous, more gregarious, growing larger, radiating out in ways that prepared them for the same dry times in which forests shrank and made way for the Savanna.... The response of elephants and hominids was the same. We began to wander, traveling literally to the ends of the earth. As the climate changed, so did we, reacting to the 'Goldilocks Effect,' moving more to the center of adaption. Not too large or too small, but just right."

Lyall Watson pleads on behalf of elephants everywhere, "It is still possible to argue that [elephants] represent the most highly evolved form of life on the planet. Compared to them, we are primitive, hanging on to a stubborn, unspecialized five-fingered state, [and are] clever, but destructive. They are models of refinement, nature's archangels, the oldest and largest land animals, touchstones to our imagination."[13]

Although the elephant's situation has improved in parts of the world due to ivory bans and reduction in human-animal conflict, poaching syndicates and corruption grow more sophisticated, more dangerous and more ruthless. People must be educated so they associate ivory with death, greed and suffering rather than luxury and fashion. One Kenyan campaign against poaching featured women wearing ivory jewelry next to photos of elephants with their faces hacked off and slogans like, "Dressed to Kill," and "Accessories to Murder." We have a long path to blaze before we can relax about the future of elephants on our planet. Much work needs to be done in solving the root cause of the poaching problem—poverty—so that poaching isn't a career of necessity for so many of the world's poorest people.

Very few human beings have the privilege of touching an elephant, experiencing a trunk taking food from your hands, feeling that one side of an elephant's ear is soft while the other side is rough, and staring close-up through their long, curly eyelashes into their deep, amber eyes, the most transformative experience. What we stand to lose if elephants are driven to extinction sharpens in focus when we get up close and personal with these incredible beings. It is as profound an experience as one can have.

Most of us accept that the ways humans live their lives affects all other living beings on our precious Earth. And most of us believe that the resources stockpiled on the planet ought to be shared among all living creatures. There have been many international treaties relating to biodiversity, most of which the Trump administration slithered away from. One key question remains: How do we insist on extending this moral kindness to other living organisms? Humans currently hold to a person-centered status, but that must change and it must change swiftly. If similar numbers of humans were being murdered as the elephants are, we would call it genocide, a Holocaust, a gruesome abomination. If we remove the prefix "wildlife" from the widely used term wildlife crime, it leaves just plain old "crime." Calling it wildlife crime insinuates a lesser level of investigation and judicial enforcement. These criminal acts must stop before it's too late for the elephants and all the other trophy animals. Many elephants have become refugees, fugitives, families with no safe place to go. The term theriocide comes to mind, a recently coined term which is the name for diverse human actions that lead to animal deaths.

Part Three

Humankind clings to our beliefs as rigidly as an elephant's shackled legs. Some of us are alarmed at the rates elephants are killed, others unaware, perhaps disconnected from the natural world. What is clear is that the status of elephants is a barometer of the ecology of our planet. Ivory doesn't fall harmlessly out of an elephant's mouth the way a child loses a tooth, as many armchair warriors on this issue believe. Getting involved is essential: elephant lives matter greatly. Sitting by is unacceptable. It is imperative that we unchain our minds from outdated views and values and do everything in our power to stop the genocide and help protect these highly evolved creatures before it is too late. They are living, breathing beings that are largely peaceful, can recognize themselves in a mirror and remember faces and voices for decades. Dame Daphne Sheldrick described elephants as a "kindred species" to humans.[14] How much more like elephants must we be before killing them equals systematic extermination?

Glossary

Affiliative Behavior—social bonding behavior or behaviors that reinforce bonds such as touching a trunk to another's mouth or putting their trunk on another's head or back in an affectionate way.

Aggregation—a group specifically made up of more than one family unit with or without associating independent adult males. Several clans can intermingle in an aggregation, usually when food and water are plentiful. Among the reasons for elephants to aggregate include better opportunities for breeding and increased ability to deter predators.

Behavioral Ecology—the study of the evolutionary basis for animal behavior due to ecological pressures.

Boma—the nighttime shelter from the elements where most of the elephants at KEP sleep. It is considered a community enclosure, a stockade or corral.

Bond Group—two or more family units who associate with one another frequently or exhibit affiliative behavior toward each other.

Bull—a male elephant.

Bullock—a long, metal rod tool to help control an elephant. They used to have hooks on the ends which often injured the elephants when used to prod them. Animal activists have advocated for them to be made without the hooks.

Census Records—record the presence or absence of each family member at a sighting.

Charging Behavior—ears close to the head, feet not kicking up dirt, beware of these behaviors!

Clan—families who share the same dry season home range, usually made up of several bond groups and numerous families, such that several hundred elephants may make up a clan.

Cow—a female elephant.

Culling—the deliberate elimination of elephants by shooting them for the purpose of population control.

Estrus—the part of the reproductive cycle in which a cow is receptive to mating.

Part Three

Ethogram—a catalog or inventory of behaviors or actions exhibited by species. The behaviors in an ethogram are usually defined to be mutually exclusive and objective.

Family Unit—one or more adult females and calves with a high frequency of association over time, who act in a coordinated manner and exhibit affiliative behavior toward one another. It is not necessary for one of each sex to be present, nor does it require that calves be present.

Fission-Fusion—the ebb and flow of a group of elephants. The fission-fusion in herds usually follows predictable patterns.

Frustrated Behaviors—shaking their head or a full body shake.

Group—any number of elephants of any age or sex moving together in a coordinated manner with no one member at a distance from its nearest neighbor greater than the diameter of the main body of the group at its widest point.

Jacobson's Organ—also known as the vomeronasal organ (VNO), is the split auxiliary olfactory organ located in the soft tissue of the nasal septum in the nasal cavity just above the roof of the mouth. It is present and functional in all snakes and lizards and in many mammals, including elephants, cats, dogs, cattle, pigs, horses and some primates. In some species it is nonfunctional. The Jacobson's organ is useful in the process of communicating chemical messages, such as readiness for sexual activity between members of the same species.

Musth—is a periodic condition in bull elephants characterized by highly aggressive behavior and accompanied by a large rise in reproductive hormones. Scientific investigation of musth is problematic because even the most placid elephants can become highly violent toward humans or other elephants during musth.

Poaching—the illegal killing of elephants and rhinos for their tusks and horns and sometimes over land use rights. Most of the tusks and horns are sold on the black market after being smuggled across international borders.

Sighting Records—records the presence of families, or portions of families, in a group that is encountered in the course of a day. Presence requires at least one member of a family to be sighted.

Submissive Behaviors—these can include backing away from another elephant or backing to another elephant, head down, sometimes putting their rear ends to face the other.

Vigilance Behaviors—elephant body language that shows they are alert and scanning their environment, such as holding their tail up and swishing it back and forth, ears out to the side, holding their head upright.

Elephant Resources and Non-Government Organizations (NGOs)

Aaranyak
www.aaranyak.org

African Conservation Foundation
www.africanconservation.org

African Elephant Research Unit
(AERU)
www.aeru.co.za

African Parks
www.african-parks.org

African Wildlife Foundation
1100 New Jersey Avenue, SE,
Suite 900
Washington, D.C. 20003
www.africanwildlife.org or
www.awf.org

Amboseli Trust for Elephants
www.elephanttrust.org

Big Life Foundation
1715 N. Heron Drive
Ridgefield, WA 98642
www.biglife.org

Born Free Foundation
www.bornfree.org.uk

Burn the Ivory
PO Box 1447
Bend, OR 97709
www.burntheivory.org

Caretakers of Environment
International
www.caretakers4all.org

Conservation Canines at
Washington University
www.conservationcanines.org

David Sheldrick Wildlife Trust
PO Box 15555
Nairobi, Kenya
www.sheldrickwildlifetrust.org

Eco Activists for Governance
and Law Enforcementat
Washington University
www.eagle-enforcement.org

Elephant Action League
*www.aidchain.co/charity/-
elephant-action-league*

Elephant Aid International
PO Box 283
Attapulgus, GA 39815
*www.elephantaidinternational.
org*

Elephant Care International

166 Limo View Lane
Hohenwald, TN 38462
www.elephantcare.org

Elephant Care Unchained
www.elephantcareunchained.com

Elephant Nature Park
www.elephantnaturepark.org

The Elephant Network
www.disappearingelephants.org

Elephant Sanctuary
27 E. Main Street, PO Box 393
Hohenwald, TN 38462
www.elephants.com

Elephant Trust
www.elephanttrust.org

Elephant Voices
www.elephantvoices.org

Elephants Alive
www.elephantsalive.org

Elephants for Africa (Botswana)
www.elephantsforafrica.org

Elephants Without Borders
www.elephantswithoutborders.org

Environmental Investigation Agency International
www.eia-international.org

Game Rangers Association of Africa
www.gameranger.org

Global March for Elephants and Rhinos
www.march4elephantsandrhinos.org

Great Elephant Census
www.greatelephantcensus.com

Humane Society International
1255 23rd Street NW, Suite 450
Washington, D.C. 20037
www.donate.hsi.org

International Anti-Poaching Foundation
1655 N. Fort Myer Drive, #700
Arlington, VA 22209
www.iapf.org

International Elephant Foundation
PO Box 366
Azle, TX 76098
www.elephantconservation.org

International Fund for Animal Welfare
411 Main Street, PO Box 193
Yarmouth Port, MA 02675
www.ifaw.org

International Ranger Federation
www.internationalrangers.org

International Union for Conservation of Nature African Elephant Specialist Group
PO Box 68200, Nairobi, Kenya
www.iucn.org/afesg

IUCN Species Survival Commission
Po Box X7, Claremont 7735
Cape Town, South Africa
www.iucn.org/ssc

Jane Goodall Institute
www.janegoodall.org

The Kerulos Center
PO Box 1446
Jacksonville, OR 97530
www.kerulos.org

Knysna Elephant Park
www.knysnaelephantpark.co.za

LAGA Wildlife Law Enforcement
www.laga-enforcement.org

Mara Elephant Project
www.maraelephantproject.org

The Nature Conservancy
www.nature.org
World Wide Office
4245 N. Fairfax Drive, Suite 100
Arlington, VA 22203–1606
www.nature.org

Northern Rangelands Trust
www.nrt-kenya.org

Over and Above Africa
www.overandaboveafrica.com

Peace Parks Foundation
www.peaceparks.org

Performing Animal Welfare
Society
www.pawsweb.org

The Project for the Application of
Law for Fauna
www.palf-enforcement.org

Protected Area Management
Solutions Foundation
www.pamsfoundation.org

Rainforest Action Network
www.ran.org

Roots and Shoots
www.rootsandshoots.org

Save the Elephant Foundation
www.savetheelephants.org

Save the Elephants
PO Box 54667, Nairobi, Kenya
www.savetheelephants.org

SOS Elephants
www.soselephants.org

South African National Parks
Honorary Rangers
www.sanparks.org or
www.sanparksvolunteers.org

Sri Lanka Wildlife Conservation
Society
www.slwcs.org

The Thin Green Line Foundation
www.thingreenline.org.au

Think Elephants International
www.thinkelephants.org

Tusk
www.tusk.org

Victoria Falls Anti-Poaching Unit
www.vfapu.org

Wilderness Foundation Africa
www.wildernessfoundation.co.za

Wildlife Alliance
www.wildlifealliance.org

Wildlife Conservation Society
1101 Connecticut Avenue NW,
7th Floor
Washington, D.C. 20036
www.wcs.org

Wildlife Direct
921 Pennsylvania Avenue, SE,
Suite 304
Washington, D.C. 20003
www.wildlifedirect.org

Wildlife Friendly Enterprise
Network
www.wildlifefriendly.org

Wildlife Justice Commission
www.wildlifejustice.org

Elephant Resources and Non-Government Organizations

Wildlife SOS
www.wildlifesos.org

Wildlife Trust of India
www.wti.org.in

Working Dogs for Conservation
www.wd4c.org

World Animal Protection
www.worldanimalprotection.org

World Elephant Day: August 12
www.daysoftheyear.com

World Wildlife Foundation
1250 24th Street, NW
PO Box 97180
Washington, D.C. 20090–7180
www.worldwildlife.org

WWF South Africa
www.wwf.org.za

August 12 is World Elephant Day. Conservationists have designated August 12 as World Elephant Day to raise awareness about conserving these majestic animals. Elephants have many engaging features, from their incredibly dexterous trunks to their extraordinary memories and cognitive abilities and complex social structures.

What Can You Do to Help?

We each have the power to educate, persuade and rally others to save elephants, which will contribute to making this a better world in so many ways.

In spite of their loud trumpeting, elephants are voiceless. Speak for them by becoming outspoken about their plight. Talk to friends, family and others, write letters to government officials, and sign petitions.

Participate in campaigns related to elephants crossing international borders. They need enough land to be able to live naturally. Elephants don't know what borders are and need to be protected as they travel the landscape. Donations, volunteering at places like KEP, helping educate others and acting as an advocate are all important to the cause.

Educate others all about elephants, their intelligence, and family-oriented herds, gentle natures.

Follow elephant-related groups on social media.

Don't sell, wear, or buy ivory or any other by-products of elephants.

Support conservation efforts worldwide; make contributions, however small, if you can.

Be aware of the plight of caged and working elephants and spread the word. Do not support facilities or circuses that engage elephants in exploitation such as elephant back riding, performing, and do not support zoos or parks that keep elephants under poor conditions. In doing so, you would be supporting a cycle of abuse.

Adopt an elephant symbolically from any of the many nonprofit elephant conservation organizations.

Get involved with Roots and Shoots and the Jane Goodall Institute.

Write for their rights—send letters or emails to your elected officials urging them to support elephant conservation and ban elephant trophies and ivory imports.

What Can You Do to Help?

If you're searching for unusual jewelry, rather than ivory choose
jewelry made from seeds, stones and nuts, great alternatives to
elephant or rhino ivory.

Help plead with hunters by educating them to understand that
shooting elephants today is endangering the species and the gene
pool of future generations of elephants.

Volunteer at the Knysna Elephant Park or another elephant park that
engages in meaningful research and who cares for their elephants
by providing the best conditions in order for them to flourish.

Chapter Notes

Chapter 2

1. Dugmore, Heather. (2019). "The Last Knysna Elephant Has a Message For People." www.businesslive.co.za.
2. *Ibid.*
3. *Ibid.*

Chapter 3

1. Veasey, J. (2006). "Concepts in the Care and Welfare of Captive Elephants." *International Zoo Yearbook* 40(1), pp. 63–79.

Chapter 4

1. Watson, Lyall. (2002). *Elephantoms.* New York. W. W. Norton and Co.
2. O'Connell, Caitlin. (2021). *Wild Rituals: 10 Lessons Animals Can Teach Us About Connection, Community, and Ourselves.* New York: Chronicle Prism.
3. *Ibid.*
4. Meredith, Martin. (2001). *Elephant Destiny: Biography of an Endangered Species in Africa.* Cambridge, MA: Public Affairs.
5. Garstang, Michael. (2015). *Elephant Sense and Sensibility: Behavior and Cognition.* New York: Academic Press.
6. *Ibid.*
7. Gardner, Howard. (1994). *The Arts and Human Development.* New York: Basic Books.
8. Watson, *Elephantoms.*
9. Raubenheimer, Erich. (2021). *Elephants, Ivory and Avarice: The Demise of a Giant.* South Africa: Malan Media.
10. Meredith, *Elephant Destiny.*
11. *Ibid.*
12. *Ibid.*
13. *Ibid.*
14. *Ibid.*
15. *Ibid.*
16. O'Connell, Caitlin. (2007). The Elephant's Secret Sense: The Hidden Life of the Wild. Chicago: University of Chicago Press.
17. *Ibid.*

Chapter 5

1. Jacobs, Bob. (2018). "The Unique Elephant Brain." www.earthsky.org/earth/elephants-unique-brain-neurons.
2. Wemmer, Christen, and Catherine Christen. (2008). *Elephants and Ethics: Toward a Morality of Coexistence.* Baltimore: Johns Hopkins University Press.
3. Moss, Cynthia J .Elephant Memories. Chicago: University of Chicago Press.
4. Lindsay, Keith, Mike Chase, Kelly Landen, and Katarzyna Nowak. (2017). "The Shared Nature of Africa's Elephants." Biological Conservation, vol. 215, pp. 260-267.
5. Foerder, P., M. Galloway, T. Barthel, D.E. Moore, III, and D. Reiss. (2011). "Insightful Problem Solving in an Asian Elephant." PLoS ONE 6(8): e23251. https://doi.org/10.1371/journal.pone.0023251.
6. *Ibid.*
7. O'Connell, *Wild Rituals.*
8. *Ibid.*

Chapter 6

1. Garstang, *Elephant Sense and Sensibility.*
2. Moss, Cynthia, J., Harvey Croze,

and Phyllis C. Lee. (2011). *The Amboseli Elephants: A Long-Term Perspective on a Long-Lived Mammal.* Chicago: University of Chicago Press.
3. *Ibid.*

Chapter 7

1. Olsen, Deborah. (N.D.). *Elephant Husbandry Resource Guide.* American Zoo and Aquarium Association Elephant Taxon Group, Elephant Managers Association and International Elephant Foundation.
2. Mumby, Hannah. (2020). *Elephants: Life and Death in the World of the Giants.* New York: Harper.

Chapter 10

1. Wemmer and Christen, *Elephants and Ethics.*
2. Kristof, Nicholas D., and Sheryl WuDunn. (2014). *A Path Appears: Transforming Lives, Creating Opportunity.* New York: Vintage.
3. Geisel, Theodor. (2004). *Horton Hatches the Egg.* New York: Random House.
4. Vidya, T.N.C. (2014). "Novel Behavior Shown by an Asian Elephant in the Context of Allomothering." Jawaharlal Nehru Centre for Advanced Scientific Research. Acta Ethologica 17(2), pp. 123–137.
5. Herman, Judith. (2015). *Trauma and Recovery: The Aftermath of Violence—From Domestic Abuse to Political Terror.* New York: Basic Books.
6. *Ibid.*
7. Bradshaw, G. A. (2009). *Elephants on the Edge: What Animals Teach Us About Humanity.* New Haven, CT: Yale University Press.
8. *Ibid.*
9. McComb, Karen, Cynthia Moss, Soila Sayialel, and Lucy Baker. (2000). "Unusually Extensive Networks of Vocal Recognition in African Elephants." *Animal Behaviour* 59(6), pp. 1103–1109.

Chapter 11

1. Wylie, Dan. (2008). *Elephant.* London: Reaction Books, Ltd.

2. Evans, Kate E., and Stephen Harris. (2008). "Adolescence in Male African Elephants, Loxodonta africana, and the Importance of Sociality." *Animal Behaviour* 76(3), pp. 779–787.
3. *Ibid.*
4. *Ibid.*
5. O'Connell, Caitlin. (2015). *Elephant Don: The Politics of a Pachyderm Posse.* Chicago: University of Chicago Press.
6. Moss, Elephant Memories.

Chapter 12

1. Rossman, Zoë T., Clare Padfield, Debbie Young, and Lynette A. Hart. (2017). "Interactions with Humans: Individual Differences and Specific Preferences in Captive African Elephants (Loxodonta africana)." *Frontiers in Veterinary Science* 4(60), https://doi.org/10.3389/fvets.2017.00060.
2. *Ibid.*
3. *Ibid.*
4. *Ibid.*
5. *Ibid.*
6. Walker, Matthew W. (2017). *Why We Sleep: Unlocking the Power of Sleep and Dreams.* New York: Scribner.

Chapter 14

1. Olsen, *Elephant Husbandry Resource Guide.*
2. Hurt, Hannah. (2018). "How African Elephant Behavior Differs When Listening to Different Moods of Music." Dissertation: University of Hull, United Kingdom.
3. Nuwer, Rachel Love. "Elephants Really Can't Handle their Liquor." *New York Times*, May 26, 2020.

Chapter 15

1. O'Connell, *Elephant Don.*
2. Aktipis, Athena. (2020). *The Cheating Cell: How Evolution Helps Us Understand and Treat Cancer.* Princeton, NJ: Princeton University Press.
3. *Ibid.*
4. *Ibid.*
5. *Ibid.*

6. Wei-Hass, Maya. "Cancer Rarely Strikes Elephants. New Clues Suggest Why." *National Geographic*, August 14, 2018. https://www.nationalgeographic.com/science/article/news-cancer-elephants-genes-dna-new-research.

Chapter 16

1. O'Connell, *Wild Rituals*.
2. Wemmer and Christen, *Elephants and Ethics*.
3. Chadwick, Douglas H. (1992). *The Fate of the Elephant*. San Francisco: Sierra Club Books.

Chapter 17

1. David Sheldrick Wildlife Trust, www.sheldrickwildlifetrust.org.
2. Wildlife Conservation Society. "Elephants." https://www.wcs.org/our-work/wildlife/elephants.
3. de Greef, Simon. "Scores of Dead Elephants Found in Botswana 'Poaching Frenzy.'" *New York Times*, September 15, 2018.
4. Hübschule in de Greef, "Scores of Dead Elephants."
5. Zafra-Calvo, N., J. Lobo, G. Prada, M. Nielsen, and N. Burgess. (2016). "Predictors of Elephant Poaching in a Wildlife Crime Hotspot: The Ruvuma Landscape of Southern Tanzania and Northern Mozambique." *Journal for Nature Conservation* 41, pp.79–87.
6. *Ibid.*
7. *Ibid.*
8. Shannon, Graeme, Rob Slotow, Sarah Durant, Katito Sayialel, Joyce Poole, Cynthia Moss, and Karen McComb. (2013). "Effects of Social Disruption in Elephants Persist Decades After Culling." *Frontiers in Zoology* 10(62).
9. Scholes, R.J., and K.G. Mennell. (2001). *Elephant Management: A Scientific Assessment for South Africa*. South Africa: Wits University Press.
10. *Ibid.*
11. *Ibid.*
12. Millet, Lydia. "Save the Elephant." *New York Times*, July 26, 2015.

13. Ani, Jerline Sheebha, and Arun Kumar Sangaiah. (2018). "Wireless Integrated Sensor Network: Boundary Intellect System for Elephant Detection via Cognitive Theory and Fuzzy Cognitive Maps." *Future Generation of Computer Systems*, vol. 83, pp. 522–534.
14. Wadey, J., L.B. Hawthorne, S. Salman, O. Nasharuddin, and P. Leimgruber. (2018). "Why Did the Elephant Cross the Road? The Complex Response of Wild Elephants to a Major Road in Peninsular Malaysia." *Biological Conservation*, vol. 218, pp. 91–98.

Chapter 18

1. Nuwer, Rachel Love. (2018). *Poached: Inside the Dark World of Wildlife Trafficking*. New York: De Capo Press.
2. Lindsay et al., "The Shared Nature of Africa's Elephants."
3. Scholes and Mennell, *Elephant Management*.
4. Leibovitz, Sarah. "How a University of Washington Geneticist (Sam Wasser) Is Saving Elephants with Poop." NPR Broadcast, July 12, 2019.
5. Kolbert, Elizabeth. (2017). "There's a New Tool in the Fight Against Elephant Poaching." *Smithsonian Magazine*, www.smithsonianmag.com/science-nature/new-tool-fught-against-elephant-poaching.
6. Nuwer, *Poached*.
7. Wylie, *Elephant*.
8. *Ibid.*
9. Garstang, *Elephant Sense and Sensibility*.
10. Wylie, *Elephant*.
11. Sukumar, Raman. (1994). *Elephant Days and Nights: Ten Years with the Indian Elephant*. London: Oxford University Press.
12. Garstang, *Elephant Sense and Sensibility*.
13. Watson, *Elephantoms*.
14. Sheldrick, Daphne. (2012). *Love, Life and Elephants: An African Love Story*. New York: Farrar, Straus and Giroux.

Bibliography

Africa Geographic. "Five Traits Elephants and Humans Have in Common," March 31, 2017. africageographic.com/blog//5-traits-elephants-humans-common.

Aktipis, Athena. 2020. *The Cheating Cell: How Evolution Helps us Understand and Treat Cancer.* Princeton, NJ: Princeton University Press.

Alexander, Shana. 2000. *The Astonishing Elephant.* New York: Random House.

Allport, Susan. 1997. *A Natural History of Parenting: A Naturalist looks at Parenting in the Animal World and Ours.* New York: Three Rivers Press.

Ani, Jerline Sheebha, and Arun Kumar Sangaiah. 2018. "Wireless Integrated Sensor Network: Boundary Intellect System for Elephant Detection via Cognitive Theory and Fuzzy Cognitive Maps." *Future Generation of Computer Systems,* vol. 83, pp. 522–534.

Anthony, Lawrence, with Graham Spence. 2009. *The Elephant Whisperer.* New York: St. Martin's Press.

Baker, Peter, and Emily Cochrane. "Trump Halted These Hunt Trophies. Elephant Lovers Will Never Forget It." *New York Times,* November 20, 2017.

Baures, Mary. 2015. *Love Heals Baby Elephants.* Cambridge, MA: Merrimack Media.

Beard, Peter. 1965. *The End of the Game.* New York: Chronicle Books.

Beirne, Piers. Crime, Vol. 3, No. 2: 44–46. (2014). Theriocide: Naming Animal Killing. *International Journal for Crime, Justice and Social Democracy.* Vol. 3, No. 2: 49–66. 2014.

Bloom, Steve. 2009. *Elephant!* London: Thames and Hudson.

Bonato, Maud. Interview by the author, March 2021.

Bradley, Carol. 2014. *The Last Chain on Billie: How One Extraordinary Elephant Escaped the Big Top.* New York: St. Martin's Griffin.

Bradshaw, G.A. 2009. *Elephants on the Edge: What Animals Teach Us About Humanity.* New Haven, CT: Yale University Press.

Buckley, Carol. 2009. *Tarra and Bella.* New York: GP Putnam & Sons.

Byock, Satya Doyle. 2014. "Morals Gone Astray." *Utne Reader,* Fall/Winter. Reprinted from Oregon Humanities.

Canby, Peter. "Elephant Watch." *New Yorker Magazine,* May 11, 2015.

Chadwick, Douglas H. 1992. *The Fate of the Elephant.* San Francisco: Sierra Club Books.

Chuma, Shepherd. Interview with the author, October 2018.

Conciatore, Jacqueline. "Going Tuskless: A Brutal Outcome of Poaching African Elephants for Their Ivory?" *African Wildlife Foundation,* May 31, 2019. www.awf.org.

Croke, Vicki Constantine. 2015. *Elephant Company.* New York: Random House.

de Greef, Simon. "Scores of Dead Elephants Found in Botswana 'Poaching Frenzy.'" *New York Times,* September 15, 2018.

Delort, Robert. 1992. *The Life and Lore of the Elephant.* New York: Harry N. Abrams, Inc.

Douglas-Hamilton, Iain, and Oria. 1975. *Among the Elephants.* New York: Viking.

Dube, Dumisani. Interview by the author, October 2018.

Dugmore, Heather. "The Last Knysna Elephant Has a Message for People." *BusinessLive.* February 6, 2019. www.businesslive.co.za.

Bibliography

Edge, Jane. "Elephant Charities: The Good, the Bad & the Ugly." *Africa Geographic,* April 17, 2015. www.magazine.africa geographic.com/weekly/issue-42/-elephant-charities-the-good-the-bad-the-ugly.

"Elephant Cognition." *Psychology Wiki,* November 22, 2017. www.psychology. wikia.com/wiki/Elephant_cognition.

Elephant Specialist Advisory Group. 2017. *Understanding Elephants: Guidelines for Safe and Enjoyable Elephant Viewing.* South Africa: Penguin Random House.

Evans, Kate E., and Stephen Harris. 2008. "Adolescence in Male African Elephants, *Loxodonta africana*, and the Importance of Sociality." *Animal Behaviour* 76(3), pp. 779–787.

Garstang, Michael. 2015. *Elephant Sense and Sensibility: Behavior and Cognition.* New York: Academic Press.

Geisel, Theodor. 2004. *Horton Hatches the Egg.* New York: Random House.

Gettleman, Jeffrey. "Elephant in Stealth Mode: A Bull Named Morgan Survives Somali War Zone." *New York Times,* March 17, 2016.

Goldberg, Jeffrey. "The Hunted." *The New Yorker,* April 5, 2010. www.new yorker.com/magazine/2010/04/05/the-hunted.

Goldman, Jason G. "The Weird Psychology of Elephants." *Scientific American,* September 28, 2012. https://blogs. scientificamerican.com.

Gowdy, Barbara. 2000. *The White Bone: A Novel.* New York: Metropolitan Books.

Gray, Richard. "Elephant Personalities Revealed by Scientists." *Telegraph,* October 28, 2012. www.telegraph. co.us/news/earth/wildlife.9638340/-Elephant-personalities-revealed-by-scientists.html.

Hakeem. A., P. Hof, C. Sherwood, R. Switzer III, L. Rasmussen, and J. All-man. 2005. "The Brain of the African Elephant." *Anatomical Record, Part* A287A:1117–1127. Wiley-Liss.

Helfer, Ralph. 1997. *Modoc: The True Story of the Greatest Elephant that Ever Lived.* New York: Harper.

Herculano-Houzel, Suzana. "The Paradox of the Elephant Brain." *Nautilus,* No. 35. April 7, 2016.

Herman, Judith. 2015. *Trauma and Recovery.* New York: Basic Books.

Holdrege, Craig. 2003. *The Flexible Giant: Seeing the Elephant Whole.* Ghent, NY: The Nature Institute.

Hullinger, Jessica. "7 Behaviors That Prove Elephants Are Incredibly Smart." *Mental Floss,* April 1, 2017. www.mental floss.com/article/55640/7-behaviors-prove-elephants-are-incredibly-smart.

Hurt, Hannah. 2018. "How African Elephant Behavior Differs When Listening to Different Moods of Music." Dissertation: University of Hull, United Kingdom.

Ihwagi, Festusa, Chris Thouless, Teijun Want, Andrew Skidmore, Patrick Omondi, and Iain Douglas-Hamilton. 2018. "Night-Day Speed Ratio of Elephants as Indicator of Poaching Levels." *Science Direct,* Vol. 84, pp. 38–44.

Jacobs, Bob. "The Unique Elephant Brain." *Earthsky,* August 12, 2018. www. earthsky.org/earth/elephants-unique-brain-neurons.

Joubert, Beverly, and Dereck Joubert. 2008. *Face to Face with Elephants.* Washington, D.C.: National Geographic Kids.

Juwa, Mac. Interview by the author, October 2018.

Kolbert, Elizabeth. "There's a New Tool in the Fight Against Elephant Poaching." *Smithsonian Magazine,* January 2017. www.smithsonianmag.com/science-nature/new-tool-fught-against-eleph antpoaching.

Komar and Melamid, with M. Fineman. 2000. *The Quest of Two Russian Artists to Save the Elephants of Thailand.* New York: HarperCollins.

Kristof, Nicholas D., and WuDunn, Sheryl. 2014. *A Path Appears: Transforming Lives, Creating Opportunity.* New York: Vintage.

Leibovitz, Sarah. "How a University of Washington Geneticist (Sam Wasser) Is Saving Elephants with Poop." NPR Broadcast, July 12, 2019.

Lindsay, Keith, Mike Chase, Kelly Landen, and Katarzyna Nowak. (2017). "The Shared Nature of Africa's Elephants." *Biological Conservation,* vol. 215, pp. 260-267.

Bibliography

Maathai, Wangari. 2007. *Unbowed A Memoir*. New York: Anchor Books.

Maathai, Wangari. 2010. *The Challenge for Africa*. New York: Random House.

Mackay, Margo. 1996. *The Knysna Elephants and Their Forest Home*. South Africa: Knysna Center of the Wildlife and Environment Society of South Africa.

MacPherson, Malcolm. 2001. *The Cowboy and His Elephant*. New York: St. Martins Griffin.

Malby-Anthony, Francoise, with Katja Willemsen. 2018. *An Elephant in My Kitchen*. New York: Pan Macmillan.

Masson, Jeffrey Moussaieff, and Susan McCarthy. 1995. *When Elephants Weep: The Emotional Lives of Animals*. New York: Delacorte Press.

Mathee, Dalene. 1984. *Circles in a Forest*. New York: Alfred Knopf.

Mbaura, Davison. Interview by the author, October 2018.

McCallum, Taffy G. 1989. *South Africa: Land of Hope*. South Africa: Amagi Publications.

McComb, Karen, Cynthia Moss, Soila Sayialel, and Lucy Baker. 2000. "Unusually Extensive Networks of Vocal Recognition in African Elephants." *Animal Behaviour* 59(6), pp. 1103–1109.

McFee, D. 2013. *Through the Eyes of Ernest: A Memoir to Honor Elephants*. CreateSpace Independent Publishing Platform.

Meredith, Martin. 2001. *Elephant Destiny: Biography of an Endangered Species in Africa*. Cambridge, MA: Public Affairs.

Miller, A., M. Hensman, S. Hensman, K. Schultz, P. Reid, M. Shore, J. Brown, K. Furton, and S. Lee. 2015. "African Elephants (*Loxodonta Africana*) Can Detect TNT Using Olfaction: Implications for Biosensor Application. *Environment Society of SA. for Biosensor Journal Application. Applied Animal Behavior Science*, Vol. 171, pp. 177–183.

Millet, Lydia. "Save the Elephant." *New York Times*, July 26, 2015.

Momsenge, Ndyebo. Interview by the author, October 2018.

Montefiore, Clarissa Sebag. 2017.

"Criminals of the Illegal Wildlife Trade." *Womankind*. Issue 14.

Moss, Cynthia. J. 2000. *Elephant Memories: Thirteen Years in the Life of an Elephant Family*. Chicago: University of Chicago Press.

Moss, Cynthia, J., Harvey Croze, and Phyllis C. Lee. 2011. *The Amboseli Elephants: A Long-Term Perspective on a Long-Lived Mammal*. Chicago: University of Chicago Press.

Moyo, Charles. Interview by the author, September 2018.

Mumby, Hannah. 2020. *Elephants: Life and Death in the World of the Giants*. New York: Harper.

Nordland, Rod. "These Elephants Have No Tusks. No Poacher Either." *New York Times*. June 17, 2018.

Nuwer, Rachel Love. "Elephants Really Can't Handle Their Liquor." *New York Times*, May 26, 2020.

Nuwer, Rachel Love. 2018. *Poached: Inside the Dark World of Wildlife Trafficking*. New York: De Capo Press.

Nyamazunza, Wilfred. Interview by the author, September 2018.

Nyoni, Fanwell. Interview by the author, October 2018.

O'Connell, Caitlin. 2007. *The Elephant's Secret Sense: The Hidden Life of the Wild*. Chicago: University of Chicago Press.

O'Connell, Caitlin. 2011. *The Elephant Scientist*. New York: Houghton Mifflin.

O'Connell, Caitlin. 2012. *An Elephant's Life: An Intimate Portrait from Africa*. Guilford, CT: The Lyons Press.

O'Connell, Caitlin. 2015. *Elephant Don: The Politics of a Pachyderm Posse*. Chicago: University Of Chicago Press.

O'Connell, Caitlin. 2021. *Wild Rituals: 10 Lessons Animals Can Teach Us About Connection, Community, and Ourselves*. New York: Chronicle Prism.

Olsen, Deborah (no date). *Elephant Husbandry Resource Guide*. American Zoo and Aquarium Association Elephant Taxon Group, Elephant Managers Association and International Elephant Foundation.

Orenstein, Ronald, Ed. 1997. *Elephants: The Deciding Decade*. Buffalo, NY: Firefly Books.

Bibliography

Owens, Mark, and Delia Owens. 2007. *Secrets of the Savanna: Twenty-Three Years in the African Wilderness Unraveling the Mysteries of Elephants and People.* New York: Houghton Mifflin.

Owens, Mark, and Delia Owens. *The Eye of the Elephant: An Epic Adventure in the African Wilderness.* New York: Houghton Mifflin.

Padfield, Clare. Interview with the author, September 2018.

Palminteri, Sue. "Breaking a Fence-Breaking Habit: Maintaining the Fences That Reduce Human-Elephant Conflict." *Mongabay,* June 2, 2017. www.news.mongbay.com.

Parkinson, Kevin. 2016. *A Plea for the Elephants.* Cape Town, South Africa: Publishing World.

Payne, Katy. 1999. *Silent Thunder: In the Presence of Elephants.* New York: Simon & Schuster.

"Perception." *Proceedings of the National Academy of Sciences of the United States of America.* www.ncbi.nlm.nih.gov/PMC3986168/. 3/25/14.

Peterson, Dale, and KI. Moarl Ammann. 2009. *Elephant Reflections.* Berkeley: The University of California Press.

Picoult, Jodi. 2014. *Leaving Time.* New York: Ballantine Books.

Pincott, Sharon. 2016. *Elephant Dawn.* London: Allen & Unwin.

Pinnock, Don, and Colin Bell. 2019. *The Last Elephants.* Washington, D.C.: Smithsonian Books.

Plotnik, Joshua M., Frans B.M. de Waal, Donald Moore, III, and Diana Reiss. 2010. "Self-Recognition in the Asian Elephant and Future Directions for Cognitive Research with Elephants in Zoological Settings." *Zoo Biology,* 29:179–191. Wiley-Liss.

Plotnik, Joshua M., and Frans B.M. de Waal. 2014. "Extraordinary Elephant Perception." *Proceedings of the National Academy of Sciences of the United States of America.*

Poole, Joyce. 1996. *Coming of Age with Elephants: A Memoir.* New York: Hyperion.

Psychology Today. "Solving the Problem for Elephants: An Interview with Cari Zuckerman on the new All Bull Elephants' Sanctuary," February 8, 2017. www.psychologytoday.com/blog/-bear-in-mind/201702/solving-the-problem.elephants.

Rossman, Zoë T., Clare Padfield, Debbie Young, and Lynette A. Hart. (2017). "Interactions with Humans: Individual Differences and Specific Preferences in Captive African Elephants (*Loxodonta africana*)." *Frontiers in Veterinary Science* 4(60), https://doi.org/10.3389/fvets.2017.00060.

Rowe, Martin. 2013. *The Elephants in the Room.* New York: Lantern Books.

Scholes, R.J., and K.G. Mennell. 2001. *Elephant Management: A Scientific Assessment for South Africa.* South Africa: Wits University Press.

Schroeder, Kathy. Interview with the author, September 2018.

Scigliano, Eric. 2002. *Love, War and Circuses: The Age Old Relationship Between Elephants and Humans.* New York: Houghton Mifflin.

Scigliano, Eric. 2002. *Seeing the Elephant: The Ties That Bind Elephants and Humans.* London: Bloombury Publishing.

Shand, Mark. *Queen of the Elephants.* London: Jonathan Cape.

Shannon, Graeme, Rob Slotow, Sarah Durant, Katito Sayialel, Joyce Poole, Cynthia Moss, and Karen McComb. 2013. "Effects of Social Disruption in Elephants Persist Decades After Culling." *Frontiers in Zoology* 10(62).

Sheldrick, Daphne. 2012. *Love, Life and Elephants: An African Love Story.* New York: Farrar, Straus and Giroux.

Shell, Jacob. 2019. *Giants of the Monsoon Forest: Living and Working with Elephants.* New York: W.W. Norton & Co.

Skinstad, Noleen. Interview by the author, September 2018.

Sukumar, Raman. 1994. *Elephant Days and Nights: Ten Years with the Indian Elephant.* London: Oxford University Press.

Sukumar, Raman. 2003. *The Living Elephants.* London: Oxford University Press.

Tembo, Elliot. Interview by the author, September 2018.

Bibliography

Tholander, Christina. Interview by the author, September 2018.

Thomason, Ron. 2006. *Managing our Wildlife Heritage*. Hartbeespoort, South Africa: Magron Publishing.

Thomson, Ron. 2016. *Elephant Conservation: The Facts and the Fiction*. South Africa: Ron Thomson Publications.

Thuppil, Vivek, and Richard G. Coss. 2015. "Playback of Felid Growls Mitigates Crop Raiding by Elephants, *Elephas maximus* in Southern India." *Fauna and Flora International*. journals.cambridge.org.

Tobias, Ronald B. 2013. *Behemoth*. New York: Harper Perennial.

Trautmann, Thomas R. 2015. *Elephants & Kings: An Environmental History*. Chicago: University of Chicago Press.

Tsuchiya, Yukio. 1951. *Faithful Elephants: A True Story of Animals, People and War*. New York: Houghton Mifflin Company.

Van Rooyen, Sias. Interview by the author, September 2018.

Veasey, J. 2006. "Concepts in the Care and Welfare of Captive Elephants." *International Zoo* 40: 63. Springer-Verlag Berlin Heidelberg and ISPA 2013. www.springer.com/article.10.1007.

Vidya, T.N.C. 2014. "Novel Behavior Shown by an Asian Elephant in the Context of Allomothering." Jawaharlal Nehru Centre for Advanced Scientific Research. *Acta Ethologica*, 17 (2), pp. 123–137.

Vipond, Alex. Interview by the author, September 2018.

Wadey, J., L.B. Hawthorne, S. Salman, O. Nasharuddin, and P. Leimgruber. 2018. "Why Did the Elephant Cross the Road? The Complex Response of Wild Elephants to a Major Road in Peninsular Malaysia." *Biological Conservation*, Vol. 218, pp. 91–98.

Walker, Matthew W. 2017. *Why We Sleep: Unlocking the Power of Sleep and Dreams*. New York: Scribner.

Watson, Lyall. 2002. *Elephantoms*. New York: W.W. Norton and Co.

Wei-Hass, Maya. "Cancer Rarely Strikes Elephants. New Clues Suggest Why." *National Geographic*, August 14, 2018. https://www.nationalgeographic.com/science/article/news-cancer-elephants-genes-dna-new-research.

Wemmer, Christen, and Catherine Christen. 2008. *Elephants and Ethics: Toward a Morality of Coexistence*. Baltimore: Johns Hopkins University Press.

Williams, J.H. 1950. *Elephant Bill*. New York: Doubleday & Company.

Wylie, Dan. 2008. *Elephant*. London: Reaction Books, Ltd.

Yee, Amy. "Female Elephants Follow in Their Mothers' Footsteps." *New York Times*. July 4, 2016.

Young, Debbie. Interview by the author, September 2018.

Zafra-Calvo, N., J. Lobo, G. Prada, M. Nielsen, and N. Burgess. 2016. "Predictors of Elephant Poaching in a Wildlife Crime Hotspot: The Ruvuma Landscape of Southern Tanzania and Northern Mozambique." *Journal for Nature Conservation* 41, pp.79–87.

Index

Index

Index

Index